The End of the War

The End of the War

Singapore's Liberation and the Aftermath of the Second World War

Romen Bose

Published by Marshall Cavendish Editions
An imprint of Marshall Cavendish International
1 New Industrial Road, Singapore 536196

Other Marshall Cavendish Offices
Marshall Cavendish Ltd. 119 Wardour Street, London W1F 0UW, UK • Marshall Cavendish Corporation. 99 White Plains Road, Tarrytown NY 10591-9001, USA • Marshall Cavendish Beijing. D31A, Huatingjiayuan, No. 6, Beisihuanzhonglu, Chaoyang District, Beijing, The People's Republic of China, 100029 • Marshall Cavendish International (Thailand) Co Ltd. 253 Asoke, 12th Flr, Sukhumvit 21 Road, Klongtoey Nua, Wattana, Bangkok 10110, Thailand • Marshall Cavendish (Malaysia) Sdn Bhd, Times Subang, Lot 46, Subang Hi-Tech Industrial Park, Batu Tiga, 40000 Shah Alam, Selangor Darul Ehsan, Malaysia

National Library Board Singapore Cataloguing in Publication Data
Bose, Romen.
The end of the war : Singapore's liberation and the aftermath of the Second War World / Romen Bose. – Singapore : Marshall Cavendish Editions, c2005.
p. cm.
Includes bibliographical references.
ISBN : 981-261-066-9

1. World War, 1939-1945–Singapore. 2. World War, 1939-1945–Battlefields–Singapore. 3. Singapore–History–Japanese occupation, 1942-1945. I. Title.

D767.55
940.5425–dc21 SLS2005033082

Printed in Singapore by Utopia Press Pte Ltd

For Brigid, Lara and Olive,

the muses in my life

Contents

Foreword

Ji hui jie zhong er zhi. All endings lead to new beginnings. This famous Chinese phrase aptly describes the creation of this book as it was on the author's last day of service with the Singapore Tourism Board (STB) that the idea for this book was conceived.

After having served as the Board's Coordinating Area Director for South Asia, the Middle East and Africa, as well as in the Mega Events Division, Romen was heading to the UK on a British Council Chevening Scholarship to do his Masters degree at Goldsmiths College, University of London.

As he walked into my room on that day, I was thinking of how Singapore's recent history could be made more accessible and appealing to numerous visitors, who were intrigued by the country's unique past and vibrant heritage. The commemoration of the end of the War in the Asia Pacific would soon be coming up and we were in the midst of organising events and activities for this historic event.

Romen, who is a keen historian and had written several books on Singapore's World War II history, was eager to help and I asked him to do some research on what we could possibly do. A month later, he came up with a wide-ranging proposal, which included the publication of this book. Clearly a journalist at heart, he had kept quiet about his plans for a "scoop" of a book and only revealed it to me once the manuscript was done! I say "scoop" because most of the book is based on recently declassified top-secret documents and interviews that will for the first time, provide answers to some of the last remaining mysteries of the end of the War.

Readers will be fascinated by the amazing secret Japanese surrender of Singapore and find out what actually happened to wartime-hero Lim Bo Seng.

I believe the ending of the War in the region is also a great beginning for books like these. With a dearth of information and research on the period, very few people, with the exception of greying veterans and some locals, know what actually happened back then in 1945. This book can change that.

In addition to the extensive details and surprising stories within its pages, the book also highlights several sites in Singapore that are intimately tied to this historic period; some sites that even most Singaporeans do not know about. Thus, books like these help highlight our unique heritage and provide visitors with a different perspective and window into our history and culture.

Many military veterans, civilians and their families plan to be in Singapore and Malaysia in 2005 to mark the 60th Anniversary of the end of the War and to remember fallen colleagues who gave their lives so that we could live ours. We owe a great debt of gratitude to these men and women who will always be remembered. It is my hope that books like these will also help recognise the role played by these heroes.

The STB along with the National Heritage Board, National Institute of Education, the British High Commission and World War II sites and museums, have planned events that will include heritage tours, commemorative exhibitions, a Veterans' Forum, public conferences and talks on the Asia Pacific War as well as promotions at Singapore's World War II museums. These activities will culminate in September 2005 with memorial services at the Kranji War Memorial, the Changi Chapel & Museum and the Sembawang Wharves.

I hope this book will provide a good reference as we seek to mark a unique chapter in our history.

Lim Neo Chian
Deputy Chairman & Chief Executive
Singapore Tourism Board

Preface

I have always held a fascination for the last days of the war in Singapore and the eventual British reoccupation. As a child, I would spend hours at the Surrender Chamber on Sentosa Island, where wax figures of Vice Admiral Lord Louis Mountbatten and his aides accepting the surrender from General Seishiro Itagaki on 12 September 1945 are frozen in time. Through the years, I have come across scraps of information and anecdotal evidence of the British recapture of Singapore and Malaya and I must thank my uncle, Mrinal Kanti Dutta, a history buff himself, who was always on the lookout for books on the war and would present me with very rare tomes on the fall of Singapore and the eventual liberation of the island.

However, it was not until I received the British Council's Chevening Scholarship in 2004 for a year's study in the United Kingdom that I was given the opportunity to go through the entire series of documents pertaining to the end of the war, ensconced safely at the National Archives in Kew. I would like to thank the Council's Errim Mahmoud and Sandra Bodestyne for their continued support and help.

I would also like to take the opportunity to thank the various individuals and organisations that have been crucial to the completion of this book: The President and Mrs S.R. Nathan; Lim Neo Chian; The Imperial War Museum; The National Archives, London; The Australian War Memorial; Dr Gareth Stanton and the Media and Communications Department, Goldsmiths College; The British Council; The Singapore Tourism Board; The National Library, Singapore; The National Archives, Singapore; C.O. Donough; Jeyathurai A.; Jennifer A.; and of course my Mum and Dad, Ajoy, Anuradha, Nita, Hari, Nisha and Anusha. A very special thank you to Brian Farrell for helping to spot the loopholes of logic and giving incisive comments on how to write a better book. I must also thank Benny Chung, my editor at Marshall Cavendish whose unflagging enthusiasm and patience led to the writing of several of the appendices in this book.

This book, on the end of the war, does not purport to be a comprehensive tome on the period nor does it attempt to reveal all that is known about the events then or even provide a social history of the times. This book is an attempt to help readers understand better what actually happened during those few months in 1945 when the war was at an end and it appeared, to the newly reinstated colonial masters at least, that the future of the peoples in Malaysia and Singapore would be determined by whichever power controlled Southeast Asia.

The End of the War reveals many secrets of the Second World War that have been hidden in highly sensitive files and long forgotten. It tries to better explain how Britain decided to retake its possessions in Malaya and Singapore and the various ways in which they went about doing this. It also sheds light on wartime heroes like Lim Bo Seng and the role he played in the clandestine Allied operations leading to the end of the war. It concludes by revealing the actual Japanese surrender in Singapore and how the Allied forces finally returned to Malaya and Singapore. A theme that recurs throughout this book is of how endings have led to new beginnings. The fall of Singapore in 1942 led to the formulation of a British policy to retake the area, as well as the creation of resistance groups and clandestine movements. The end of the war led to the beginnings of nationalism and the eventual demands for independence and the creation of independent countries less than two decades after the Japanese surrenders.

It is hoped that this patchwork of vignettes into the various aspects of the period will stimulate greater discussion among a younger generation of readers and encourage more research into a very chaotic but historically significant point in time.

As veterans return to these sites over the next few years to commemorate events and remember fallen comrades, I hope that many who read this book will come forward and give their perceptions and tell their stories of the end of the war.

In conclusion, let me apologise to and thank those who have contributed to this book but whom I have forgotten to mention. I remain solely responsible for any errors or mistakes within this book. Should you have comments or if you have more information or leads for a future edition, please send me an email at romen@hotmail.com.

Romen Bose
14 July 2005

Chapter 1

Introduction

4 September 1945.

It was a still morning in the seas off Singapore. There was not even a breeze about as he stood on the deck of the ship. All he could see ahead of him were the grey hulks of warships that filled his view of the harbour. Sweat dripped down his chin as the coolness of the dawn evaporated and the early rays of the rising sun foretold the sweltering day ahead.

He had waited since dawn, dressed immaculately in a white, open-collared shirt, pressed khaki field uniform and polished boots. The dress sword at his side glinted in the morning light. As the ship gently rocked in the wake of the larger vessels, he took a sip of the tepid tea that had been proffered hours earlier, idly wondering whether he would still be a free man when this day was over.

Before him lay the might of the British Royal Navy. A naval cruiser and several destroyers had converged at the agreed rendezvous point just outside Keppel Harbour, their large guns all trained at the city. The sea now glittered with the oily slicks discharged by these behemoths as they lay anchored, floating and waiting. The sound of their engines created a dull throb in the still air. There was clearly a sense of anticipation in the air. It was as if the last scene from an epic play were about to begin, the cast of characters now gathering off stage, just before everyone would be cued to their places and the curtains raised.

The British had come to Singapore to take back what, they claimed, had rightfully belonged to them. They were here in force and no one expected these victors to be magnanimous.

How the tables had turned.

Less than three years before, he had been at the forefront of a conquering army that had liberated the Asiatic peoples all the way from Burma to the islands of the South Pacific. The Imperial Japanese Army had been the vanguard of a new East Asia Co-Prosperity Sphere, welcoming an era where the peoples of Asia would rule themselves, under the guidance of the Chrysanthemum Throne, of course. The Showa era was to herald untold successes for the Japanese peoples and lead to a glorious reign.

Instead, the Second World War had led to huge defeats and millions killed. Defeat after defeat had demoralised the imperial army and led to starvation and abject poverty throughout the empire. No longer could Japan hold its head up high. Vast areas of the homeland had been destroyed and the enemy had succeeded in routing most of the Japanese army.

He had lost many friends and colleagues in the last three years; too many to count, too many to mourn over. Even here, where only the stories rather than actual experience of the horrors of the Burma Campaign had filtered through, there was a deep sense of foreboding that the end was near.

Southeast Asia was to be the last stand before the enemy took the fighting to the home islands. It was supposed to be the last big battle before Armageddon. But it never came.

All the suffering, the torture of the local populace for information on fifth columnists, the quelling of resistance groups and the planning for a spirited defence of Malaya had all come to naught.

Two horrific bombs dropped on Hiroshima and Nagasaki meant the end of the war had arrived and along with it the humiliating result of having to surrender to the enemy.

As he stood on board the Japanese submarine chaser flying a black and white surrender flag in Keppel Harbour, General Seishiro Itagaki was angry. Angry that an empire as great as Japan had been defeated. Angry that despite the huge numbers of lives lost, the cause he had fought for all his life was now relegated to the dustbin of history. Angry that his commander-in-chief, Field Marshal Count Hsiaichi Terauchi, had refused to surrender to the Allied forces, feigning ill health. And angry that he would have the humiliating task of surrendering his country's forces at a location which had symbolised the empire's victory over its enemies only three years before.

Itagaki had served in the Kwangtung army in China in 1936 and celebrated the creation of the Japanese puppet state of Manchukuo with Emperor Isenjiro Pu Yi (in *pinyin*, Aixin Juelo Puyi) as its titular head. Itagaki became minister of war in Prime Minister General Hideki Tojo's military cabinet of 1941 and commanded the 17th Area Army in Korea. As Japan's fortunes began to wane, he ended up commanding the 7th Area Army in Singapore and was in charge of all Japanese forces in the area when Japan announced its unconditional surrender on 15 August 1945. Less than three years after that date, Itagaki would be hanged as a war criminal[1].

But that would be in the future. For now, Itagaki waited aboard the chaser, pacing nervously and refusing to talk to his naval counterpart who stood calmly to one side.

Vice Admiral Shigeru Fukudome, Commander of the 10th Area Fleet, was much more of a character. Described as an opportunist, Fukudome was very ambitious and always sought to further his own career and objectives at the expense of fellow officers. Even now, he was looking for ways to ingratiate himself with the new masters of Singapore in an attempt to save his skin and hopefully earn himself a position in a post-war Japanese government. He was intelligent, talked freely, and appeared to be "a markedly superior Japanese officer". Even though he understood English, he had chosen to converse through an interpreter at the upcoming meeting with the British in order to give himself time to think of appropriate responses to questioning. However, unbeknownst to him, a top-secret cable from Washington earlier in the day had revealed to British commanders that Fukudome had been director of the 1st section (Plans and Operations) of the Japanese naval staff at the time of the attack on Pearl Harbour. He was one of the officers principally responsible for planning the destruction of the American fleet and was regarded by the Americans as a war criminal[2].

In ending up at Singapore, Fukudome's track record had not been entirely spotless. In late March 1944, just before the battle in the Marianas for the islands of Saipan, Palau and Truk, Fukudome had been in a plane crash in the Philippines. He was Admiral Yamamoto's successor as Chief of Staff for the combined fleet, and had been carrying the battle plans for the Japanese fleet but lost them in the crash. The documents were retrieved from the crash site by Philippine resistance fighters and smuggled to the Americans, who then translated them with the help of two Hawaii-born Nisei soldiers—Japanese Americans who had signed up to serve in a special unit in the US army. General Douglas MacArthur later sent the translation to Hawaii where this "operational-level coup" greatly aided Admiral Raymond Spruance a few weeks later as he met the Japanese at the Battle of the Philippine Sea, a major defeat for Japanese naval aviation that saw the loss of more than 400 Japanese aircraft and the severe crippling of three Japanese aircraft carriers[3].

These two men, with two very different pasts, would now hand over the entire Japanese force in Singapore to the British.

The Allied forces had called for this hasty meeting on board a warship only five days before. The Japanese had expected the British to take over the Malayan peninsula before heading to Singapore but it was now clear that the British had made a lightning dash to Singapore to recapture the island first. Itagaki was still not sure if the meeting was to arrange for a surrender or if it would be the surrender itself. The one thing he was sure of was that, after the meeting, he would clearly be living on borrowed time.

Suddenly, the *HMS Sussex* began signalling Itagaki's vessel. The submarine chaser drew alongside the large cruiser and Itagaki and Fukudome were invited aboard[4].

In true British naval tradition, the two Japanese general officers were piped aboard the *Sussex*. The decks of the *Sussex* and the surrounding escort warships were filled with curious officers and ratings, all trying to get a good look at the historic event unfolding before their eyes.

The two men, followed closely by their staff officers, were introduced to the captain of the *Sussex* and escorted to a small cabin where they were disarmed. There, they were made to wait until the representatives of Vice Admiral Lord Louis Mountbatten, the Supreme Allied Commander, Southeast Asia (SACSEA), were ready to meet them.

The meeting was to be held in the Admiral's Dining Room. The rectangular room, normally used for meals, had been cleared of all its glass and accoutrements in order to fit a long table covered with green cloth. As a psychological ploy, the row of chairs intended for the Japanese delegates

The Allied Generals: Posing for an official picture in the cramped Admiral's Dining Room on board *HMS Sussex*, after General Itagaki signed the terms of agreement for the surrender of Singapore on 4 September 1945 are (left to right, seated) Lieutenant FP Donachie, Major General EC Mansergh, Brigadier General ND Wingrove, Lieutenant General Sir AFP Christison, Vice-Admiral CS Holland, Captain CFJ Lloyd Davies and Major General H R Hone.

General Itagaki, Commander of the 7th Japanese Area Army, signing the initial surrender terms on board *HMS Sussex*, 4 September 1945. Itagaki is being assisted by his chief of staff, Lieutenant Colonel Itoga, as Staff Officer Captain Onoda looks on.

was kept some distance away from the table in order to make them feel uncomfortable and prevent them from leaning onto the table or using it effectively.

As the Japanese waited in the anteroom, Mountbatten's army representative, Lieutenant General Sir Alexander Frank Philip Christison, General Officer Commanding (GOC), 15th Indian Corps, entered the dining room. Christison, who had served in the Burma Campaign and who would end his career as a General Aide-de-Camp to the British King George VI, would lead the proceedings[5].

He was followed by Rear (later Vice) Admiral Cedric Swinton Holland, Mountbatten's naval representative, who had led the top secret emergency dash to recapture Singapore. By his side was Major General Eric Carden Robert Mansergh, Commander of the 5th Indian Division, who would be leading the first Allied division in the reoccupation of Singapore.

Rounding off the group was Major General Sir Herbert Ralph Hone, the civil administration officer who later would set up a post-war British military administration in Singapore.

Christison was relieved that Itagaki had turned up for the meeting. He had feared that the general would change his mind at the last minute and put up a struggle. As the British fleet in the harbour was not loaded for an assault, Japanese resistance would have meant the wholesale destruction of the Allied forces gathered off the coast of Singapore.

At 11.00am, the Japanese officers were summoned to the Admiral's Dining Room. Itagaki and his aide led the delegation as they marched into the room and stood at attention. They saluted and bowed to the Allied generals but remained standing until instructed to sit down.

The atmosphere was very tense and the air was filled with expectation. Security was tight—a marine was posted at the doorway—and for a moment, there was pin-drop silence as each side sized up the other.

Not giving Itagaki a chance to begin, Christison cleared his throat and spoke through his interpreter. He asked the Japanese officer for his name, rank and appointment and Itagaki responded[6].

Christison: Are you entitled to speak for the Field Marshal Count Terauchi, Supreme Japanese Commander, Southern Region, on Army matters?

Itagaki: Not entirely for the whole area, but only for the landings in the Singapore area.

Christison: Do you know the Terms of Agreement signed in Rangoon?

Itagaki: I know of the Agreement signed in Rangoon and, furthermore, I have complied with what I ought to have done in Singapore with regard to this Agreement.

Christison then asked Fukudome to identify himself and asked whether he had Terauchi's authority to discuss the Japanese surrender. Fukudome, smiling and winking, responded in kind.

Christison: Do you abide by the Imperial decision to cease hostilities and are you prepared to carry out the orders of the Supreme Allied Commander, South East Asia?

Itagaki: Yes, I am quite prepared.

Although he appeared meek, Itagaki, from the start, wanted to ensure that his men would not face the wrath of the victorious Allies. When asked what his plans were, he asked for the Japanese troops to be segregated away from the Allied troops.

Itagaki: For future plans, we wish to avoid possible clashes between the Allied Army and consider our forces should be as far away as possible. I am now constructing temporary barracks in the following areas: (1) West of Island, in Jurong–Choa Chu Kang; (2) East of Island, between Singapore–Changi Roads from Ulu Bedock–Simpang Bedock (Ulu Bedok–Simpang Bedok) Bugis Estate–Honyeyang Estate (Bugis Estate–Hougang Estate);—which I should like to use. As a temporary construction is not yet completed at present, our Headquarters will be in the Raffles College.

However, for the British commanders, the bigger concern was the level of violence and lawlessness in Singapore during the phoney surrender, the three weeks between the announcement of the Japanese surrender and the British arrival in Singapore to reoccupy Malaya. Christison was worried that his troops would have to quell riots.

Christison: Is there any sabotage, looting or local civil disturbance taking place in the Singapore area?

Itagaki: With regard to the maintenance of law and order there are no riots of a serious nature but there is every sign of possible looting and some sort of violence of a small nature which is under the guard of our Forces now and we have also suspicions certain Societies are being formed but we are taking every possible step to suppress them. We are also collecting information about them.

Christison: I rely on General Itagaki to keep law and order until my Forces take over.

He then told Itagaki that Mansergh's troops would be landing in Singapore the next day at Keppel Harbour and the wharves. Rear Admiral Holland instructed Fukudome to use Japanese minesweepers to sweep the channel ahead of the Allied troops to ensure a clear path into Singapore. The waters around Singapore were still unsafe.

Fukudome: ... Inside Keppel Harbour all is safe. Boom still exists and is visible above water... Since the beginning of this year the Americans came over and dropped magnetic or other mines in the areas coloured red and blue on the chart. The channels are quite safe but outside these, everything is uncertain.

Asked about the occupants of Keppel Harbour, Fukudome said there were no warships there although there were submarines.

Fukudome: At present there are no Naval boats in Keppel Harbour. There are two German submarines in Keppel Harbour... only guarded by Japanese guards.

The British officers ordered the Japanese delegates to keep the harbour clear of all ships during the landings on 5 September. Christison gave Itagaki a copy of the *de facto* surrender agreement, the *Instructions to the Japanese Forces under Command or Control of Japanese Commanders Singapore Area* (see "Appendix F: Part 1") which he asked Itagaki to study before signing.

The Japanese were caught completely off-guard. Itagaki and Fukudome were not expecting to sign anything. Moreover, they had to translate the document and understand it fully before agreeing. For four hours, Itagaki and Fukudome were holed up in the ante-room with their staff officers Lieutenant Colonel Itoga, Captain Onoda and their two interpreters as they went over the terms of surrender[7].

The Japanese forces on Singapore island and in Malaya were to be treated as "surrendered personnel" rather than as prisoners of war. This would mean that the Allied forces, with their limited troops and resources, would not have to set up special prisoner of war camps and guard the Japanese as prisoners. The Japanese would be disarmed but could continue to wear uniforms and badges of rank. Japanese commanders would remain responsible for the maintenance and discipline of their own troops, for public order, for the protection of banks, and for the feeding of civilians in territories that had hitherto been under their control.

Essential services such as light and water were to be maintained and guarded until Allied forces had assumed control; aircraft would be grounded and remain so. No demolitions would be permitted; and damage to bridges, waterways, railroads, telegraphs and telephones, stores of food, and cattle belonging to civilians had to be prevented. To implement these instructions, the Japanese would be allowed guards of 100 men for military stores, dumps and vehicle parks, for dock installations, for bulk holdings of cash, and for Japanese hospital patients who could not be moved.

The Japanese were to also provide the location of fortifications, camps of Allied prisoners of war (POWs) or internees, aircraft and airfields, weapons and ammunition. The status of broadcasting stations, radar and signal equipment, rolling stock, workshops, harbour facilities, war materials and food stocks were also to be reported. Charts of minefields and booby traps were also demanded. All documents, records, ciphers and codes would be handed over together with nominal rolls, orders of battle, lists of medical supplies, shops used by the Japanese and stocks of petrol and oil. A final clause insisted that all requisitioned or stolen goods and property were to be restored.

In addition, the Japanese were ordered to submit a list of all the graves of Allied troops and civilian internees. All Japanese flags, emblems and memorials other than graves were to be removed before the 5th Indian Division landed the following day.

These were unacceptable demands. Itagaki had to act to ensure that he was able to negotiate a more conditional surrender. On returning to the conference table, he was insistent that the Japanese view prevail. One of the main clauses he wanted amended was the instruction for the Japanese forces to be reduced immediately and marched to the mainland. Itagaki argued that no quarters existed there, north of Johor Bahru.

Itagaki: ... The present situation is that we are just removing to the Jurong district and the temporary barracks are only half-finished. If we are to be ordered to the mainland, it would make a terrible mess of everything. If possible, we should like to be given a certain amount of time in which we could prepare for the secondary movement.

He said it was difficult to maintain law and order on the mainland in view of the actions of certain elements, chiefly communists, and suggested they should be concentrated on the Indonesian islands of Munda and Bintan.

However, Christison would not compromise. This was a surrender and not a treaty negotiation. He promptly told Itagaki that the Japanese 46th Division was still armed and would be able to defend itself in a move to the mainland. Mansergh noted that the 46th Division would be allowed to keep only small arms but would be disarmed once the 5th Indian Division took over responsibility for the area. Moreover, as the Indonesian islands Itagaki mentioned were part of Dutch territory, Christison said the Dutch would have had to agree to the proposal first. Until then, Japanese forces would have to move to Johor.

Itagaki also wanted to remove the clause prohibiting reprisals against anti-Japanese resistance and guerrilla forces.

Itagaki: We do not take reprisals for anything that has happened in the past, but in the future, it will be difficult for us to distinguish if they are really guerilla (*sic*) forces or whether they are unattached and are persons who are attacking us from purely personal motives. We will have to protect ourselves and it is difficult for us to discriminate.

Christison: These guerilla (*sic*) forces will be in uniform and will wear a uniform like this (he produced an officer wearing the uniform) and they will wear a beret with three stars like this one.

Fukudome: We can give you an actual incident where, after the cessation of hostilities, a person wearing that cap approached Japanese Naval personnel and told them to help the Allies now (that) the war was over. He was in possession of a machine gun. He called himself a Communist. It happened in the southernmost part of the Malayan Peninsula, and he tried to get the Japanese to join his party. It is difficult for us to distinguish that sort of person.

Holland: How can you guard against this sort of thing? Such acts were only committed by individuals and not by battalions.

Christison:	This is the general policy. Such personnel will be treated by you as though they were Allied Forces. They all know hostilities have ceased and any hostile acts by them shall be resisted by you and the individual handed over to us.
Itagaki:	It will be difficult for any Japanese Army personnel to resist a person who carries arms.
Christison:	We are leaving you the 46th Division until our arrival. You can take what action you like against hostile acts. Call on General Mansergh if you want any help.

There was no option but to accede. Itagaki and Fukudome reluctantly agreed to the terms.

The only clause where the Japanese won a reprieve was on the issue of saluting and the surrender of swords. The Japanese delegates refused to budge on the point, insisting that as these were not terms outlined in Rangoon, they needed permission first from Field Marshal Terauchi, Commander-in-Chief of the Japanese Southern Army. As such, the clause was held in abeyance but was nonetheless implemented shortly after the reoccupation.

Mansergh also issued additional orders to Itagaki to ensure that the 5th Indian Division could take over quickly[8]. Orders issued to the Japanese commander of Singapore island instructed every member of the "Japanese forces and puppet forces" that still remained on the island to wear a white armband. Mansergh also ordered all Japanese wives, families and members of the "Japanese comfort corps" to accompany their various formations during the withdrawal from the island. However, hospital staff were to remain on duty and the Japanese were instructed to leave a guard or sentry at all buildings that were vacated in order to prevent looting during the transition period.

At about 4.00pm, the two Japanese officers again left the dining room as the instrument was retyped. At 6.05pm, a little more than seven hours after the meeting first began, General Itagaki and Vice Admiral Fukudome signed the surrender agreement and handed over close to 96,000 Japanese troops in Singapore to less than 10,000 Allied troops on the seas off the island.

Fukudome, who had smiled and winked at the enemy commanders during the meeting and was at pains to convey his goodwill, smiled and saluted as he left the room, continuing his efforts to ingratiate himself with the British commanders. Itagaki, however, appeared to be a broken man. He wept as he walked out of the room, no longer a general but a "surrendered enemy personnel".

And so came the actual surrender of Japanese forces in Singapore on 4 September 1945. This almost-secret surrender was never publicised. In the following days, even major British newspapers did not mention the Singapore surrender but only reported that British forces were nearing Singapore. The British Government and Allied media were more concerned with the official surrender of the Japanese in Singapore's City Hall on 12 September 1945. It did not matter that Japanese forces in Southeast Asia had already effectively signed a surrender of troops in the region on 28 August 1945 in Rangoon. The drama and pomp of the official surrender were important in order to show that the British had returned and were in full control, even if the 4 September ceremony on the *Sussex* had already signalled their return to the region in force, with the strategic and symbolic recapture of Burma and Singapore.

Mountbatten's strategy for the reoccupation of British territories in Southeast Asia was to create an impression of a takeover by superior forces. If the Japanese were made to believe that they were outnumbered, they would be less likely to consider a counterattack. More importantly, it would help to instil order and calm among the recently liberated Asian populace, who had remained in a power vacuum for almost a month during the so-called phoney surrender period between the surrender of the Japanese and the arrival of Allied forces to enforce a reoccupation.

Singapore, being Britain's jewel in the Far East and the symbolic site of its defeat at Japanese hands in 1942, had to be retaken at speed and with as much pomp and pageantry as possible. The reoccupation of Singapore was so crucial to British strategy that it occurred four days before the recapture of the rest of Malaya. The official surrender ceremonies could be held later and it was only after the Allied troops landed on the beaches of Morib and Sepang on the mainland that Mountbatten had his moment of glory on the steps of City Hall.

The famous images of Mountbatten accepting the Japanese surrender from Itagaki in the City Hall chambers are what most people would identify with from that time. The official surrender ceremony, however, would never have taken place had the signing and agreement on board *HMS Sussex* not happened. Within a day of the *Sussex* surrender, 35,000 Japanese troops were transported off the island to be housed in prisoner camps in southern Johor.

Although the events of 12 September 1945 closed the chapter on the Japanese military domination of Asia, they also marked the beginnings of the communist insurgency in Southeast Asia. The British were not completely prepared to resume control of the region and the resulting phoney surrender period led to huge communal clashes between the Malays, Chinese and the Indians. The communist-inspired Malayan People's Anti-Japanese Army (MPAJA) killed those whom they accused of having collaborated with the Japanese forces—and later those identified as non-sympathisers—in their bid to form a communist state. Where once the races were able to live and work side-by-side under British rule, this period of lawlessness and retribution, accentuated by the years of Japanese repression, planted some of the seeds of hatred and contempt each ethnic group held towards the other, a problem that would plague the post-war road to independence.

Like many other aspects of the end of the war in Singapore and Malaya, the proceedings of the Japanese surrender on board *HMS Sussex*, although partly reported in Allied newspapers of the time, have long been forgotten and are remembered by only a select few who were intimately involved in the top-secret recapture of British possessions in Malaya and Singapore at the end of the Second World War.

The events that led to the signing on board *HMS Sussex* are also just as mysterious and intriguing and go to the heart of explaining what actually happened in the closing days of the war and how Singapore and Malaya came to be liberated in September 1945.

Using highly sensitive documents and files that have only just been opened to the public, close to 60 years after the event, this book traces some of the most secret operations and plans undertaken to liberate Singapore and Malaya, revealing the last remaining secrets of the end of the war in Singapore and Malaya.

From the top secret TIDERACE operations to retake Penang and Singapore, to the final fate of secret agents like Lim Bo Seng, the story of the liberation of Singapore and Malaya has its foundations in the fall of Singapore on 15 February 1942.

Endnotes

1 Ammentorp, Steen. "Biography of Seishiro Itagaki". *The Generals of WWII.* [Internet]. Accessed 28 January 2005. Available from: <http://www.generals.dk/general/Itagaki/Seishiro/Japan.html>.

2 *SMC 857/17, No 74490 AK3, 17 September 1945, WO203/2308.* London: The National Archives.

3 Harrington, Joseph D. *Yankee Samurai: The Secret Role of Nisei in America's Pacific Victory.* Detroit: Pettigrew Enterprises, 1979. 190–91, 195–97.

4 *Letter of Proceedings – OPERATION TIDERACE. 18 September 1945, ADM116/5562.* London: The National Archives. 3.

5 Ammentorp, Steen. "Biography of Sir Alexander Frank Philip Christison". *The Generals of WWII.* [Internet]. Accessed 28 January 2005. Available from: <http://www.generals.dk/general/Christison/Sir_Alexander_Frank_Philip/Great_Britain.html>.

6 *Verbatim Report at Meeting on board* HMS Sussex, *4 September 1945, between Representatives of the Supreme Allied Commander, Southeast Asia, and Representatives of Field Marshal Count Terauchi, Supreme Japanese Commander, Southern Region. 3408/E.I.14232/45, 27 October 1945, ADM116/5562.* London: The National Archives. 1–14.

7 *Instructions to the Japanese Forces under Command or Control of Japanese Commanders Singapore Area. 4 September 1945, ADM116/5562.* London: The National Archives. 1, Appendices A, B, C, D.

8 *Orders of the Commander Occupying Force to the Japanese Commander of Singapore. 31 August 1945, WO203/2308.* London: The National Archives. 1–2.

Chapter 2

The British Pacific Policy and the End of the War

The fall of Malaya and Singapore in 70 days with the loss of close to 125,000 British and Commonwealth troops along with a huge amount of war material was an enormous blow to the British war effort. More importantly, the loss of the major supplier of the world's rubber and tin meant that they would have to find other sources for these crucial materials of war.

Although Britain had been forcibly ejected from Southeast Asia and moved slowly in developing a Pacific strategy, one thing remained clear after the devastating defeats in late 1941 and early 1942. It did not see the discontinuation of the British presence in Southeast Asia as the end of imperial rule[1] but as a setback. Many held the view, expressed in 1945, by then British foreign secretary, Sir Anthony Robert Eden, that there was "not the slightest question of liquidating the British empire"[2].

Regardless, just as in the First World War, Britain could not hope to triumph without American assistance. However, because American pre-war foreign policy was anti-imperialist by nature, getting their help in recapturing former British colonies would be a real challenge. More importantly, the war against Germany was viewed as much more crucial with the majority of Allied forces and material headed for the European theatre. Nonetheless, the appointment of Lord Louis Mountbatten as the Supreme Allied Commander, Southeast Asia (SACSEA), at Quebec in August 1943 put Britain in a position to restore its place as a great power in Southeast Asia[3].

The biggest challenge facing British planners lay in how to deploy its meagre resources against the Japanese. With the loss of its colonies, the situation in Southeast Asia seemed bleak with Eden noting that, "there was nothing for it but to wait and hold our end up as best we could, leaving most of the talk and proposing to others", namely the Americans[4].

However, the surrender of the Italian navy in September 1943 and the disabling of the German battleship *Tirpitz* helped free up British naval forces from home waters and the Mediterranean, allowing British military planners to take a fresh look at Southeast Asia.

British Prime Minister Winston S Churchill was also keen to recapture British possessions in Southeast Asia, hoping that if the inhabitants of these territories saw the British as liberators, they could expunge the shame of defeat and rebuild the British Empire. During 1944, Churchill, supported by the Foreign Office and Southeast Asia Command (SEAC), argued with the British chiefs of staff for an attack against north Sumatra, codenamed Operation CULVERIN[5].

Lacking adequate intelligence on Japanese troop strength in Malaya and Sumatra, the chiefs strongly disagreed, with many feeling it better to send land and air forces to Australia, in support of the American flank towards the Philippines and Formosa (Taiwan). Also, American planners were concerned about CULVERIN, which some felt might undermine the position of General Douglas MacArthur, the newly appointed Supreme Allied Commander of the Southwest Pacific Area.

Throughout 1944, the differences in opinion between Churchill and his chiefs left senior British military leaders frustrated. During discussions on plans for Southeast Asia, Churchill kept insisting on operations against the tip of Sumatra and refused to look at anything else. As these meetings dragged on endlessly, Field Marshal Sir Alan Brooke, the chief of the Imperial General Staff, wrote in his diary that Churchill had:

> ... lost the power of giving a decision. He finds every possible excuse to avoid giving one. His arguments are becoming puerile, for instance he upheld this evening that an attack on the tip of Sumatra would force a withdrawal of Japanese forces in northern Burma and would liquidate our commitment in this area. We have conferred for 7 hours!!! with him today to settle absolutely nothing. Nor has he produced a single argument during the whole of that period that was worth listening to. I am at my wits' end and can't go on much longer[6]!

By 10 August 1944, with recent successes in Imphal and Kohima, a strategy for an amphibious landing at Rangoon, codenamed Operation DRACULA, was approved by Churchill and the chiefs of staff. The plan would require American assistance in terms of air support and assault shipping but was accepted as it avoided a prolonged campaign in northern Burma[7].

However, Churchill continued to vacillate on the issue of the kind of offensive to take in the rest of Southeast Asia. As the war dragged on in Europe, the timetable for defeating Japan was once again extended, showing clearly the need for Soviet help. The Allies had hoped to start moving resources to Southeast Asia by the end of 1944 but with the failure of Operation MARKET GARDEN in Arnhem in September, and the Ardennes offensive in December, planners predicted that Germany would not be beaten before the winter of 1945[8]. The setback at Arnhem immediately removed crucial resources from DRACULA. The US joint chiefs of staff diverted two infantry divisions, scheduled for the Pacific in May 1945, to the European theatre.

By June 1945, the bloody battle for Okinawa had increased the pressure on US military and civilian leaders to bring the war to a quick end. With intelligence reports calculating between 30,000 to 60,000 troops moved to the Japanese islands to defend the homeland, plans for the invasion of Kyushu and Honshu were developed, codenamed Operation CORONET and Operation OLYMPIC, respectively. However, before the British could commit to an all-out effort in attacking the Japanese homeland, they needed to recapture Southeast Asia.

Cut off from the rest of the Japanese empire, the strategic value of the Japanese Southern Army in Southeast Asia had been greatly reduced by December 1944, after the loss of Leyte in the Philippines. Still, even though the Japanese forces were lacking munitions and men, staff planners at SEAC and the Joint Intelligence Committee (JIC) correctly anticipated that the Japanese would attempt to delay the advance of the British for as long as possible in Burma, Malaya, Indochina and Siam[9]. In an effort to divert Allied forces away from the homeland, the Japanese ordered a division from Sumatra to reinforce Siam and a division from Celebes to reinforce Singapore. In March 1945, the Japanese also assumed military control of French Vichy Indochina and reinforced it with three divisions. The commander-in-chief of the Southern Army, Count Hsiaichi Terauchi, had already based himself in Saigon in late 1944. The JIC predicted that it would take at least another 12 months to force a collapse of the Japanese position in Southeast Asia.

The British reached Rangoon in May 1945, successfully executing a scaled-down version of Operation DRACULA (Operation MODIFIED DRACULA). With the Japanese in retreat, SEAC planners began drafting an amphibious assault plan for the west coast of Malaya codenamed Operation ZIPPER, which was scheduled for September 1945. The plan called for the capture of advanced naval and air bases on Phuket island in Thailand (Operation ROGER) and Penang island in Malaya (Operation JURIST) before the activation of Operation ZIPPER. The invasion of Singapore island, codenamed Operation MAILFIST, would then occur relatively soon after ZIPPER was launched, by which time the Allied troops who had landed on the west coast would have forced the Japanese into retreat down the Malayan peninsula.

However, SEAC Intelligence reports indicated that ZIPPER and MAILFIST would face an uphill challenge as the Japanese were already planning a strong defence of Malaya:

> With the fall of Rangoon, it has become increasingly evident that the Japanese anticipate an early assault on Malaya itself. Consequently, a considerable strengthening and allocation of troops is now taking place, including the reported arrival of up to four battalions from SIAM, although in view of the size of the garrison in SIAM, it is possible that these troops originally came from F.I.C. (French Indochina) In addition, elements of 37th Division are reported to have arrived in Bangkok from F.I.C. in early July. The possibility arises, therefore, that this division is also in transit to MALAYA... The garrison in MALAYA... will probably be further reinforced by the retention there of all troops arriving from N.E.I. (Netherland East Indies).... It is obvious that the Japanese regard SINGAPORE as our ultimate objective, but it is difficult to say which they consider the most likely area for the initial assault...[10].

Intelligence indicated the Japanese had more than 24 infantry battalions and 75 tanks in Malaya amounting to more than 59,000 troops. This, they believed, would rise to 29 infantry battalions, or about 72,000 troops, and 75 tanks by ZIPPER's D-day[11]. To counter this, ZIPPER called for the massing of the 5th, 23rd, 25th and 26th Indian Divisions, the 3rd commando brigade and one parachute brigade of the British 6th Airborne Division, amounting to more than 100,000 troops. Even so, British intelligence expected "formidable opposition to coastal landings at major bases is likely to be presented by base forces and guard forces consisting of naval shore-based troops, roughly equivalent to our marines"[12].

However, this planning went into a tailspin with the dissolution of the British coalition government on 23 May 1945 in preparation for a general election in July 1945. The first shock came with the sudden announcement by the intervening caretaker government for the quick release of personnel serving in the various theatres of war. This, compounded by the fact that the War Office planned to reduce the army's overseas tour of duty by four months, left planners frustrated. In an exchange with the chief of Imperial General Staff (CIGS), the commander-in-chief of the Allied Land Forces in Southeast Asia, Lieutenant General Sir Oliver Leese, noted that the planned tour of duty reduction, codenamed PYTHON, would reduce forces for ZIPPER and MAILFIST from seven to six divisions. In addition, heavy cross-posting of officers and men between all divisions in Burma would also be necessary to replenish the depleted ZIPPER divisions mounted from there, causing a "considerable strain on all formations since they will have to reorganise concurrently with their task of completing the annihilation of the Japs in Burma"[13]. As there was no way to repatriate officers and other ranks whose tour of duty would end just before ZIPPER, these troops would have to stay in India and Burma for several months before they could be sent home, creating morale and discipline problems. In order to defuse the situation, Mountbatten and the commander-in-chief, India, Field Marshal Sir Claude Auchinleck, agreed to suspend the implementation of PYTHON for troops taking part in ZIPPER.

To further ease the manpower situation, the chiefs of staff noted that only once Singapore was captured would priority be given to the creation of a Commonwealth force for the invasion of the Japanese isles[14].

As a result, British participation in the American-led CORONET and OLYMPIC was based on the premise of a quick recapture of Malaya and Singapore, with strategic planners indicating that Allied forces would have to face close to 96 Japanese divisions in the final fight for the Japanese home islands. Although Churchill gave his approval for ZIPPER and MAILFIST, the assault phase of ZIPPER and the entire MAILFIST plan was never carried out as the war ended very abruptly. By then, Churchill was also out of government with Clement Attlee taking over as prime minister.

American President Harry Truman's decision to drop the atomic bomb on Hiroshima on 6 August 1945 and a second bomb on Nagasaki on 9 August 1945 resulted in the Japanese surrender on 15 August 1945.

The sudden surrender meant that SEAC planning for the amphibious invasion to recapture their possessions in Southeast Asia had quickly been superseded by events. They would now have to move fast in order to reclaim their territories from the surrendering Japanese before a power vacuum developed.

On 4 August 1945, Mountbatten's American deputy, Lieutenant General Raymond Wheeler, on learning from his chief that the Americans were about to end the war shortly, ordered SEAC planners in Colombo to come up with a plan to recapture Singapore ahead of a modified ZIPPER, which would now be carried out sans heavy armaments and assault troops and without the Singapore component[15]. The recapture of Rangoon in May 1945 and the decision by Mountbatten to advance directly to Malaya, instead of first seizing Phuket, made it unnecessary to implement ROGER. Singapore would have to be recaptured as the primary objective as fast as possible, as part of a separate plan. So, a top-secret plan was hatched specifically to capture Britain's most prized possessions in the Far East. The emergency reoccupation of Singapore (SHACKLE)[16] and Penang (FLASHLIGHT) would involve a large naval and air force with the 5th Indian Division and the 3rd commando brigade. Wheeler noted that this new top-secret plan, codenamed TIDERACE, should not interfere with ZIPPER but rather spearhead the recapture of Southeast Asia. He concurred with his planners that it was crucial to reoccupy Penang first before taking Singapore:

> On strong representations of Commanders-in-Chief, I agreed that the first phase of this operation was to reoccupy FLASHLIGHT... in order to provide a firm advanced naval and air base, from which to advance to SHACKLE[17].

The planners rushed out an outline plan for TIDERACE in less than four days. The 30-page document outlined the plan to "occupy SINGAPORE as soon as possible after the capitulation by the Japanese government, securing as a preliminary measure an advance anchorage and all-weather air base"[18].

It noted that once the capitulation of the Japanese in Singapore had been negotiated,

> ... it is essential that the occupying forces arrive as quickly as possible and in the maximum possible strength for the maintenance of law and order and for purposes of prestige. It follows, therefore, that the occupying forces

> should be at least one division in strength, with maximum show of naval and air forces. Furthermore, this division should arrive as a whole or at least be concentrated on the island by the evening of the day on which the landing takes place[18].

Planners stressed the importance of capturing Penang first as "the advanced anchorage and air base should include an airfield which can be used in all weathers as a staging base for the fly in of the 5th Division to SINGAPORE, if required. This condition is met only at PENANG where the airfield is all-weather and believed to be in good condition"[20].

X-day would mark the date on which the operation would begin. On X+12, the force, to be mounted from Ceylon and Burma, would arrive off Penang and a demonstration by Liberator aircraft from Rangoon, including leaflet-dropping, would take place. A cruiser with two destroyers would then proceed to a position approximately two miles off Fort Cornwallis. Known as Operation JURIST, the sub-plan to retake Penang would see SACSEA's representative and the naval force commander, who would already be on board, negotiate the surrender of the Japanese forces there. On the completion of negotiations, the naval force commander would then be transferred to a destroyer, which would remain in Penang while the cruiser headed down to Singapore.

Meanwhile, a minesweeping force would start clearing a channel in the Straits of Malacca. The cruiser with SACSEA's representative would then arrive at Phillip Strait in the morning of X+14, passing through the swept channels. The Japanese garrison commanders would then be ordered out to the ships where negotiations would be carried out for the surrender of the garrisons in Singapore and Malaya[21]. Should this prove successful, the 5th Division would then land on Singapore at dawn on X+15, with the first objective being the Keppel docks and Kallang Airfield. As soon as the docks were occupied, the remaining convoy would be signalled in.

Should the Japanese put up a strong resistance, the plan called for the force to abandon the operation and await the beginning of ZIPPER, which would have a small assault force. TIDERACE was to be an occupying force and was thus not equipped to deal with any significant resistance.

Rear (later Vice) Admiral Cedric Holland was appointed the naval force commander and SACSEA's naval representative who would take the Japanese surrender in Singapore.

SACSEA's military representative was to be Major General Mansergh, general officer commanding (GOC) of the 5th Indian Division, the force that would reoccupy Singapore. The 5th Division, which had been serving in Burma, would temporarily report directly to headquarters, Allied Land Forces Southeast Asia (HQALFSEA), and later to the 15th Indian corps HQ, headed by Lieutenant General Christison.

> Thus, the reoccupation of Malaya would take place in three phases. Phase one would be the recapture of Penang island (Operation JURIST). Phase two would be the recapture of Singapore (Operation TIDERACE) by the 5th Indian Division and phase three would be the landing of the ZIPPER forces in the Port Dickson–Port Swettenham area in accordance with the original ZIPPER plan to reoccupy the rest of Malaya[22].

With the Japanese surrender on 15 August 1945, planning for TIDERACE went into overdrive.

Rear Admiral Holland held several planning meetings to work out the forces needed for TIDERACE. The first part of the operation would be to get the necessary force into Singapore at the earliest possible moment. The force, once landed, would need to complete three objectives: first, to "show the flag" and assume control from the Japanese; second, to deal with the prisoners of war (POWs) and internees; and third, to disarm and contain the Japanese forces[23].

SEAC planners were also concerned about the way Allied troops were to treat Japanese forces and outlined several broad considerations that would have to be taken into account in determining this policy[24], namely how the local population would deal with the continuation of Japanese rule after the Japanese surrender announcement but before the British resumed control; the need to impress upon the Japanese the strength of the Allies and the magnitude of the Japanese defeat as well as the need to raise the morale of the local population.

The problems of internal security would also require urgent attention, and much information would have to be gathered to obtain an adequate estimate of conditions. The immediate relief and early repatriation of Allied POWs would be the first call upon TIDERACE's resources. The treatment of Japanese prisoners were also a concern:

> A further problem is the treatment to be accorded to the surrendered Japanese and to Japanese civilians remaining in occupied territories (this will presumably have to be covered in surrender orders). Closely connected with this is the necessity to bring home both to the Japanese and to local populations the magnitude of our victory. Propaganda organisations and film and photographic units will have to cover the Japanese surrender and ensure that the maximum worldwide publicity is given both to it and to the successive acts of liberation by Allied forces[25].

Holland, however, only saw a very limited role for himself as SACSEA's naval representative and Naval Force Commander in that he "stated that his responsibilities in this operation only extended until Commander 5th Division was established ashore and was satisfied that he had secured the island of Singapore"[26]. Therefore, most of these considerations of policy towards Japanese forces and surrendered Japanese personnel were left to Major General Mansergh and the various departments at SACSEA.

Holland did not see the usefulness of clandestine resistance groups operating in Malaya like Force 136 in helping to contact the Japanese in Malaya or in helping the 5th Indian Division gain control of Singapore. With the Japanese defeat, the thinking was that the Japanese would no longer put up a resistance so there was no need for clandestine forces. However, the eventual threat that Force 136 was crucial in stemming, as will be seen later, did not originate from the Japanese. As a result of Holland's approach, Major General William RC Penney, SEAC's Intelligence Director, instructed the head of 'P' division (Clandestine Operations) that Force 136's "... role during the occupation was to supply information and to keep the guerrillas quiet"[27].

Holland also noted that the phasing in of the 15th Indian corps HQ, which would take charge of Mansergh's 5th Indian Division, did not concern TIDERACE. This disregard for the setting up of the corps HQ to command the ground troops in Singapore meant Holland was to be surprised later when, just before the surrender proceedings, instead of Mansergh, Christison turned up to accept the Japanese surrender as Mountbatten's military representative.

Setting the date for X-Day also proved a formidable challenge as this was dependent on when General MacArthur would take the Japanese surrender in Tokyo. It was only after the Tokyo surrender that any other official surrender could take place. When it became clear that the surrender ceremony in Tokyo Bay would take place on 2 September, the go-ahead was given for TIDERACE's X-Day. The constantly changing date for the Tokyo surrender meant X-Day was postponed three times before it was finally fixed as 21 August 1945[28].

However, with X-Day set for 21 August, British convoys would only arrive in Malayan waters on 2 September at the earliest. They would not be able to take over from the Japanese in Singapore until 5 September. Worse still, ZIPPER would only be implemented on 9 September. As Emperor Hirohito announced Japan's surrender on 15 August, this meant that most of Malaya and Southeast Asia would remain in a power vacuum for close to a month; the time that it would take TIDERACE and ZIPPER to be implemented.

Appreciating the need to shorten this phoney surrender period, Mountbatten, on 20 August, a day before X-Day, sent a signal in the clear to Japanese Field Marshal Count Hsiaichi Terauchi, commander-in-chief of the Southern Army, in Saigon:

> You are to send a representative or representatives with plenipotentiary powers to meet my Chief of Staff at RANGOON on Thursday, 23 August, to arrange the orderly surrender of all Japanese land, sea, air and auxiliary forces in the area of your command. Your plenipotentiaries are to bring your official seal of office and your written, signed and sealed authorisation that they are fully empowered to act on your behalf.
>
> These representatives are to travel in not more than two unarmed aircraft to be provided by you. These aircraft are to be painted all white and are to bear upon the side of the fuselage and top and bottom of each wing green crosses easily recognisable at 500 yards[29].

The representatives were ordered to bring details on the strengths and locations of troops and equipment, charts of all minefields and swept channels, airfields, aircraft, location and status of Allied POWs, submarines, ships, stocks of food, petrol, hospitals, rubber stocks and radio stations in the region. As instructed, the Japanese acknowledged receipt of this signal through a broadcast on Saigon Radio that was repeated every hour for six hours on 22 August 1945.

Now the stage was set for the first surrender meeting in Rangoon—but the decision to allow a phoney surrender period in Malaya would come to haunt British forces. The clandestine resistance movements built by the

Special Operations Executive's Force 136 in the jungles of Malaya would now become a formidable force to be reckoned with, marking the start of insurgent problems for the returning British.

Endnotes

1 Baxter, Christopher. "In Pursuit of a Pacific Strategy: British Planning for the Defeat of Japan, 1943–45". *Diplomacy & Statecraft,* vol. 15, no. 2, June 2004. 253–277.

2 Eden, Anthony R. *Minute for Churchill, PREM 4/31/4.* London: The National Archives, 8 January 1945.

3 Baxter, 2004. 254.

4 Eden, Anthony R. *The Eden Memoirs: The Reckoning.* London: Cassell, 1965. 425–426.

5 Baxter, 2004. 256.

6 Brooke, Field Marshal Alan F. "Diary Entry for 8 August 1944". *War Diaries 1939–1945: Field Marshal Lord Alanbrooke.* London: Weidenfeld and Nicolson, 2001. 578.

7 Baxter, 2004. 258.

8 Ibid. 261.

9 *Japanese Strategy and Capacity to Resist, JIC(45)136(0)(Final), 28 April 1945, CAB 81/128.* London: The National Archives.

10 *Estimate of Enemy Situation and Reaction to Operation ZIPPER, No.35094/ GSI(a)(iii), Main HQ ALFSEA, 17 July 1945, WO 203/4489.* London: The National Archives.

11 Ibid. 5.

12 Ibid. 3.

13 *Personal for CIGS from LEESE infm Supreme Allied Commander and C-in-C India, TAC 3503, 170800 June 1945, WO 203/2158.* London: The National Archives.

14 *Portal, Minute, COS(45)124. CAB 79/33.* London: The National Archives, 11 May 1945.

15 *For Mountbatten From Wheeler, KANMO 237, 110945Z August 1945, WO 203/2158.* London: The National Archives.

16 In order to preserve operational security, key locations were referred to in code in the planning and operational documents. Singapore was referred to as SHACKLE, while Penang was codenamed FLASHLIGHT.

17 Ibid.

18 *Outline Plan for Operation TIDERACE, 8 August 1945, WO 203/2157*. London: The National Archives.

19 Ibid. 1.

20 Ibid. 2.

21 Ibid. 6.

22 *ALFSEA Operational Directive No. 7, 10146/G(O)1, 12 August 45, WO 203/2308*. London: The National Archives.

23 *Aide Memoire on Japanese Capitulation, Conference Secretariat Minute 5/212, 11 August 1945, WO 203/2158*. London: The National Archives.

24 Ibid.

25 Ibid. Appendix B: 3.

26 *Minutes of a Meeting of TIDERACE Planners Held in Hut 121G HQSACSEA at 1030 Hours on Sunday 12 August 1945, TR/001/A, WO 203/3104*. London: The National Archives.

27 Ibid. 2.

28 *TIDERACE Postponed, August 251215Z, C.IN.C. E.I.F., WO 203/2307*. London: The National Archives.

29 *From Admiral Lord Louis Mountbatten SACSEA For Field Marshal Count Terauchi, Commander Japanese Southern Army, 201341Z August 1945, HS1/328*. London: The National Archives.

Chapter 3

Clandestine Forces

Much has been said about the role of the Special Operations Executive (SOE) in clandestine operations in Southeast Asia during the Japanese occupation. As the battles raged during the Malayan Campaign, SOE's Orient Mission, led by Basil Goodfellow, had trained groups that were left behind enemy lines in a bid to help build resistance and carry out sabotage missions against the Japanese.

In the last days before the fall of Singapore, the SOE also began training Chinese nationalists who would help resist the Japanese onslaught. Training was also carried out for Chinese communists, who had been released from British jails in Singapore and Malaya, forming small brigades of fighters who had initially put up token resistance against the Japanese when they invaded the island.

By late 1942, however, these Chinese nationalists and communists had taken to the jungles of Malaya and begun organising themselves as a guerrilla army. The SOE trained and put behind enemy lines a total of some 365 Chinese communists, including a Special Intelligence Service (MI6) team with a wireless set. However, the sets available in 1942 were not powerful enough to transmit to the SOE Far East Operations base in India and the groups simply disappeared into the Malayan jungle.

Although Lieutenant Colonel (later Colonel) Frederick Spencer Chapman was commander of the 11 European groups which the Orient Mission had planted in enemy-held Malaya in early 1942, nothing had been heard from them for more than a year. With the loss of Malaya, two Orient Mission officers, Captain (later Major) Richard Neville Broome and Major (later Colonel) John Davis, based themselves in Sumatra to maintain contact with clandestine groups operating in Malaya. Following the Japanese occupation of Sumatra, they sailed a native junk across the Indian Ocean to India where they joined SOE's India Mission. The India Mission, led by Colin Hercules Mackenzie and Gavin Stewart, later became known as Force 136[1].

The India Mission initially lacked both men and materials and was attempting to build a base of recruits. It initially operated out of Calcutta. However, with the creation of the Malayan Section, operations moved to Meerut. While in Calcutta, Broome and Davis spent their time unsuccessfully searching for Chinese, Indians and Malays who had escaped from Singapore. Amongst those interviewed were hundreds of Chinese seamen stranded by the war[2]. Many were illiterate and others simply unsuitable. None of the men were willing to go back into Japanese-occupied Malaya. Then, they met a young Straits-born Chinese businessman named Lim Bo Seng.

Lim Bo Seng and Operation Gustavus

Lim was born in China on 27 April 1909. He and his family migrated to Malaya when he was a boy. In 1925, when he was 16, the family moved to Singapore. There, he continued his studies at Raffles Institution and in 1928 passed his Senior Cambridge Examinations. He then furthered his studies at the University of Hong Kong.

Like many overseas Chinese of his time, Lim was a Chinese patriot. In the 1930s, when Japan's actions in China became increasingly hostile, Lim, who was now back in Singapore, became active in raising funds for anti-Japanese activities.

He was violently anti-Japanese and during the 70 days leading to the fall of Singapore he had mobilised thousands of Chinese into the Civil Defence Corps. Many of them would lose their lives once the Japanese took over, massacred by their new rulers in the infamous *Sook Ching* operation just days after the British surrender. Lim escaped and turned up in Calcutta where he joined the SOE team. Taking advantage of his top-level contacts with nationalist government officials in Chungking, Lim made two trips to China

John Davis and Lim Bo Seng: Davis and Lim worked very closely during the GUSTAVUS operation.

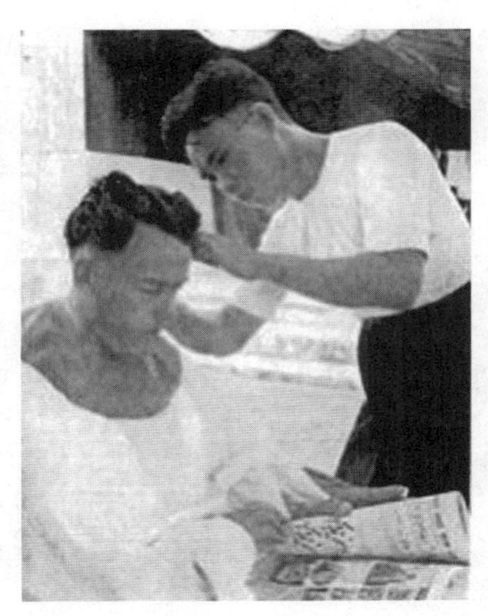

Richard Broome: Having a haircut after the war.

to elicit support. A number of Malaya-born Chinese University students soon began to arrive in Pune for training. This group was codenamed DRAGONS.

Lim's top-secret personnel file, held in the MI6 archives and sealed for the last 60 years, was only declassified in January 2005. Among other things, it showed the trips to Chungking were not only a recruitment exercise but also involved an undertaking of a more personal nature[3].

Lim was director of Hock Ann & Co Ltd, one of several companies forming the Brick Selling Agency. The group sold bricks and material to the British in Singapore prior to the fall of the island. The Royal Navy had placed an order with the Brick Selling Agency for material worth $40,000 (Straits Settlements Dollars) and collected it prior to Singapore's fall. As a result of the quick defeat in Malaya, no payment had been made. In Chungking, Lim approached the British embassy in an attempt to get the money due to him.

The embassy contacted the former Malayan surveyor, who confirmed the contract to the senior surveyor, Ceylon and India. However, the Malayan surveyor noted that the contract was for only $4,447 (Straits Settlements Dollars). Moreover, he "regretted that payment could NOT be made except to the duly authorised agent of the Brick Selling Agency. If Mr Lim could produce a Power of Attorney, or similar instrument, authorising him to collect credit for the Brick Selling Agency, the matter would then be given consideration" [4]. It was further noted that Lim was director of "one of several companies forming the Brick Selling Agency, but as the bricks were sold by several companies of the agency, the matter could only be settled through the agency and NOT through a separate firm"[5].

As the bricks sold were actually solely from his company but transacted through the Brick Selling Agency, Lim was obviously frustrated that the monies owed to his company would not be paid. In the meantime, he had been placed in the Malayan Country Section (MCS) of the India Mission and Major FS Crawford, an agent at the Section, informed the embassy that there would be a "reply drafted after talk with Lim". With plans for insurgent operations in Malaya, Crawford recollected that Lim agreed to drop his demand for compensation until after the war[6]. The issue was given very short shrift after the war and correspondence in the files at the National Archives in London indicate that the matter was not raised further but was instead dropped quietly, without any mention being made to Lim's family or the remaining companies of the Brick Selling Agency[7]. As a result, the compensation owed to Lim and the agency has remained outstanding for more than 60 years.

Lim was interviewed by Lieutenant Colonel Basil Gerritsen Ivory, the officer who is believed to have headed the SOE's Chungking outfit. Ivory, along with the MCS in India, determined that Lim would be recruited as a senior member of the MCS Chinese Section and employed in the field as an agent.

Lim's rate of pay was set at RS 300 per month, increasing to RS 1,000 per month when he was in the field. Force 136 then undertook to look after the education of Lim's brother, who was studying in Calcutta, and paid him a monthly stipend of RS 300.

Designated agent No. BB 192, Lim went under the aliases of Tan and Tang, with the most common being that of Tan Choon Lim[8]. In signals to headquarters however, Lim was only referred to as 192, in order to protect his identity and that of his family. Lim was married to Gan Choo Neo and had seven children as well as an extended family who were still in Japanese-occupied Singapore.

In his enlistment record, it was noted that Lim's dependants would be entitled to a Major's pension when his death was established. In a signal to the Finance section after the war, the MCS noted that, "In a minute dated 20/9/43 and initialled by Col Ivory, it is stated that in the event of death, he (Lim) is entitled to Major's pension payable either as a lump sum or as an annual payment. This would be payable from the date of death, less any sums paid out thereafter"[9]. However, this simple pension would become a major issue after the war.

After being reunited with his brother in Calcutta, Lim joined forces with Davis and Broome. As soon as the nationalist Chinese Kuomintang (KMT) agents had been chosen, they had to be trained for their dangerous and specialised work. One of the agents Lim recruited was Tan Chong Tee. Tan (Ah Lim/Lim Song/Lim Soong/Lim Shu/Tan Tien Soong/Tan Thiam Seng) was born in Singapore in 1916 and had studied at the Kheng Cheng Primary School and Swatow Public Middle School in Singapore before attending the Chungking National University of Art:

> Upon the outbreak of the Second World War, I was furthering my studies in Chungking. Hearing that the Japanese had penetrated Malaya, causing untold suffering to numerous families, I decided to sacrifice my studies and respond to the call of the Central Government of China for volunteers to go to India for training in intelligence work. Accompanying me in the pioneer batch to depart from Chungking were Lim Mong Seng alias Tan Choon Lim (Lim Bo Seng)... We arrived at Calcutta by air and were received by Major Goldfarer (the liaison officer for Force 136). The next day, we departed by train for Poona (Pune), and from there by military transport to the Sungari Hills (Singarh Hills near Singarh Fort) for training. The training staffs were Captain Davies (*sic*), Captain Broome and many others[10].

By this time, Mackenzie, as one of the leaders of the India Mission, was also concerned about what should be done with the SOE-trained communist guerrillas that had been left behind in the Malayan jungles in January 1942. The India Mission decided to work with the guerrillas but adopted the stance that until plans were made to retake Malaya, the communists should be restricted to mounting attacks from their jungle bases, leaving the Japanese holding the towns. In the urban areas, where they had fomented industrial disputes prior to the war, they would continue to do so and carry out sabotage. This policy towards the communist guerrillas and the eventual supplying of weapons to the communist-backed Malayan People's Anti-Japanese Army (MPAJA) would, after the war, help the MCP in their armed insurgency against their wartime ally and colonial master.

The first step in rebuilding a British clandestine presence would be to insert a party of agents back into Malaya to make contact with the communists and to find out if Chapman and his stay behind parties were still alive. The first operation launched in Malaya was codenamed GUSTAVUS I. The party, consisting of five nationalist Chinese, was led by Davis. On 24 May 1943, the first group of Force 136 landed on the beaches off Lumut. After bumping into a Malay man and woman upon stepping ashore, Davis hid in a rubber estate and sent out the Chinese agents to make contact one at a time. An ethnic Hokkien Chinese man named Wu Chye Sin (Goh Meng Chye/Ah Ng) was chosen to go first not only because he was very keen and resourceful but because his dialect was commonly spoken in the area. He was dressed as a destitute and his cover story was left to his discretion.

Wu found a rubber-tapper overseer named Tan Kong Cheng (Kong Ching) and his wife, "to whom he had spun his hard-luck story, only to be told uncompromisingly that he did not speak or look the part. He changed his ground accordingly and, after 24 hours of almost non-stop talk, these people became his staunchest friends and agreed to go to all lengths to help him once they were assured he was not a guerrilla—of whose extortions they appeared to be very much afraid"[11].

Another of one Davis' agents, Lung Chiu Ying (Ah Loong/Ah Long/Ah Ying/Ah Eng), had chosen to get work at a coffeeshop in order to gather information and meet the other agents. He found himself at a shop in Segari market near the bus station. Very understaffed, the owner offered him $10 (Straits Settlements Dollars) a month as "under-coolie"[12]. In half-an-hour, he was at work, with the proprietor having promised to obtain the necessary paperwork. One of his first customers was Wu, who was surprised to see Lung established so quickly. Lung was happy with the arrangement and the owner of the shop also turned out to be a good friend of Tan Kong Cheng.

In the meantime, Li Han Kwang (Lee Han Kwong/Lee Tsing/Lee Ah Cheng), Davis' third agent, crossed by boat to Pangkor island to start making arrangements for a boat to take Davis out to the submarine rendezvous (RV) point:

> He crossed over without difficulty, but once there, his apparent aimlessness was noted by a Malay policeman, who questioned him. Being unable to give any satisfactory answers, Tsing (Li Han Kwang) blustered indignantly and insisted on being searched. Fortunately, though dressed in his oldest clothes, he had $60 in his pocket, and this re-assured the policeman, as the poorer a Chinese was in Malaya at that time, the more suspect he was. Nevertheless, Tsing was arrested and taken to the police station, where he insisted he was able to obtain a guarantor. He was allowed to go unescorted to find one. He went straight to the shop of a Toochew (*sic*) he had met on the boat. With some hesitation, the man sent a coolie to the police station to vouch for Tsing. The Malay corporal would not accept the guarantee, but let Tsing go, saying that he would make a very thorough investigation the next day. The Toochew then introduced Tsing to the only person who could really help him—the unofficial headman of the village, Choy (Chua Koon Eng)[13].

Once Chua was persuaded to help, he set about creating a proper cover for Li. He introduced Li as the son of an old acquaintance and set him up as a fishmonger. The next day, Li returned to report to Davis with a present of fresh fish. Within a week, he had gotten so effective that his new firm had already sent two consignments of fish down the coast. It would obviously be much easier to keep RVs if it could be combined with legitimate trading. However, to do this, it was necessary to borrow a boat from Chua and to get his help in arranging the trading voyage. It was impossible not to tell Chua the real reasons for the trip and, on being told, he agreed to take responsibility for all shipping arrangements. Chua also told Li he was in touch with 800 guerrillas in Setiawan. Li then arranged to meet Davis and sail from Pangkor on 25 June 1943 in order to make GUSTAVUS' first RV.

With GUSTAVUS I landed and operational, GUSTAVUS II was infiltrated into Malaya. This second group consisted of Broome and three other Chinese agents: wireless operator Liang Yuan Ming (Lee Choon/Lee Chuen), agent Yi Tian Song (Chan Siak Foo/Tan Shi Fu/Tan Sek Fu) and Tan Chong Tee. Although GUSTAVUS II reached Malaya, "Davis considered the presence of more than one European an embarrassment at that stage, (so) it was decided that he alone, with Lee Chuen, Ah Lim and Sek Fu should go in on the next sortie"[14]. Davis returned to Colombo with GUSTAVUS II and returned to Malaya on 27 July 1943 on GUSTAVUS III. On 12 September, Broome arrived in Malaya on GUSTAVUS IV.

By this time, the network in Malaya had expanded considerably, noted Broome:

> The initial success of our organisation in Perak was entirely due to Ah Ng (Wu Chye Sin), whose outstanding ability, good sense, courage and initiative made him the key man from the beginning. In a way, this was unfortunate, in that the other men relied on him and visited him far too much. After launching himself as a relative of Tom (Tan Kong Cheng) at Segari, he quickly gained a great deal of influence both there and in Lumut, and before long had started a business in Ipoh. This business was a shady concern of mushroom growth similar to many that have sprung up since the occupation. It dealt in rice, lubricating oil, gold, etc., all articles which are unlawfully traded in and mostly smuggled. It brought about the most valuable contacts, including Japs, who like making money on the side. Many people with a certain amount of 'pull' were thus compromised and available to us. The locally recruited newspaper man, Lee (Moh Wing Pun), was installed as Ng's (Wu) manager in the Ipoh office and Ah Lim (Tan) became the Lumut representative[15].

Davis was more blunt about Wu's business venture, where the "(e)mphasis was on a 'get rich quick and no questions asked' basis"[16]. Broome noted that:

> ...the extent of Ah Ng's (Wu) achievement before the collapse may be judged by the fact that he was chief owner of a motorboat operating between Singapore and North Malaya and also had a lorry and private car. He was on good terms with several high-ranking Chinese detectives, some of whom were satisfactorily compromised and who expected to warn him of any impending action by the Japs. Ng himself was well aware of his danger through the connection with Bill (Chua Koon Eng) and was always trying to clear himself of this embarrassment, but the fact that we had had to rely on Bill in the initial stages put a burden on the whole of our organisation which could never be shaken off[17].

The field operatives were always short of funds and in March 1944, Lim Bo Seng would finally leave his hideout in the jungle to help sort out this problem[18]. However in October 1943, Lim Bo Seng was still safely ensconced in Colombo, training more field agents and operators for future operations in Malaya. On 1 November 1943, the *o24*, a Dutch submarine commandeered for use by Force 136, surfaced off Sembilan island in the Straits of Malacca to land the GUSTAVUS V party led by Lim. In country, Lim was to be known as Tan Choon Lim. Many of the SOE's wireless sets were too heavy (450lbs) to be carried into the jungle camps and had to be buried. So, when Lim arrived with two 30lb sets, they were prized assets. Much of the supplies Lim brought along were lost as they were transported ashore. As the guerrillas needed arms, medicine, vitamins and money, these items were to be included in the next shipment. However, after the January 1944 RV, most of the following ones would be missed, leading to a huge shortage of funds and supplies.

Davis noted that Lim arrived in camp at the end of November, having travelled by car. His stores were all left at Jenderata to be brought up when possible as the Japanese were very active throughout the Bidor and Telok Anson areas at the time[19].

By January, a representative from the headquarters of the communist Anti-Japanese Union/Force (AJUF) turned up to negotiate a working agreement. A two-day conference was held with Chang Hong, an elected representative of the MCP on the one side and Davis, Broome and Lim as the "military representatives of the Allied C-in-C (commander-in-chief) Southeast Asia (who were) fully empowered to cooperate with any anti-Japanese party in Malaya"[20]. Chang Hong was in reality an alias for Lai Teck, the Secretary General of the Malayan Communist Party (MCP), who had come in disguise to negotiate the agreement with the British. Lai Teck was accompanied by the MCP's Perak State Commissar, Chin Peng (also known as Chen Ping or CTP), who would succeed Lai Teck as Secretary General of the MCP and launch the Communist Insurgency five years later[21].

By this time, Davis and Broome had managed to contact Chapman, who walked into their camp with members of the communist guerrillas in tow on Christmas Day 1943. Now all three, along with Lim, would plan the next moves.

With the agreement of the MCP, Force 136 concentrated their efforts on getting their wireless transmitters up to camp and operational, raising finance and "strengthening our organisation on the plains"[22].

However, due to heavy Japanese air activity and the proximity of the SOE's Belantan camp to the plains of Tapah and Bidor, it was decided to move into a *Sakai* (an aboriginal tribe) camp, on the lower slopes of Gunung Batu

Puteh. They finally located the camp at the house of the village headman, Pa Kasut (literally 'Father Shoe'), with the camp then known as Pa Kasut.

By January 1944, Davis noted the network in the plains had been well laid-out and established:

> Tsing Li was installed in a small fish business at Pangkor with several partners and was helped by Bill (Chua), who was friendly and fatherly towards him. His job was to maintain our sea RVs by junk. Unfortunately, he proved quite unfitted for this job and Ng (Wu) had to involve himself with Bill a great deal in getting right his mistake. It was this that led to Bill's knowing far too much about our whole organisation. After I arrived, Tsing was left merely vegetating in Pangkor with nothing to do... Ah Tsing did very well at the beginning and was responsible for the organisation of the successful junk service for RVs. Later, however, owing to his bull-headedness and lack of common sense, he became dangerous and had to be taken off this work, so that he was doing nothing for us till the collapse. His escape was a fine piece of work and saved Ying's (Lung Chiu Ying) life. Unfortunately, he blotted this record by intrigue and general bad behaviour in camp, which can be only partly excused by the very trying circumstances we lived in...
>
> ...Ying, after starting as a coffeeshop boy in Segari... later became our chief RV keeper and did the job—despite the failures—with very great courage and resource. His cover was always bad, because, although he had all the necessary papers, he had no specific employment; at the end Ng (Wu) was negotiating to set him up in a wine shop in Ipoh.
>
> Sek Fu, who was the last out before Tan (Lim), was installed as owner of a sundry shop in Tapah, and had a manager who was not employed by us or in our secrets. He was nervous at first but carried on very well. Previously he had spent some time tucked away in a rubber estate near Ipoh with Lee's (Moh Wing Pun) father, but it had not proved possible to launch him at that time and he had returned to camp[23].

Broome noted that Tan Chong Tee, "did very well when set up as Ng's (Wu) agent in Lumut but had little opportunity to show his ability, since he was engaged in settling down and had little else to do until the collapse. Was loyal and cheerful throughout"[24].

The network, according to Tan, consisted of an interior and exterior section. The interior was headed by Davis at Pa Kasut's camp and the exterior consisted of field agents stationed in Ipoh, Lumut and Pangkor[25]. Everything began to fall in place with the arrival of Lim Bo Seng, and Tan was ecstatic at the prospect of working again for Lim:

> Ultimately in the beginning of March 1944 the headquarters of the Organisation was established at Ipoh with the arrival of the Leader Tan Choon Lim (Lim), who came from India in December 1943. The principal objects of the organisation were to: 1. Unite with the Resistance Army, 2. Transfer materials and personnel into the interior, 3. Establish a wireless station and 4. Maintain sea communication...
>
> ... Maintenance of sea communication, which entails the meeting of submarines by our sailing boats to bring in materials, money, jewellery, etc., is the lifeblood of our organisation. With certain misunderstanding(s) between Lee Ah Cheng (Li Han Kwang) and Capt. Davies (*sic*), Ah Long (Lung Chiu Ying) was sent to assist the former. The main work of going out to sea was subsequently performed by Ah Long.
>
> From May 1943 all the objects originally mapped out were proceeded with successfully according to plan, and in March 1944, I was informed by our leader Tan Choon Lim that the first stage of our mission can be stated as successfully completed, and we were asked to carry out the second stage, i.e. organisation and propaganda.
>
> Owing to lack of funds, the activities were confined to Perak... Goh Meng Chye (Wu Chye Sin) was sent to Singapore by our Leader to raise a big sum in order to enable representatives to be sent to other states. The persons who were to have been approached in Singapore were Soh Hun Swee, Ong Pia Teng, Koh Chee Peng, etc[26].

From the base at Pa Kasut's camp, Broome was pleased with the progress being made but realised that something had to be done to improve their financial situation:

> When Tan (Lim) arrived, he immediately applied himself to the problem of raising money. He had three old friends in Malaya of whom he had great hopes, one being Soh Hun Swee and the others a banker and a schoolteacher whose names I forget. He described the three people to Ng (Wu) and provided him with means of recognition, and Ng then made a trip to Singapore to see them. He reported on his return that Hun Swee was non-committal and clearly frightened to do anything, but he had had much more success with one of the others and hoped on a subsequent visit to make an arrangement to actually get some money. Tan was greatly disappointed to hear about Hun Swee, in whom he had put great faith[27].

Tan Chong Tee (left) and his leader, Lim Bo Seng (right): Tan heard Lim being tortured in Batu Gajah Prison and subsequently confirmed Lim's death on 29 June 1944.

With finances very tight, Davis, Broome and Chapman were heavily reliant on the RV drops which would have brought in much needed funds, in the form of gold bars and coins, as well as medical supplies. However, Broome and Davis were both unable to make the February and March RVs due to enemy activity and illness. As a result, Lung was sent to make the RVs but failed to make contact.

So by March 1944, Force 136's financial situation in Perak state was very bleak. Lim, who had until then been in the jungles with Davis, Broome and Chapman, decided to go into town, according to Broome:

> The decision to let Tan (Lim) go out was taken with great reluctance but was in my opinion a correct one. There was no reason at that time to fear any danger, and things appeared to be going very well. Tan could obviously do a great deal of good by going out, whereas in the jungle he was merely wasting his time. The plan was that he should spend as short a time as possible in Ipoh and try and arrange a safe hideout whence he could direct our organisation without being two days journey away in the jungle; he had great hopes of finding a place on a rubber estate belonging to a friend of his on the Cameron Highlands road... In the middle of March Tan left camp to join Ng (Wu) in Ipoh. The reasons for this step were:

a) Ng was having difficulty in getting our projected financial backing and Tan felt his personal touch was necessary.

b) Tan was worried over Ng's business which was absorbing too much of Ng's time and was, Tan thought, being run on far too unstable lines despite high profits.

The plan was Tan's own and we only agreed after long discussion. It seemed to us, however, an essential move if we were to make any progress at all. Tan was accordingly installed in a house (No. 12, Conoly Road) in Ipoh as Ng's uncle. Again, we were reluctantly compelled to centralise far too much on Ng. The reasons for this were as before, i.e., Ng was the only man capable of fixing the necessary passes, which had to be done by personal influence and judicious bribery. It was intended that Tan should return to camp as soon as he had put things straight below[28].

As Davis later admitted:

We were, at this time, under the grave misapprehension that the attack on Malaya would come in summer 1944 and therefore considered our intelligence system should be speeded up even to the extent of taking risks which would not otherwise be warranted[29].

Things, however, began to go seriously wrong shortly after Lim settled in Ipoh. As a result of a counter-espionage operation in January 1944, the Japanese had captured a communist guerrilla, who revealed the existence of a clandestine Allied network operating on Pangkor island. Many post-war accounts and authors claim that Lai Teck, who was a triple agent working for the British, Japanese and the MCP, was the one who revealed Lim's identity and the existence of the Ipoh network. However, Chin Peng, Lai Teck's successor, refutes this allegation:

It has been claimed that Lai Te (Lai Teck) had learned of Lim's identity at the Belantan meeting the previous December and, as a result, was able to identify him to the *Kempeitai* (Japanese secret police). As I alone escorted Lim, under his alias, to Belantan, attended all sessions of those negotiations and stayed with Lai Te the entire time he spent at the camp, I know this particular conjecture to be baseless. I personally did not learn of Lim's true identity until immediately after the war. Even then, I did not consider the information important enough to pass on to anybody. Lai Te, therefore, could never have been able to identify Lim for the *Kempeitai*. The reality is, Lim Bo Seng was betrayed by one of his own men[30].

By mid March 1944, the Japanese had begun a full-scale counter-espionage operation on Pangkor island and were searching all sea-going vessels. Although Li Han Kwang was on the island, the Japanese missed him and were unable to locate the RV boat as it had sailed out with Lung to make the March RV in order to collect more funds and supplies. Lung, however, returned empty-handed and went to see Lim before he headed to the Pa Kasut camp to report to Davis and Broome. Tan, who was based at Lumut, also went to see Lim with the same information. The missed rendezvous meant no new funds would be forthcoming for at least another month. So, Lim sent Wu back to Singapore once again in the hopes of getting more funds.

However, in late March, the *Kempeitai* placed a detachment of more than 200 Japanese soldiers on Pangkor. The *Kempeitai* were also involved in anti-espionage activities and on the afternoon of 21 March, *Kempeitai* counter-espionage teams began searching all the islands around Pangkor. The next day, Pangkor was surrounded, but Li managed to escape.

By 23 March, unable to trace Li or Chua on Pangkor, Tan left Lumut and contacted Lim, who told him that Lung had already visited him and that Pangkor was surrounded by Japanese. Tan recalls the circumstances:

> Ah Long (Lung) also stated that while he was at Pangkor, a demand was made by someone for $25,000 (Straits Settlements Dollars), which was promised by our organisation to the Resistance Army (AJUF) but the demand for the money was not carried out in the manner arranged by us. Chua Koon Eng, our Pangkor representative, was stated to have asked the man to come the next day, on which day (23 Mar) Koon Eng went away from Pangkor. In view of the circumstances, I advised our Leader to leave Ipoh, but he considered it advisable to remain until he heard from Goh Meng Chye (Wu), whom he said he (had) sent to Singapore to raise funds. I was instructed to go to our firm, Kian Yick Chan (Chop Kian Yick Chan, 77, Market Street, Ipoh), to await news of Goh Meng Chye[31].

By 24 March, the *Kempeitai* had tracked Chua down and arrested him at Teluk Murrek. This was the beginning of the end. Chua confessed and implicated Li in the spy ring. The Japanese laid a trap for Li (who had already escaped from Pangkor by then) and, using Chua as bait, captured him shortly after. Under duress, Li was forced to confirm Chua's story but managed to avoid adding anything to what the Japanese already knew.

Then, using Li as bait, the *Kempeitai* held back further arrests of the other Chinese members in the hopes of getting at the British masterminds. Li had been taken to Ipoh and detained at the *Kempeitai* headquarters, where some Japanese soldiers, Chinese detectives and a few 'comfort' girls lived in a large house. Li was treated very well. The Japanese were hoping to get more details through kindness and perhaps turn him. He was not locked up—although he was kept under constant guard. On 26 March, Li made a daring escape:

> He was being looked after by two women when one of the Japanese wandered into the room stark naked—a Japanese habit. This outraged the natural Chinese modesty of the girls to such an extent that they walked out of the room, thus giving Tsing (Li) his chance. He got up, too, as if it had been already agreed, and said he was going to have a bath and got away through the bathroom window, climbing from the second storey to the street. He then ran wildly down the street and jumped into a taxi, telling the driver to go towards the main road. As soon as he could, he told the driver he was an escaping guerrilla. The driver responded magnificently and shouting *"Tai ka ting pau"* (We're all of us of one blood) proceeded at full speed to Bidor, where Tsing immediately entered the jungle, first borrowing his fare from the local AJUF guides. Tsing knew nothing of the fate of the others, beyond hearing one of the detectives say he had to go to Tapah, which may have meant he was after Sek Fu (Yi Tian Song)[32].

However, the next to be captured would be Tan:

> A few hours after the disappearance of Ah Cheng (Li Han Kwang), the Japanese found out about his abscondment and searched all rendezvous. They arrived at Kian Yick Chan to find (*sic*) Goh Meng Chye (Wu), but unfortunately they found me there. I suspected that something was wrong and planned to escape. I reached the Teng Ah Hotel at 10.00pm but was immediately followed by armed guards. Being unarmed I was unable to offer a fight. Determined to sacrifice myself, I sent word through the waiter to Mok Kee (Moh Wing Pun), a member of the Organisation, of my arrest. Within five minutes of my arrest, Mok Kee and Sek Fu (Yi), who happened to be in Ipoh, were accordingly informed, and they in turn immediately informed our leader[33].

Yi, who happened to be in Ipoh, was then alerted by Moh, who told him of Tan's arrest:

> Moh Wing Pun (in charge of the liaison post at No. 4, Clare Street, Ipoh) received information from Ah Seng, a waitor (*sic*) employed in the Oriental Hotel, Ipoh at about 10.30pm on the same night, that Lim Soong (Tan) was being arrested. He immediately conveyed the message to Chan Siak Foo (Yi Tian Song) (in charge of the liaison post, Chop Yee Kee Chan, No. 65 Main Road, Tapah), who at the time (was) staying at Yan Woh Lodging House, Hale Street, Ipoh. He (Moh) also called on Chan Choon Lim (Lim Bo Seng), our officer-in-charge, at his residence, No. 12 Conoly Road, Ipoh, to make the same report and ask for his instructions.
>
> By this time, the reason of Lim Soong's arrest was not known yet. So Chan Choon Lim instructed him (Moh) to go into this matter, find out what had really happened and make an effort to save Lim Soong. Moh was also instructed to tell Chan Siak Foo to report the matter to the headquarters at the mountain of Bidor as quickly as possible and to inform Ah Loong (Lung Chiu Ying) not to come down from the mountain...
>
> Moh Wing Pun had lost no time to carry out the above instructions. On the morning of March 27, the next day, he found out that Chop Kian Yik Chan, our organising centre, No. 77 Market Street, Ipoh, had been raided and closely watched by the enemy. Upon receiving Moh's report on the above and after some considerations, Chan Choon Lim decided to escape by car with Moh Wing Pun as driver. They were unfortunately stopped and arrested at a junction near the 7th milestone of Jalan Gopeng.
>
> Siak Foo (who was returning to Tapah before heading to Bidor) was arrested at his post... on the early morning of 28 March 1944. Wong Kwong Fai (Wu Chye Sin) was arrested at Kuala Lumpur while on his way back to Ipoh from Singapore on 31 March 1944. He determined to end his own life by crashing his head against the wall in the lock-up at the Kuala Lumpur Police Station. His attempt, however, was unsuccessful though he collapsed with a fractured wound on the head bleeding profusely[34]...

Davis, Broome and Chapman meanwhile remained unaware of what was happening in Ipoh:

> About 20 March Ying (Lung) brought us a letter from Tan (Lim) saying that Ng (Wu) had left for Singapore to continue his financial discussions. He also told us that Bill (Chua), the night before, had had a mysterious visit from two men claiming to be AJUF representatives and demanding money with menaces. Bill was said to have kept his head and not disclosed his relations with AJUF. This visit was mysterious and alarming, because Bill had been for

> a long time our chief agent in Pangkor for financing the guerrillas. It seems clear now that his two visitors were working for the Japs[35].

It was now time for the April RV but, as the two previous ones had failed and Japanese patrols had been stepped up, it seemed unwise for Broome, Davis or Chapman to go[36]. Thus, Lung left on 29 March to keep the rendezvous. That same evening, he was back in camp with Li, whom he had met on the way. Obviously, there had been a disaster:

> On hearing Tsing's (Li) story we immediately, with C.T.P.'s (Chin Peng) help, sent out messengers to warn Tan (Lim) and Sek Fu (Yi). We could do nothing for Ng (Wu) in Singapore or for Lim in Lumut, the only hope for them was a warning via Tan, if we could reach him in time. The messengers went out repeatedly but were unable to find either Tan or Sek Fu at the addresses given or to hear any word of them. Clearly we were much too late[37].

Chua, who had cooperated fully with the Japanese, was released shortly after, noted Broome:

> Bill (Chua) was released and is now back in his business in Pangkor under strict Jap control. All the junks in Pangkor are now owned by a firm under Bill's direction.
>
> In assessing Bill's culpability in this matter, it should be borne in mind that he helped us loyally and enthusiastically from the beginning. He was not chosen by us as the result of careful consideration, but came into our orbit entirely fortuitously. Had he chosen, he could have ruined our whole venture at the start; instead he decided to help and did so. We always took it for granted that he would break down if arrested[38].

Even if Broome could forgive Chua's actions, it was his confession that had led to the destruction of Force 136's network in Perak and Lim Bo Seng's capture and eventual death. In captivity, Tan Chong Tee revealed the privations they faced:

> In spite of terrible torture, we refused to speak for the time we were arrested, but after three days we were shown the evidence of Lee Ah Cheng (Li). We then realised that the organisation was smashed. We decided therefore that we should not sacrifice needlessly, and we hoped that one of us might live through the torture to clear our names[39].

Tan could hear Lim being interrogated. He noted that "the Japanese tried to force Lim to cooperate with them but he refused. They even got his friends in Singapore to come over to persuade him, but he was not moved.... Instead, he reminded the rest of us to remain firm and not to surrender to the Japanese"[40].

On 24 April, Lim Bo Seng, Yi Tian Song, Moh Wing Pun and Tan Chong Tee were transferred to the Batu Gajah Jail and placed in cells on the second floor. Lim protested against the ill-treatment of POWs by refusing food. He asked that his portion of sweet potatoes be distributed to the rest of his comrades[41]. After 20 days, Lim, Moh and Tan were struck by dysentery. "Through the ill treatment of the Indian Dresser and the casualness of the Indian Doctor..."[42], Lim was bundled up in an old blanket and left without food and water in an empty room meant for dying prisoners. For the next three nights, Lim held on, dying in the early hours of 29 June 1944. His remains were buried in a pauper's grave on the outskirts of the jail.

In 1995, Tan Chong Tee penned his memoirs on Force 136. Written 50 years on, Tan described vividly his role at Lumut and the death of Lim[43]. However, Tan confessed that in his post-war report to Davis and Broome, he had covered up details on Wu Chye Sin's womanising and several other indiscretions prior to the destruction of the network and did not report Moh Wing Pun's 'traitorous' confessions to the Japanese. Although Tan did finally tell Davis about Moh's breakdown under interrogation and Tan's belief that Moh had collaborated with the enemy, Davis did not act on it.

Clearly, there are discrepancies in Tan's initial statement in 1945 and in his memory of those events 50 years later. Now, 60 years on, it is not easy to tell which version is more closely related to fact or who the actual traitors were. Wu was very highly regarded by Davis and Broome, as was Moh. Regardless, all these members of Force 136, with the exception of Chua Koon Eng, will always be viewed as heroes.

By January 1945, Davis, from the jungles of Perak, was forced to signal Colombo (Force 136 headquarters) that the network had been destroyed[44]. Although Davis, Broome and Chapman claimed no knowledge of what happened to Lim, Davis' signal on 4 February 1945 left no doubt as to the reason for the collapse:

> From DEE (Davis): 192, NG, TSING, SEK FU, LIM arrested late March, owing collapse of BILL (Chua) under arrest[45].

Lim Bo Seng's funeral in Singapore, December 1945: It would take more than 3 years before Mrs Lim would receive the pension promised to her husband.

No trace was left of Lim and his network of agents in Perak and it would be more than a year later, after the Japanese surrender that much of what happened would come to light.

With the end of the war, Force 136 was keen to find out the fate of its ill-fated GUSTAVUS mission members in Perak. Frantic signals were sent from Colombo to field operatives in Malaya to track down Lim Bo Seng and his agents.

By 28 August 1945, Tan Chong Tee, Wu Chye Sin and Yi Tian Song were released by the Japanese. Tan rushed to Penang and got in touch with Force 136 elements there who flew him to Singapore. After some confusion, Tan met with the SOE Singapore head, Derek Gill Davies, who was then able to ascertain what actually happened.

Signals in Lim Bo Seng's file show that by 30 August 1945, Force 136's Perak outfit was busy looking for traces of Lim. By 6 September, brief reports were filtering in from Perak and it seemed very likely that Lim was still very much alive and Tan might have been wrong:

> Report on my demand to KEMPEI chief for return of our agents captured PERAK March 44. Members of KEMPEI say that the men were captured at Gopeng. LIM BO SENG entered BATU GAJAH Prison 29th July '44. Released 25th August 45[46].

However, the next day, it was all too clear that Tan was right:

> AH HAN back from IPOH. Jap story mainly true. LIM BO SENG died of dysentery in hospital[47].

Force 136's MCS was in shock. One of their key operatives was now confirmed dead. They needed more details and had to locate Lim's remains before relaying any message to his family:

> Try locate LIM BO SENG's grave. Record statements witnesses his fate. Do not inform his wife yet[48].

Tan along with Gill Davies and an Anglican priest, the headmaster of St. Andrew's School where Lim's sons were studying, called on Mrs Lim. It was a devastating blow for a family that had survived the hardships of war and occupation, only to be confronted with the worst news of all.

In a signal to Force 136 HQ, Gill Davies outlined the deprivations the Lim family were facing and the need to provide urgent closure:

> Have had most distressing meeting with Mrs Lim Bo Seng. Complete family have suffered terribly at hands of Japanese.
>
> Eight male members missing. All property ruined and very large financial loss.
>
> Have given Mrs Lim 5000 rpt 5000 dollars. I must have some guidance what compensation I can pay as the people cannot be left to starve. Lims estimate their losses at 1,000,000 rpt 1,000,000 dollars.
>
> Am putting pressure on Japanese through Army to find out exact fate of Lim Bo Seng. Would stress importance of quick and generous settlement.
>
> Emphasise fully-recognised valuable service rendered by Lim Bo Seng to British prior to fall Singapore and afterwards with this force. Also, he had outstanding claim on British naval contract[49].

Lim's family was not the only one affected. On returning home, Tan also discovered that his mother had died. His elder brother had also been killed in February 1942, leaving behind his sister-in-law and four children who were living in abject poverty. Tan asked Davies for money to feed his family and for housing for the children but there was not much that Davies could do[50].

Compensation for Lim Bo Seng's family would not be straightforward. Lim's brother, who was still studying in Calcutta, found that his stipend had been stopped, leaving him no money to live on. An urgent signal from the MCS to Force 136's finance section called for the immediate resumption of the payments.

Force 136's finance section did not appreciate the nature of the compensation or why Lim was to be treated so specially:

> Fixed procedure in all cases is to cease payment salary and allotments six months after person reported missing on present information. Regret unable authorise any further payment to nominee (Lim's brother).
>
> Who authorised Gill Davies pay Mrs Lim Bo Seng 5000 dollars. Realise that in hardship cases small immediate payments necessary pending final decision liquidation committee but this is equivalent of nearly pounds 600 rpt pounds 600 sterling at present rate.
>
> Loss sustained by Lim family is not SOE responsibility. HQ are only responsible compensations in respect of death Lim Bo Seng when this has been confirmed[51].

In several more signals, SOE's Group B finance section dressed down Gill Davies for making the $5,000 payment and noted that, "In view Gill Davies payment to wife of nearly 600 pounds sterling, no further payments can be made until full facts known and award determined by liquidation committee" [52].

Gill Davies and the MCS were incensed at the rulebook attitude taken by their financial section. Over the next few months there were more signals to Colombo and more refusals.

Although the finance section did not appear to appreciate Lim's contribution, the Chinese nationalist government did. By December 1945, they had voted an *ex-gratia* payment of $400,000 (Chinese nationalist dollars) to Mrs Lim for services rendered by her husband. More importantly, memorial services for Lim, attended by thousands, had been held in Ipoh and Kuala Lumpur and would now be held in Singapore, sponsored by the British Military Administration. Yet, payments of a military Major's pension, promised to Lim when he signed on, had not been paid to Mrs Lim.

Under pressure, the finance section agreed that they would only pay Mrs Lim $4,632 extra as full and final compensation, after deducting the amount paid by Gill Davies earlier. No mention was made of a pension or compensation for the Brick Selling Agency contract[53].

By 11 December 1945, the Chinese nationalist government in Chungking had issued a citation appointing Lim Bo Seng posthumously to the rank of Major General, asking the British legation to hand the citation to Lim's family in Singapore. This was a further embarrassment to Force 136, who still could not iron out Lim's compensation. The MCS finally hit out in a signal to the finance section, referring to the agreement signed by Ivory in 1942:

> Contract initialled by Col Ivory rpt Ivory calls for compensation either in form Majors pension to widow or at discretion force 136 lump sum equivalent to such pension
>
> Majors pension pounds 170 rpt 170 plus pounds 36 for each child total for wife and seven children pounds 422 rpt pounds 422 per annum... Equivalent is over pounds 6200 rpt 6200...
>
> ... Surely record sheet not rpt not necessary for decision in view of tariff fully documented...
>
> ... This is not a case of compensation to an agent, fulfilment of a contract in which one party has come to be recognised as the Chinese foundation of Sino-British resistance in Malaya and the other party has become identified with British rule in Malaya. Request urgent re-consideration. The imagination boggles at the nature of the uncommon enthusiasms of Lim rpt Lim Family, Chinese and British Community if your proposed settlements is even mentioned in such circles[54].

This stiff opposition from the MCS prompted the finance section to cable London for support, claiming that the payment had been "ridiculed" by the country section. As there was no progress, Davis intervened and convinced the finance section that an annuity should be purchased for the duration of Mrs Lim's life and for 15 years more in the event of her death. Although Mrs Lim should have rightfully received £422 a year, the finance section finally agreed to recommend a pension of only £400[55]. The section then submitted this revised proposal to London on 10 January 1945 with the suggestion that payment of the pension begin on 1 January 1946. None of this was made known to Mrs Lim, who would eventually end up with a pension of only £400 a year.

However, the actual determination of how the pension should be paid and the logistics of it was not easily settled. It would take special intervention by the successors to the SOE to ensure that Mrs Lim received the £400 annually. In the end, the pension payment was only approved in January 1947, with the British government providing compensation almost three years after Lim had died and long after everyone else had recognised his contributions[56]. Compensation for the $40,000 Brick Selling Agency contract remains outstanding.

Today, Lim Bo Seng is viewed not only as a nationalist Chinese hero but a Singaporean hero as well. His sacrifice for Singapore is mentioned in modern-day secondary school history textbooks and he is treated as a national hero by Singaporeans despite Lim having really fought for Britain and the nationalist government in Chungking. Yet 60 years on, although he is valorised by a country that did not even exist at the time of his death and is remembered by the nationalist government in Taiwan, Lim Bo Seng has been forgotten by the organisation and the empire for which he gave his life.

Force 136 Operations

Many other SOE operations, including sabotage missions, were more successful. The SOE carried out numerous operations, landing agents in Malaya with teams operating in every state by the end of 1944 (see map on page 50). Down under, their Australian counterparts, with former Orient Mission member Lieutenant Colonel Ivan Lyon at the helm, carried out one of the most successful sabotage raids against Japanese shipping in Singapore in 1943. Operation JAYWICK has become legendary in special operations circles, where Force 'Z', under Lyon's command, sailed from Darwin to Singapore in a fishing boat, and then using specially designed fol-boats, sneaked into Singapore's Keppel Harbour and stuck limpet mines on the hulls of numerous ships. This resulted in the destruction of more than 50,000 tonnes of enemy shipping.

However, the following year, in an attempt to carry out a similar operation in Singapore Harbour, Lyon and his men were killed while fleeing through the Indonesian islands. Although Operation RIMAU succeeded, Lyon's Force 'Z' was effectively destroyed.

Nonetheless, the build-up of agents and supplies in the Malayan jungles continued. Through numerous night-time airdrops and operations like

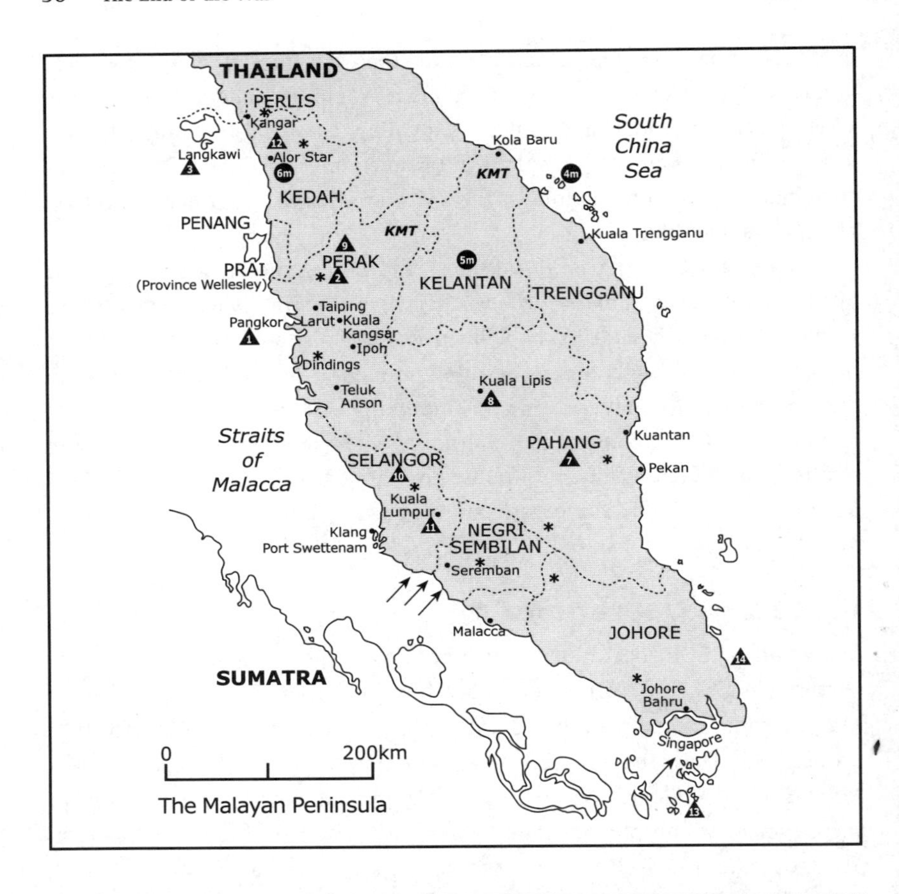

1 GUSTAVUS/REMARKABLE	7 PONTOON	13 RIMAU
2 John Davis's camp & radio	8 BEACON	14 CARPENTER/MINT
3 MULLET	9 EVIDENCE	* MPAJA
4 OATMEAL	10 GALVANIC	***KMT*** Kuomintag
5 HEBRIDES	11 Major Ian MacDonald's party	m Indicates a Malay based party
6 FUNNEL	12 Major Pierre Chassé's party	↗ Operation ZIPPER

Force 136's drop zones and infiltration points for its various operations in Malaya.

Based on a map reproduced with permission from:
Gough, Richard. The Jungle was Red. Singapore: SNP Panpac, 2003.

CARPENTER and FUNNEL, Force 136 grew considerably in size. By 1945, Force 136 was involved in the planning for ZIPPER and felt the clandestine units in Malaya could play a key role in the reoccupation.

In his signals to Colombo, Davis emphasised the urgency for a quick decision on the role of Force 136 in ZIPPER. Mountbatten had raised the issue in Whitehall as early as July 1944 and his views were put to the War Cabinet in a secret memorandum on 9 December 1944. Mountbatten pointed out that the cooperation of any local resistance in Malaya would depend on Britain's post-war plans for that country and these should be explained to the population beforehand.

His view was that a favourable atmosphere needed to be created to assist the setting-up of a future post-war administration and "our agents" would need general guidance on the subject. However, despite pressure from Mountbatten, the British Government was not prepared to commit itself publicly to any post-war solution. As far as Force 136 was concerned, it simply had a military, not political, objective to fulfil.

From March 1945, there was a great effort to build up the necessary guerrilla forces for ZIPPER but this was not a priority until the success of Operation MODIFIED DRACULA in May. Although the plan was to divide Malaya into eight sections, roughly corresponding with MPAJA's eight regiments, there was also a need to coordinate the Malay guerrillas and Chinese nationalist resistance forces as well.

It was estimated that 300 men of all ranks would need to be infiltrated, together with arms, supplies and wireless sets. In addition, due to the questionable loyalty of the MPAJA, gurkha support units would also be needed to protect the agents and their Drop Zones (DZs). All this created not only a huge demand on resources but also the need to find a solution to the problems of resupplying the agents on the ground during the monsoon and obtaining enough aircraft to fly the sorties needed[57].

Eventually, SACSEA provided a general outline of the part the MPAJA would be expected to play in ZIPPER, now pencilled-in for the first week in September. Apart from ambushing Japanese columns, the resistance should seize all bridges, railway stations and power stations to prevent them from being destroyed by the Japanese.

The plan for ZIPPER, when it finally emerged, consisted of three main operational areas, namely the Malayan states of Johor, Perak (where Davis was based) and Selangor, the last of which would cover the city of Kuala Lumpur and the proposed invasion beaches of Sepang, Morib and Port Dickson. As all west coast road and rail communications ran through these states, control by the guerrillas would effectively isolate the Japanese throughout Malaya. The first Force 136 party (GALVANIC) to land in Selangor in May 1945 was led by Lieutenant Colonel Douglas Keith Broadhurst, a pre-war police officer in Malaya[58].

However, as the end drew nearer, racial tensions began emerging. The murder of SOE's two Chinese nationalist operators by the communists highlighted the very complex political situation that laid below the surface in Malaya. In Chinese communities in Malaya, communist supporters of Mao Tze Tung (in *pinyin*, Mao Zedong) were forced to co-exist with their sworn enemies, the KMT, who were supporters of the nationalist government in China. Within this political mix, the communist MPAJA guerrillas had agreed to support the return of the British, while some more radical guerrilla leaders wanted to seize power and install a Chinese communist government[59].

Meanwhile, there was growing support amongst Malays for the new, Japanese-sponsored Malay nationalist movement. The Malays had their own views about the post-war future of Malaya and believed that they should have special rights and privileges as the original inhabitants of the country. This did not include power sharing with the Chinese. At that point in time, very little was known in SEAC about the Malay nationalists, who, with Japanese encouragement, wanted independence from Britain and were prepared to resist the return of British troops to Malaya. With the help of the Japanese chief of staff in Singapore, several Malay leaders formed an organisation for the independence of Malaya. It was called Kesatuan Rakyat Indonesia Semenanjung (KRIS), or the Union of Peninsular Indonesians, and it sent three representatives in July 1945 to meet with Indonesian nationalist leader Sukarno.

Two months earlier, Japanese officials in Singapore had discussed the implementation of Indonesian independence. Following that meeting, the Malay Lieutenant Colonel, Ibrahim Yaacob, was urged to convene a meeting at the Station Hotel in Kuala Lumpur on 17 August 1945 to support Indonesian independence and get Malaya included in that new state. However, opposing these groups were the SOE's anti-Japanese Malay guerrillas in north Malaya. For instance, near Kuala Lipis, SOE's BEACON party had the support of the local Malay District Officer, Che Yeop Mahideen, who promised to recruit 500 volunteers. A second party, MULTIPLE, located east of Raub, had 250 armed Malays but was under threat from a hostile local MPAJA patrol. In the state of Pahang, 750 Malay guerrillas had the support of the Sultan. Ironically, the Sultan had also been nominated by the Japanese-sponsored Malay nationalist movement to head their government in a post-war independent Malaya[60].

In June 1945, the simmering racial tensions between the Malays and Chinese finally exploded, with disastrous consequences in west Johor. Although the tension between the Malays and Chinese was not new, it dramatically increased when the British-trained and mainly Chinese resistance guerrillas began demanding taxes, supplies and intelligence from Malay *kampongs* (villages) and towns. These were interspersed with reports of Malay women being kidnapped to work in guerrilla camp kitchens while others were molested or used as comfort women[61].

Although some Malays joined the MPAJA voluntarily, others were obviously conscripted. In what appeared to have been a campaign of terror throughout the countryside, the MPAJA killed any Malays and Chinese suspected of collaborating with the Japanese and destroyed their homes. Many people simply disappeared—particularly Malay policemen, government officials and district and village headmen. The bodies that were eventually found showed signs of extreme torture and mutilation[62].

Two MPAJA regiments involved in the Johor clashes were the 3rd at Segamat and the 4th covering Kota Tinggi, Johor Bahru and Muar. In May 1945, a Malay headman who had refused to collect the MPAJA taxes was abducted by the Kangkar guerrillas while on his way to Yong Peng. His body was never found[63].

Retaliatory raids by gangs of Malays and Chinese against one another led to the loss of innocent lives. As clashes spread, Chinese refugees fled into adjoining areas, bringing with them stories of Malays on the march attacking Chinese communities, cutting women and children down with knives. Malays repeated stories of arrogant communist guerrillas butchering or beheading Malays. Some captured by the MPAJA were drowned, others scalded to death with hot water or given the water treatment until their stomachs distended.

The communal violence in the absence of any real and effective authority led the Malays to form *kampong* defence groups, which in June 1945, became the foundations of the Sabilillah army led by Kiyai Salleh Abdul Karim. Members of this group eventually collaborated with the Japanese in attacks against the MPAJA detachments in Asam Bubok, killing the MPAJA leader Seng Nga[64].

SACSEA's lack of understanding of the complex political situation in Malaya became apparent when, in an attempt to defuse this racial conflict, the RAF dropped leaflets on 20 July, in both Malay and English, warning that those responsible for the violence would be severely dealt with when the British returned. As there were no leaflets printed in Chinese and the British were arming the Chinese resistance groups, it was obvious the message was meant only for the Malays. The leaflets strengthened the Malay view that the Chinese and MPAJA had the support of the British, thereby encouraging those uncommitted Malays to support the Japanese-sponsored KRIS[65].

By the end of July, Mackenzie realised that an effective plan for the use of Force 136 in the reoccupation had to be drawn up. In a top-secret paper to Captain GA Garnons-Williams, Head of 'P' division (Clandestine Operations) at SEAC, Mackenzie noted that members of Force 136 in the field should be attached as small liaison detachments on the staff of the various formations and units involved in ZIPPER and TIDERACE. They would then be able to advise on local conditions, provide updated intelligence and most importantly, "control local guerrilla units through the British Officers in the field in accordance with the Senior British Officer's requirements"[66].

Force 136 had infiltrated 77 British officers in-country and these men had set up 40 wireless transmitting (WT) stations throughout the country. Mackenzie felt that ZIPPER and TIDERACE commanders would benefit from Force 136 help as they would be able to clear drop zones and airfields for the reception of airborne units while providing guards and patrols on vital lines of communications. Force 136 could also provide a nucleus for the creation of a disciplined police force to prevent civil disturbances and looting as well as distribution of foodstuffs and other essential commodities. The WT stations could also be used for the passing of instructions "for the Senior British Officer concerned to local authorities, including possibly enemy units and formations"[67].

However, the main contribution of these clandestine forces would be to help fill a power vacuum, should it occur—clearly a prophetic prediction of events to come:

> Whilst it is understood that every effort will be made on the part of the military authorities to ensure that there is no hiatus in the handover from the Japanese to the British, it is pointed out that if such a hiatus does occur, the above-mentioned British Officers and WT sets will be available; and that it will be possible for them to receive instructions from higher authority[68].

In meetings with Rear (later Vice) Admiral Cedric Holland, who had just started planning for TIDERACE, it was clear that Force 136 did not have a role in Singapore. SEAC planners also did not see a need to activate Force 136 as no lag time was expected between the surrender of the Japanese government and the reoccupation by British forces. Therefore, 'P' division instructed Force 136 to "stay where you are". Moreover, General Douglas MacArthur did not want the British to appear as if they were taking the surrender of the Japanese and ordered Mountbatten not to accept the surrender of any Japanese forces before MacArthur himself did so on 2 September 1945. Mountbatten's acceptance of this edict and the resulting power vacuum in Malaya proved a serious miscalculation on the part of the returning British forces.

By the end of the first week of August 1945, John Davis, who was still in Perak, received a signal informing him that the Japanese surrender was imminent and providing directions outlining the role Force 136 was to take in the matter:

> The general policy is to keep resistance forces concentrated in their areas and as much under the control of Allied officers with them as is possible. Every effort will be made to avoid clashes between resistance forces and Japanese forces.
>
> Personnel of clandestine organisations in the field will be prepared to carry out the following tasks when required. In order to carry out these tasks, clandestine organisations will continue to remain under cover.
>
> a) To provide local intelligence particularly with regard to action taken by the Japanese to comply (or otherwise) with surrender orders.
>
> b) To provide topographical and other local information to the Allied occupational forces when these arrive.
>
> c) To provide guides and interpreters to Allied occupational forces.
>
> d) In certain cases to establish contact with Allied POW (prisoner of war) Camps.

e) In the event of continued Japanese resistance in certain areas, or failure to comply with surrender orders, to concert the action of resistance forces with the operations of Allied Forces as required by the Allied Commander concerned.

As a last resort, if either means of establishing contact with Japanese commanders fail, clandestine organisations may be required to establish contact in accordance with instructions to be given at the time[69].

Clearly, Force 136 personnel were to remain where they were. Davis, like most other members of the MCS, was enraged. In a signal to Colombo, he noted it was unreasonable to:

> ... expect the guerrillas to remain half-starved in the hills while the Allies leisurely took over the administration from the Japs.... The MPAJA expect and await specific orders and not vague directives.... I am satisfied that 3,000 armed guerrillas with Force 136 parties would obey reasonable orders.... They must be fully-equipped, rationed and used by us... and be given the full share in the honours of victory.... The matter is very urgent and there is a serious risk of a disastrous anticlimax[70].

'P' division realised that the "stay where you are" instructions placed Force 136 in an untenable position and, appreciating that the nationalist takeover of the Netherlands East Indies could be repeated in Malaya, rescinded the order on 23 August.

SEAC signalled John Davis that while avoiding clashes with the Japanese, the MPAJA in conjunction with Force 136 officers should take over responsibility for ensuring law and order in those areas not occupied by the Japanese. They should also prevent the MPAJA from seizing power. Field officers were told to contact local Japanese commanders to reestablish a British presence but not to "receive any surrenders". Meanwhile, they were to gather intelligence about any POW camps in their area and the condition of any airfields.

When they learnt that the ban on entering towns and villages had been removed, MPAJA HQ instructed its eight regiments to move into towns evacuated by the Japanese. There, the guerrillas formed a two-tier authority. On the township level, they developed People's Committees which nominated representatives to attend State People's Congresses. These Congresses became responsible for the rescue of refugees, communications and general security.

The Japanese, however, remained responsible for law and order.

However, this peaceful takeover would change quickly in Singapore as the Allied commanders had ordered all non-essential Japanese troops to gather in the southern part of the Johor state. Once the MPAJA 4th Regiment guerrillas in south Johor learnt that the Japanese were withdrawing from Singapore city, they ignored Force 136 instructions and moved across the causeway to base themselves at the Singapore Japanese Club, located on the site of present-day Selegie Complex.

As the Naval Force Commander for TIDERACE, Rear Admiral Holland did not see the need for Force 136 help in Singapore and Malaya during the operation; the gap in power was viewed as minimal. SEAC planners clearly did not expect such savage violence to break out and were taken by surprise when the communal clashes spread throughout the peninsula. As a result of Holland's decision not to use clandestine forces to control the rebel elements of the MPAJA, Force 136 officers remained where they were and were unable to act in the chaos that ensued in Singapore.

The reduction of the number of Japanese troops in the city led to outbreaks of violence and anarchy. Against a background of public jubilation that Japan had been defeated, the Malay guerrillas and MPAJA raided army depots for weapons. Collaborators were hunted down and their bodies left hanging from trees. Mistresses of the Japanese had their heads shaved, and were paraded and spat on before being beaten or stabbed to death by the crowds. Revenge, retribution, summary executions and fear swept through the city[71]. Records of the communal violence that rocked the island were not kept by the Japanese as it was not seen as an attack against them but more as clashes among locals. As such, many of the killings and disappearances went unreported and forgotten in the chaos of the last days of Japanese rule.

In desperation on 25 August, when an appeal to SEAC and Force 136 officers to cooperate in maintaining law and order failed, the Japanese commander issued a proclamation banning demonstrations and meetings of more than 500 people. This was ignored, and law and order in the city collapsed[72].

SEAC was of the view that the Japanese would be able to maintain effective control in Malaya despite Japan's surrender. However, the communal violence that was sweeping across Malaya meant that only the MPAJA was in control in many towns and villages throughout the peninsula. There was no way in which SEAC could help restore order in Malaya despite appeals from the Japanese. SEAC could only instruct the men they had in Malaya, namely, the 77 SOE operatives in-country. These operatives did not have any military force or weapons with which to maintain order. Force 136's main armed force was the MPAJA, which was effectively controlled by the MCP. Until SEAC landed its own troops, Force 136 had to rely upon the goodwill of the MPAJA under the agreement signed in December 1943. This meant that Force 136 officers in-country were powerless to stop rebel elements of the MPAJA from exacting revenge on the Malay population.

Moreover, the head of Force 136 in Malaya, Colin Mackenzie, was concerned for the safety of his men. They were based with the communist guerrillas during the vacuum between the Japanese surrender and the initial arrival of Allied forces as part of TIDERACE, planned for 3 September, which was still more than a week away. The bulk of forces would only arrive with ZIPPER, which was slotted for 9 September. Although the MCP was a banned organisation at the outbreak of the war, it was the only resistance group with sufficient size and manpower in Malaya. The MPAJA consisted mainly of Malaya-born Chinese whose status was inferior to the Malays, with very few having citizenship in the country. Obviously, the Chinese communists had increased in influence during the war years and the Chinese would expect a better deal from the returning British. Unless this were guaranteed to some extent, some local MCP leaders might rebel. In a signal to London on 24 August, Mackenzie asked for a statement that would help British liaison officers in any discussions with the communist guerrillas[73].

As the request dealt with a better deal for the Chinese in post-war Malaya, it was seen as a civil affairs matter, and the War Office's civil affairs department wanted to discuss the future with the Malay rulers first. A frustrated Mackenzie became more worried that the delay could be misunderstood by the MPAJA and that its reaction would not only place his men in serious danger but that a British military response would then damage post-war relations.

While the questions were being debated in Whitehall, the MCP leaders in Malaya took matters into their own hands, meeting and agreeing on a post-war manifesto. As the Royal Marines were coming ashore on Penang on 3 September 1945, the MCP published its manifesto for post-war Malaya with a demand for a democratic government in Malaya and Singapore with all races having the opportunity to vote and obtain the rights of citizenship.

The MCP had temporarily abandoned their plans of armed insurrection and national liberation for one of self-government. However, the days of submissive colonial peoples were clearly gone. The MCP would not be happy as a subject of colonial rule, with the demand for independence from Britain, clearly the next logical step.

In the four weeks since the Emperor of Japan's surrender announcement, Japanese authority in most of the territories under SEAC had effectively slipped to local nationalist organisations. In Malaya, by agreement with SEAC, some 70% of towns and villages were controlled by the communists. The remainder was held either by the KMT, Malay Home Guard or, in some cases, the triads[74]. The Japanese had recorded 212 attacks against their military units, police or strategic installations. Apart from 63 Japanese and 31 Malay policemen killed, a further 357 Malay policemen had disappeared, their bodies never to be recovered[75].

The role given to the MPAJA following the Japanese surrender was that they should control towns and villages not occupied by the Japanese. However, some units took over towns regardless of whether the Japanese were there or not. For some 12 weeks after the surrender, Force 136 personnel were the only authority in many of these villages until the military or civil government eventually took over. There were numerous confrontations between Force 136, the MPAJA and the Japanese during this period but in general the MPAJA held to their side of the bargain.

When the 25th Indian Division eventually reached Kuala Lumpur on 13 September, they found Davis and elements of Force 136 already established in the city. Although the MPAJA had earlier signed an agreement with Davis, Broome, Chapman and Lim to assist the return of British administration and to use the MCP's peaceful popular front strategy, they were deemed as a potential threat to British colonial strategy. On 12 September 1945, while some of the leaders of the MPAJA were basking in the glory of the official Japanese surrender at the Municipal Building in Singapore, Headquarters Allied Land Forces Southeast Asia issued curt instructions to the MPAJA that their operational role had ceased and they were to hand over their weapons and disband.

Despite many people in Malaya welcoming the return of the colonial masters, it was the MPAJA who were seen as the real liberators, not the British. When the army moved into some areas and the People's Committees were disbanded, some guerrillas felt their moment of triumph had been stolen by the returning British. Having spent years starving in the jungles and fighting the Japanese, they now found themselves facing fresh British and Indian troops who were still looking for the war. The soldiers' high-handed treatment of these resistance heroes led to numerous misunderstandings, which included the MPAJA fighters being roughly treated by Indian troops who mistook the MPAJA fighters for Japanese soldiers[76].

In his memoirs 60 years on, Chin Peng, who took over as the secretary general of the CPM in 1948, claimed that the ethnic violence was not caused by the communists:

> As early as July—before the first of the two atomic bombs dropped on Japan—Japanese troops, disguised as AJA (Anti-Japanese Army) guerrillas, went to a mosque in Johore and slaughtered a pig. This immediately inflamed Malay sentiments and they turned on the local Chinese villagers. Datuk Onn Bin Jaafar was at this time the district officer for Batu Pahat under the Japanese administration. Trouble spread from Batu Pahat to Yong Peng. The Malays were armed with *parang panjang*—the long knife. The Chinese villagers who became their targets were unarmed and desperately called on the AJA for support. We could not ignore their predicament and ordered in units of our army as a protection force. The British liaison officers (Force 136), who frankly didn't understand the root causes of the problem and were not prepared to listen, tried to prevent us from going. We ignored them. In the end, many liaison officers had no option but to move with us. We set up a line and told the Malays not to cross it. The Malays, believing their magic amulets would shield them from bullets, charged our lines. We shot. Some dropped. The rest hesitated, then retreated. We chased them into nearby *kampongs* and confiscated every *parang panjang* we could find. The major attack in the Batu Pahat area resulted in our forces actually arresting Datuk Onn and his assistant. In the event, Datuk Onn helped bring the violence to an end by speaking to the Malays. It was a very emotional time and nobody was willing to listen coolly to details of how the racial trouble began. The killing was on a very large scale. At least 1,000 died. Naturally, propaganda had it that the MPAJA was the primary cause. This is patently untrue. In numerous other racial instances at this time, Chinese bandits were the culprits. The CPM, of course, was blamed for their activities as well. Teluk Anson and Ayer Kuning were areas that suffered this way[77].

For many, however, it is hard to accept Chin Peng's denial of involvement in the racial massacres during the phoney surrender.

The idea behind having clandestine operations in Malaya was to destabilise Japanese rule and defensive preparations in the country while providing effective intelligence for British forces planning to recapture Malaya. Although Force 136 was effective on both these counts through the agreements signed with the MCP and other smaller resistance groups, the limitations on its size and the separate agendas of the MCP and various other resistance groups meant that Force 136 did not have an effective force with which to control these groups once the war was over.

As long as the Japanese occupied Malaya, the MCP, the Chinese nationalists and the Malay resistance groups would put aside their differences and adopt the common aim of ousting the Japanese Imperial Army. However, once it became clear that the Japanese were on the way out, individual communal and political agendas began to resurface. The MCP, who agitated for greater political rights for Chinese in Malaya, a communist China and a communist state in pre-war Malaya, began to pursue their ideology again. The Chinese nationalists, who had worked with the communists in China and Malaya during the war, once again became their sworn enemies in the fight for China's future in the Malayan peninsula. The Malay nationalists were also now agitating for an independent Malaya under Malay rule and did not want the Chinese to have a greater say in Malayan politics; many had already joined up with Japanese groups willing to continue the struggle against the British. These separate and antagonistic agendas came to a head once Japanese control was removed as each group sought to fill the power vacuum. As Chin Peng notes:

> ...When there is talk about Malay units being pro-Japanese, Westerners again invariably fall into the easy trap of over-simplification. When we, as communist guerrillas worked with the British, none of us, for a single moment, considered ourselves pro-British. We were allies, but we had our own agenda. Likewise, following Japan's capitulation, a different set of circumstances presented themselves to us as far as the defeated army was concerned [78].

SEAC and Force 136 were in no position to control these disparate agendas, which had begun to surface during the phoney surrender period. Force 136, an espionage organisation, was obviously unable to quell the racial tensions and clashes that were emerging in the country. Although they were able to harness the various groups during the occupation, once their common goal had been achieved, it was impossible to get these groups to band together again. More worrying, the weapons that Force 136 had provided to these resistance groups would now be used against the local population and eventually against the British during the Emergency.

SEAC had not expected such a violent reaction from the various ethnic groups in the country. The interrupted transition of power from the Japanese to the British in Malaya meant that pre-war racial and political tensions, which had been controlled by earlier authorities and subsumed under a common goal during the Japanese occupation, was given free reign during the five weeks of the phoney surrender. The outpouring of ethnic violence and racial hatred in those few weeks, which were finally squelched upon the return of the British, had given elements within the MCP a taste of raw power and control. Such communal violence, almost unheard of before the war and now unleashed for such an extended period, would revisit the country less than three years later with the Communist Emergency of 1948.

Endnotes

1 Gough, Richard. *The Jungle was Red.* Singapore: SNP Panpac, 2003. 5.

2 Ibid. 5.

3 *Lim Bo Seng's Naval Contract, P.F. 146/8, Chungking, 19 October 1945, HS 9/1341/6.* London: The National Archives.

4 Ibid.

5 Ibid.

6 *KYBOC V COSEC NR 906, 15 November 1945, HS 9/1341/6.* London: The National Archives.

7 *Mr Tang. (Lim Bo Seng), HS 9/1341/6.* London: The National Archives.

8 Force 136 members in this chapter will be referred to by their given names, with aliases in brackets. Where they are referred to by their aliases (i.e. in quoted text), their given names will appear in brackets. *Ed.*

9 Ibid.

10 *Record of Activities of Tan Chong Tee (ZA/4), 27 September 1945, HS 1/107.* London: The National Archives.

11 Chapman, Colonel F. Spencer. *The Jungle is Neutral.* London: Chatto & Windus, 1949. 236.

12 Ibid. 236.

13 Ibid. 237.

14 Ibid. 239.

15 *Report on GUSTAVUS, HS 1/107.* London: The National Archives. Appendix D: 1.

16 *Report on OPERATION GUSTAVUS/PIRATE, HS 1/107.* London: The National Archives. 1.

17 *Report on GUSTAVUS, HS 1/107.* London: The National Archives. Appendix D: 2.

18 Ibid. Appendix D: 1.

19 Ibid. 2.

20 *Report on OPERATION GUSTAVUS/PIRATE, Record of Conference Held at Camp, 30–31 December 43, HS 1/107.* London: The National Archives. 1.

21 Chin Peng. *My Side of History.* Singapore: Media Masters, 2003. 100.

22 *Report on GUSTAVUS, HS 1/107.* London: The National Archives. 2.

23 *Report on OPERATION GUSTAVUS/PIRATE, HS 1/107.* London: The National Archives. 2.

24 *Report on GUSTAVUS, HS 1/107.* London: The National Archives. Appendix D: 4.

25 *Record of Activities of Tan Chong Tee (ZA/4), 27 September 1945, HS 1/107.* London: The National Archives. 1.

26 Ibid. 2.

27 *Report on GUSTAVUS, HS 1/107.* London: The National Archives. 2.

28 Ibid. 3.

29 *Report on OPERATION GUSTAVUS/PIRATE, HS 1/107.* London: The National Archives. 2.

30 Chin, 2003. 106.

31 *Record of Activities of Tan Chong Tee (ZA/4), 27 September 1945, HS 1/107.* London: The National Archives. 3.

32 *Report on GUSTAVUS, HS 1/107*. London: The National Archives. Appendix D: 3.

33 *Record of Activities of Tan Chong Tee (ZA/4), 27 September 1945, HS 1/107*. London: The National Archives. 3.

34 *Chan Siak Foo, Wong Kwong Fai, Ho Wing Pun Report on Incident Leading to Arrest, 9 September 1945, HS 1/107*. London: The National Archives. 2.

35 *Report on GUSTAVUS, HS 1/107*. London: The National Archives. Appendix D: 3.

36 Chapman, 1949. 259.

37 *Report on GUSTAVUS, HS 1/107*. London: The National Archives. Appendix D: 3.

38 Ibid. Appendix D: 3.

39 *Record of Activities of Tan Chong Tee (ZA/4), 27 September 1945, HS 1/107*. London: The National Archives. 3.

40 Pang, Augustine and Angeline Song (eds.). "Meet Singapore's James Bond". *Chee Beng's Start Page*. 1998. [Internet]. Available from: <http://ourstory.asia1.com.sg/war/lifeline/bond7.html>.

41 Ibid.

42 *Record of Activities of Tan Chong Tee (ZA/4), 27 September 1945, HS 1/107*. London: The National Archives. 3.

43 Tan Chong Tee. *Force 136: Story of a WWII Resistance Fighter*. Singapore: Asiapac Books, 1995.

44 *Signal Sheet, HS 9/1341/6*. London: The National Archives.

45 Ibid.

46 Ibid.

47 Ibid.

48 Ibid.

49 *KBOC V COSEC NR. 432, 2 October 1945, HS 9/1341/6*. London: The National Archives.

50 *Letter to John Davis, 2 October 1945, HS 1/107*. London: The National Archives. 1.

51 *KYBOC V COSEC NR 1616, 4 October 1945, HS 9/1341/6*. London: The National Archives.

52 *KYBOC V COSEC NR 1994, 6 October 1945, HS 9/1341/6*. London: The National Archives.

53 *SRL 362/363, 10 December 1945, HS 9/1341/6*. London: The National Archives.

54 *From Kuala Lumpur, 13 December 1945, HS 9/1341/6*. London: The National Archives.

55 *SRL NO 637/8, 10 January 1945, HS 9/1341/6*. London: The National Archives.

56 *CAOG 9/337*. London: The National Archives.

57 Gough, 2003. 104.

58 Ibid. 114.

59 Ibid. 130.

60 Ibid. 131.

61 Ibid. 131.

62 Ibid. 131.

63 Ibid. 131.

64 Ibid. 132.

65 Ibid. 132.

66 *J.P.S. 180, G.25/4387, 6 August 1945, HS 1/328*. London: The National Archives. 1–3.

67 Ibid. 1.

68 Ibid. 1.

69 *Direction of Clandestine Operations after Japanese Capitulation, C.S.300.4/M, 15 August 1945, HS 1/328*. London: The National Archives. 1.

70 Gough, 2003. 141.

71 Ibid. 159.

72 Ibid. 159.

73 Ibid. 159.

74 Ibid. 160.

75 Ibid. 159.

76 Ibid. 170.

77 Chin, 2003. 127.

78 Ibid. 128.

Chapter 4

The Early Surrenders

In the week after the 15 August announcement of Japan's surrender, an uneasy silence prevailed as signals traffic among Japanese forces in Malaya came to a standstill.

Signal officers at SEAC, keen to implement TIDERACE, desperately needed to contact General Seishiro Itagaki, Commander of the 7th Area Army in Singapore, but all signals sent had been ignored by the Japanese forces.

Mountbatten had been so concerned that Singapore would not surrender that he sent out an urgent directive to all his commanders that should the circumstances warrant it, an urgent naval force should be launched at a moment's notice, ahead even of TIDERACE to recapture Singapore and Penang. Although there would be no assault troops as part of this new operation, tentatively codenamed TROPIC, Mountbatten called on the Allied Air commander-in-chief to provide sufficient air cover and transport to help achieve the objectives of the operation[1]. Although this plan was clearly impractical and was never carried out, the fact that Mountbatten would even have considered such an urgent recapture showed his high level of anxiety regarding the retaking of Singapore.

> At SEAC headquarters in Kandy, Captain Frank O'Shanohun, a recently-arrived SEAC Staff Signals Officer, was sent to Mountbatten at his residence in Peradeniya to tell him that Itagaki was not responding to SEAC signals, and to ask for further orders. They were joined by Colonel

(later Brigadier General) John Anstey, the Deputy Head of the SOE India Mission (Force 136). Mountbatten was silent for some moments then commented generally, "Well I suppose someone should go to Singapore and find out what he proposes to do". Turning to Anstey, he asked, "Who do you suggest we send?" There was a pause for a full minute following which Anstey turned to O'Shanohun and asked, "Are you doing anything at the moment?"[2].

As O'Shanohun recalls, he was to be dropped by Liberator aircraft on the Singapore racecourse at dawn. A small team of doctors would accompany him with about two tons of medical supplies and food[3].

When I left, we were still signalling the Japanese that Mountbatten was sending a senior British officer, me, to discuss the arrival of the British task force. However, in spite of repeated signals in clear, the Japanese did not reply so I had no idea what to expect once I landed.

It was that grey moment before daybreak when we arrived over Singapore (on 19 August 1945). There were no enemy fighters. No flak. Everything appeared quiet. As we overflew Singapore (I)sland, we saw the occasional fires as the kampongs began to wake up. The city was blacked-out but the racecourse was soon identified. As we passed over we could see it was empty. No apparent enemy reception committee.

After the aircraft circled once, I sat on the slide and waited. Then the green light came on. I felt a hard tap, more a push, on the back by the dispatcher and I was down that slide and into the dawn sky. Looking around me as I hung beneath the parachute's silk canopy, the city appeared asleep and I could see its empty blacked-out streets, which would have been bustling before the war. It was all rather eerie. Three minutes later, I hit the ground hard, some distance from the main stand.

A bit shaken, I stood up and discarded the parachute harness and looked around. I was alone in the middle of the racecourse without a Jap in sight. Then, as I began to walk towards the main stand, I saw movement as a Japanese officer stepped out of the shadows. This was it!

I kept on walking towards him and as I drew closer I saw a white band around his sleeve. A little later, when I heard the drone of the returning Liberator, I ran back and laid out white panels to show it was safe for the others to drop. After negotiating with the Japanese, one of the first places we visited was Sime Road civilian internment camp. I was soon told quite sharply by the crusty civilian doctors that I could take my medical team away. After more than three years in a Japanese camp, they knew all the internees' medical problems, I was told. "Just give us the medical supplies," they said, "and we can do the job ourselves"[4].

On 18 August, the day before O'Shanohun's arrival in Singapore, Itagaki had gone to Saigon to meet with Field Marshal Count Hsiaichi Terauchi, where he was told in no uncertain terms to obey the surrender instructions of the Allied commanders. Itagaki had initially baulked at Terauchi's order to surrender and an early landing by Allied forces might have precipitated the stubborn Itagaki into ordering his 70,000-strong Singapore garrison and the 26,000 men in Malaya to resist. Worse still, a plan to massacre all the prisoners might have been carried out[5].

On 20 August, Itagaki met O'Shanohun in Singapore and, later that day, Itagaki signalled Mountbatten that he would abide by his emperor's decision and was ready to receive instructions for the Japanese surrender of Singapore. The next morning, close to a week after the Japanese emperor's announcement, newspapers in Singapore were allowed to carry the text of the emperor's speech, confirming what many already knew from listening to All India Radio broadcasts from Delhi on forbidden shortwave radios that had been hidden away. On 22 August, Itagaki held a meeting with his generals and senior staff at the 7th Army headquarters at Raffles College in Bukit Timah. He told his men that they would have to obey the surrender instructions and keep the peace.

That night, more than 300 Japanese officers and men committed suicide. Others deserted and travelled to Sumatra to join the anti-Dutch freedom movement or went over to the MCP in Johor with their weapons to continue the fight against the British[6].

On 19 August, a team of Japanese envoys had left Tokyo to discuss the surrender arrangements. Led by Lieutenant General Kalabi Takashiba, vice chief of the imperial Japanese army staff, they went to General Douglas MacArthur's headquarters in Manila. As the Tokyo team set off to see MacArthur, a personal representative from the emperor left to instruct General Hyotaro Kimura, commander of the Japanese Burma Army to surrender the Japanese forces there[7].

Plans were soon being made too, covering the surrender of Japanese forces in Java, New Guinea, the Solomons and those opposing General Chiang Kai Shek's (in *pinyin*, Jiang Jieshi) forces in western Hunan province. MacArthur agreed with British requests that the Japanese in Hong Kong surrender to the British Royal Navy's Rear Admiral Cecil Harcourt. On 20 August, Lieutenant General Sir Montague George North Stopford, General Officer Commanding (GOC), 12th Army, ordered Kimura to make surrender arrangements.

Following Mountbatten's signal to Terauchi on 20 August, a Japanese delegation from Terauchi's headquarters in Saigon, led by his chief of staff (CoS), Lieutenant General Tokazo Numata, arrived at Ingahado Airfield outside Rangoon on 26 August, for talks before the signing of a preliminary surrender agreement. Terauchi was unable to attend any of the surrender negotiations, having recently suffered a stroke that had left him partially paralysed. Mountbatten's earlier date of 23 August for the Burma conference was thus pushed to 26 August in order to allow enough time for Terauchi's staff to make the logistical arrangements to attend the conference.

Six Spitfire fighters and a light spotter plane escorted the two silver-painted Japanese Topsy aircraft as they landed. The Japanese planes bore the specially agreed-upon green cross code markings on the underside of their wings.

Numata, short, and wearing black-rimmed glasses, had served as the CoS of the Japanese 2nd Area Army in the Celebes before being appointed as CoS of the Japanese Southern Army in 1944[8]. Accompanying him was deputy chief of staff (DCoS) Admiral Kaigyo Chudo, who had commanded the 8th Section of the Japanese Navy General Staff and had been involved in the aborted plans to invade Australia[9]. Dressed in drab khaki uniforms, the two were accompanied by staff officer Lieutenant Colonel Moro Tomuria. The collars of their open white shirts were worn outside their tunics, their high field boots were immaculately polished, and all carried swords. They did not salute.

While the 22-strong Japanese team was being taken to a nearby tent to be searched for poison and weapons, a security team of British sergeants searched the aircraft. The delegation was then marched across to where Major General George William Symes, GOC, Southern Burma, was waiting to receive them. After a brief introduction, the Japanese were then driven to their accommodation by military policemen in three station wagons with the blinds drawn down. They were followed by an army three-tonner carrying their kit and rations of corned beef, rice, cucumber and raisins, which they had brought with them. The Japanese accommodation was enclosed by barbed wire and floodlit at night.

As the talks began in the Throne Room of Government House, it soon became clear that the Japanese team had come to negotiate and comment on Mountbatten's terms of surrender, rather than to sign it.

Lieutenant General Sir Frederick Arthur Montague Browning, Mountbatten's CoS, led the Allied team. Serving as the GOC of the British 1st Airborne Division in North Africa from 1941 to 1943, Browning was GOC of the 1st Airborne Corps in Northwest Europe in 1944. Later that same year, he took over as Deputy General Officer Commanding (DGOC) of the 1st Airborne Army over Northwest Europe. Once the European sector was freed, he was attached to SEAC command for the closing chapter in the Pacific[10].

Irritated by the delays, Browning acted quickly and firmly. He allowed no discussion whatsoever of the actual terms laid down and allowed only questions of clarification and amplification. It took three long, drawn-out meetings with the Japanese delegates before a final draft was agreed upon. The preliminary agreement, originally to have been signed at 6.00pm on 27 August, was eventually signed at 1.00am on 28 August. Instructions were then sent to all Japanese senior field commanders through Terauchi to forthwith obey and assist the British commanders of the reoccupying forces.

The Throne Room of Government House, with the Union Jack, the Stars and Stripes, and the nationalist Chinese, Dutch and French flags draped from its balconies, and specially fitted with 12,000 candle power floodlights, "looked like a Hollywood film set!"[11].

For the signing ceremony, a small table and three hard-backed chairs were set out for the Japanese, facing a long table for the Allied generals. Both sides had inkwells, pens and pencils but, significantly, only the Allies had erasers.

The three Japanese, Numata, Chudo and Tomuria, marched with dignity to the table, took off their caps and stood stiffly at attention while the press photographed them. The Allied delegates then entered the room from under a huge Union Jack.

Browning, dressed in a jungle-green bush shirt, came in last and sat down at the centre of the long table. After he had explained the terms of the agreement, Browning's deputy director of intelligence, Brigadier General John Gerald Nicholson, took the papers over to the Japanese. Numata took off his glasses before looking through the documents and then quickly dipped a pen into the inkwell and signed. Beside him, Chudo and Tomuria sat at attention, looking straight ahead with faces devoid of expression. The papers were returned to Browning who signed them, and then passed back to Numata for the affixing of Terauchi's seal. In less than 20 minutes, the ceremony was over.

The Burma conference was in effect the Japanese surrender of Southeast Asia. The terms listed in the appendices of the agreement set out how the Japanese would surrender but Mountbatten was at pains to make sure it was not portrayed as such because MacArthur was to have the honour of the 'first surrender' at Tokyo Bay while Mountbatten was to have his own moment of glory with the official surrender in Singapore on 12 September. However, in a top-secret memo to his chiefs, Mountbatten admitted the significance of the Rangoon Agreement:

> The Japanese representatives signed at RANGOON a document which was in effect but not in name an instrument of surrender covering S.E.A.C. area, although, in order to comply with instructions I received from the Supreme Commander for the Allied Powers (MacArthur) not to sign any surrender papers before the TOKYO event, the document has been called a local 'agreement'[12].

Typhoons raging over Japan forced a delay in MacArthur's arrival to take the overall Japanese surrender. However, on 26 August, a massive American fleet sailed into Sagami Bay, just outside Tokyo Bay. After hurried preparations by engineers and communications specialists, MacArthur finally landed at Atsugi airfield on 30 August, together with leading elements of the American 11th Airborne Division.

The formal instrument of surrender of the Emperor of Japan, his government and his people was signed on a mess table on board the American battleship *USS Missouri* at 10.30am on Sunday, 2 September 1945. MacArthur was flanked by Lieutenant General Jonathan Mayhew Wainwright, who had surrendered the American forces to the Japanese at Corregidor, as well as by Lieutenant General Arthur Ernest Percival, former GOC, Malaya Command, who had surrendered the British and Commonwealth forces in Malaya to the Japanese in 1942.

With the official Japanese surrender over, it was now imperative for SEAC to not only take the surrenders in Malaya and Singapore but to reoccupy the territories urgently. Permission to execute Operation TIDERACE was given. The question now was how soon the British would be able to recapture Malaya and whether these non-assault-loaded forces would face fierce resistance from the Japanese army there.

Endnotes

1 *Operational Directive No. 37, OD/201/37, 15 August 1945, WO203/2308.* London: The National Archives.

2 Gough, Richard. *The Jungle was Red.* Singapore: SNP Panpac. 148.

3 Ibid. 150.

4 Ibid. 151.

5 Corr, Gerard. "The War was Over—but Where were the Liberators?". *The Straits Times Annual 1976.* Singapore: Times Publishing Bhd. 49–52, 156.

6 Ibid. 51.

7 Fursdon, Major General Edward. "Without Saluting the Japanese Came to Bargain but Soon the Sun Set on Their Empire". *The Daily Telegraph*, 12 August 1985. 11.

8 Ammentorp, Steen. "Biography of Takazo Numata". *The Generals of WWII.* [Internet]. Accessed 28 January, 2005. Available from: <http://www.generals.dk/general/Numata/Takazo/Japan.html>.

9 Dunn, Peter. "Was there a Japanese Invasion Planned to Occur between Townsville and Brisbane in Queensland during WW2?". *Australia @ War.* [Internet]. Accessed 28 January 2005. Available from: <http://home.st.net.au/~dunn/japsland/invade02.htm>.

10 Ammentorp, Steen. "Biography of Sir Frederick Arthur Montague Browning". *The Generals of WWII.* [Internet]. Accessed 28 January 2005. Available from: <http://www.generals.dk/general/Browning/Sir_Frederick_Arthur_Montague/Great_Britain.html>.

11 Fursdon, 1985. 11.

12 *Mountbatten to Commanders in Chief, SAC(45) 14411, 29 August 1945, WO203/4917.* London: The National Archives.

Chapter 5

Operation TIDERACE

As he made last-minute preparations to implement TIDERACE, Rear (later Vice) Admiral Cedric Holland was keen to ensure that the recapture of Singapore was carried out quickly and efficiently.

A naval man through and through, Holland's father had also been an admiral in the Royal Navy with a long illustrious line of naval officers preceding him. With a sharp, hooked nose and a quick wit, Holland, known as 'Hookey' to his friends, had served his country in the First World War and was the British naval attaché for Western Europe, based in Paris from 1938 to 1940. At the outbreak of the Second World War, he was put in command of the *HMS Ark Royal.* In June 1940, he joined *HMS Hood* and *HMS Foxhound* as part of Force 'H' in Gibraltar, where he acquitted himself admirably in the negotiations and operations against the French fleet at Oran. Promoted to the rank of Rear Admiral in 1942, he was Director of Signals at the Admiralty until 1943, when he was transferred to the East Indies fleet. On 1 June 1945, Holland was again promoted, this time to the rank of Vice Admiral.

A year away from retirement at the age of 56, Holland was handpicked in early August 1945 by Admiral Arthur Power, the Commander-in-Chief of the British East Indies Fleet, to lead TIDERACE as the Naval Force Commander to recapture Singapore and act as the SEAC Naval Representative in accepting the initial Japanese surrender of Singapore aboard a warship in the city's harbour.

However, the Japanese had yet to agree to this initial surrender ceremony. The agreement signed in Rangoon only listed the official ceremony on 12 September and no mention was made of this separate agreement. As a result, the Japanese were caught unawares when on 30 August, Holland signalled the Japanese with instructions for meeting his delegation:

> The commanders of the Japanese Naval and Army forces at Singapore are to meet representatives of the Supreme Allied Commander Southeast Asia on board *HMS SUSSEX* at 0200 G.M.T. on 4 September, in position latitude 01 degs. 10′, longitude 103 degs. 30′...
>
> ... The craft carrying the Japanese commanders will fly a large white flag. It is to have no ammunition or explosives on board and the breach blocks of its guns are to be removed before it reaches the rendezvous. No other shipping is to be within 10 miles of the rendezvous[1]...

In addition, the signal instructed the Japanese commanders to bring lists showing the position of all shipping, charts showing all minefields, berths occupied by ships and all obstacles to navigation. Maps were also requested showing the locations of all gun positions, fortifications and troops on the island as well as the positions of prisoner of war (POW) camps, dumps, stores, and radar and wireless equipment.

The *HMS Sussex* sailed from Trincomalee on 31 August 1945 at 11.30am at 16 knots. Major General Ralph Hone, head of the Civilian Administration Service Malaya (CAS (M)), had come aboard the ship the night before. On receipt of a signal from Vice Admiral (later Sir) Harold Thomas Coulthard Walker, Second-in-Command of the British East Indies Fleet (EIF), who was leading operation JURIST, Holland increased the speed of the fleet to 25 knots and headed for Penang[2].

However, just as this first force was leaving Trincomalee, the first British airmen had already 'retaken' Singapore.

Flight Lieutenant FL Andrews and Warrant Officer NS Painter from 684 Squadron, based in the Cocos Islands, were carrying out a photo-reconnaissance mission over Johor when suddenly the sustained roaring note of the engines changed in tone. Anxiously, Andrews scanned his instrument panel for an indication of what was wrong and diagnosed a fault in the constant speed unit.

Although the crew were not in immediate danger, they were faced with a difficult decision. Should they try to fly back across the Indian Ocean with the possibility of being forced to ditch, or risk a landing in Singapore? Although the war had ended, it was still unclear whether the Japanese in Singapore and Malaya would surrender peacefully. After some debate, they agreed to risk a landing.

Selecting the pre-war civilian aerodrome at Kallang, Andrews nosed the Mosquito plane down and then circled the area cautiously, trying to spot any danger before going into a final approach. There did not appear to be any craters in the landing strip and the Japanese, who had been watching the plane's circuits, made no aggressive gestures.

Armed soldiers ran out to meet the taxiing aircraft and Andrews and Painter followed the directions of the flag-waving marshals quite apprehensively, placing the Mosquito in a camouflaged dispersal bay. A few tense moments followed as the Japanese soldiers and airmen tried to make each other understood. However, the situation improved when an interpreter appeared, followed by a cheering crowd of prisoners of war (POWs) who had been working at the airfield. Arrangements were made for two of the POWs, who happened to be a British Royal Air Force (RAF) engineering officer and a fitter, to service the Mosquito. Although it was a type they had never seen before, the two managed to repair the constant speed unit. The two airmen spent a night as guests of their enemies, answering questions from the POWs who wanted news of the war. Although Allied doctors had been air-dropped into the Changi area on 30 August, the two airmen were the first British soldiers to land in Singapore. A terse signal was sent to SEAC informing them of the situation:

> From F/Lt. F.L. ANDREWS and W.O. PAINTER N.S. who made a forced landing at the COLON (Kallang) airfield SINGAPORE at noon today. Message reads: "Landed Colon airfield today due engine trouble"[3].

The next day, the Mosquito flew out of Singapore, ending the unofficial reoccupation of Singapore on 1 September 45.

The *HMS Sussex* along with part of the TIDERACE convoy arrived at Penang at 4.30pm on 2 September.

Late in the evening, Holland met with Vice Admiral Walker, who informed him of the Japanese surrender of Penang and handed over the Japanese minefield charts and other information brought up by Japanese officers from Singapore.

British naval forces had already been around Penang island for days. On 27 August, Vice Admiral Walker, aboard *HMS Nelson*, had led a British Task Group, which included *HMS Ceylon*, the escort carriers *HMS Hunter* and *HMS Attacker*, three destroyers and two Landing Ships Infantry (LSIs), out of port in Rangoon and set a heading for Penang, arriving there the next day.

During the 26 August discussions in Rangoon, Lieutenant General Numata, Field Marshal Count Hsiaichi Terauchi's chief of staff (CoS), had already cabled the 10th Area Fleet of the Japanese Southern Army in preparation for Walker's arrival:

> British naval units arriving off Penang, Sabang and possibly off West coast of Malaya, North and East coast of Sumatra forenoon 28 August. Aircraft and suicide craft ordered not to attack. Japanese guarantees security within harbour and coastal waters. British minesweepers commencing operations off Penang, Sabang, Malacca Straits and subsequently Singapore probably 28 August. Cooperate in supplying fresh water and vegetables to British fleet[4].

On the afternoon of 28 August, Walker met with junior Japanese naval and military representatives from Penang and made them sign an undertaking that no attack would be made on the British fleet off Penang[5]. This document was in effect another Japanese surrender, five days before the ceremony at Tokyo Bay.

After three more meetings, where the British forces ferreted out details on Japanese dispositions and locations in Malaya, Walker was poised to accept the Japanese surrender of Penang on the morning of 2 September 1945. However, when the Japanese representatives boarded the *Nelson*, their senior representatives were nowhere to be found. This was because the naval commander of Penang, Rear Admiral Jisaku Uozumi, had not yet received permission from Terauchi to sign the documents. Upon Walker's insistence, Uozumi eventually turned up for the meeting along with the Japanese Deputy Governor of Penang, Shigeru Mochinaga.

Uozumi was no stranger to the British Admiralty but Walker was surprised to see him wearing the British Distinguished Service Cross and Allied Victory Medal for his part as an ally in the First World War[6]. Serving as the captain of the Japanese cruiser *Haguro* in 1942, Uozumi had seen action at the Battle of the Java Sea where the remnants of the British and Dutch naval forces after the fall of Singapore and the Dutch East Indies faced superior Japanese naval forces in a last stand. The encounter ended with the almost total destruction of the Allied fleet. Uozumi had also served as a senior officer on the Japanese naval staff before being appointed naval commander of Penang island in August 1944. Ironically, the ship that he had commanded in victory barely two years before was sunk by the British East Indies fleet on 16 May 1945, just 45 miles southwest of Penang. Stepping on board the *Nelson*, Uozumi had clearly accepted the fate of the Japanese forces in Malaya. He apologised profusely but said he still had not received permission to sign the terms[7].

Walker, visibly upset, made the two Japanese representatives sign an undertaking that they would comply with the instructions of the British commanders following which Uozumi and Mochinaga departed on their naval vessel. A few minutes later, the Japanese vessel returned to the *Nelson*. On their way back to Penang, Terauchi had finally signalled Uozumi with his permission to sign. Thus, at 9.15pm on 2 September 1945, Uozumi and Mochinaga signed the surrender of Penang[8].

At 8.00am the following day, 480 British Royal Marines, known as Force Roma, landed on Penang island[9]. As the marines moved through the island to take over Bayan Lepas airfield and other installations from the Japanese, food riots broke out. The riots were eventually quelled but it was a clear sign of things to come[10].

Only at this point of the reoccupation did Terauchi cable Mountbatten with the message that he was agreeable to the Singapore shipboard discussions but not necessarily the signing of a surrender agreement:

> I presume the proposed conference to be held on board a warship on 4 September at Singapore is aimed to discuss the moving of a part of your forces as arranged in the preliminary agreement concluded at RANGOON. If this is the case I am ready to send my staff to attend the conference[11].

At 6.30am on 3 September, the *Sussex* sailed from Penang and contacted the TIDERACE convoy coming from Rangoon about two hours later. Up until then, everything was going according to plan. Then, the confusion began.

As part of SEAC's planning, the 15th Indian Corp was set to take over the land advance into Singapore. Lieutenant General Sir Alexander Christison, who had served in the First World War and had taken over temporarily as General Officer Commanding (GOC) of the British 14th Army in Burma, was appointed GOC, 15th Indian Corps.

As such, the 5th Indian Division, which was to take the surrender of the Japanese in Singapore, would now come under the 15th Indian Corps. The 5th Indian Division was led by Major General Eric Mansergh, who had served for many years in India and was fluent in Urdu. He had led the 5th Division in Burma as part of Operation MODIFIED DRACULA and now his division had been tasked with the Singapore surrender.

Christison, who had been at the surrender negotiations in Rangoon while the 15th Indian Corps was being reorganised, believed that as GOC, he would be the SEAC army representative and would now take the formal surrender of the Japanese, while his subordinate Mansergh would command the military reoccupation of Singapore. This meant that Holland would be both the SEAC naval representative and the naval force commander, and Christison would be the SEAC army representative and the military force commander while Mansergh would now be acting under his command instead of as the SEAC army representative.

Accordingly, before leaving Rangoon with the convoy on 28 August, Christison cabled Holland:

> I have assumed function of military force comd for operation TIDERACE vice comd 5 Ind Div now under my comd. Sailing with my Tac HQ in RMT DILWARA with first convoy. Propose come aboard *HMS SUSSEX* on arrival at KEPPEL Harbour unless you particularly require me aboard earlier.
>
> Procedure agreed here (Rangoon) yesterday as follows. On our arrival KEPPEL Harbour special Japanese liaison officer from Field Marshal COUNT TERAUCHI to Gen ITAGAKI will be summoned aboard *SUSSEX* where he will give us the situation and we as joint force commanders will give him our orders for ITAGAKI. As soon as we are satisfied we will put 5 Div ashore. NO landing to be permitted until leading tps 5 Div are established ashore. Please signal me to Naval HQ RANGOON your agreement above plan[12].

However, this message did not reach Holland before he departed Trincomalee and so he was unaware of the change in representatives when Holland's ship met the Rangoon convoy on 3 September. Thus, Holland was upset when he saw Christison board his ship:

> Here the General Officers Commanding of the 15th Corps and 5th Indian Division were transferred from SS DERBYSHIRE and DILWARA to *HMS SUSSEX.* It was not clear why the General Officer Commanding of the 15th Corps required a passage in *HMS SUSSEX*, since there had been no official signal from SACSEA nominating him as the Supreme Allied Commander's Army representative in place of the General Officer Commanding the 5th Indian Division[13].

Holland was unhappy that Christison had joined the party as an uninvited guest, one who would now outrank him at the negotiations with the Japanese. In his report, Holland questioned the need for having such high-level representation at the Corps level and the added complexity this entailed:

> The introduction of a corps headquarters at a later stage in the planning was a considerable complication, and served no useful purpose. 'TIDERACE' was a Divisional operation, and it was on that level that negotiations, entry and the development of the Island should have been executed[14].

More urgently, Holland had already signalled instructions to the Japanese before his departure from Trincomalee and Christison's contradictory instructions to the Japanese representatives in Rangoon over the Singapore surrender arrangements at the last minute had caused confusion on the Japanese side as the signal from Holland's Staff Officer to SACSEA HQ indicated:

> May have difficulty over PARLEYS on 4 September as BS3 (Vice Admiral Walker on board *HMS Nelson* in Penang) has been given a letter signed by the Japanese Army and Naval Commander at Singapore stating "They are not allowed to negotiate directly with the CINC British East Indies representative before the formal agreement is made between the SACSEA and the Supreme Commander of the Japanese Forces in the Southern Region". I have asked BS3 to inform Singapore that Conference on board *HMS SUSSEX* is being held by representatives of SACSEA and is for the purpose of arranging details based on the general agreement signed at Rangoon[15].

Furious, Holland held meetings with Mansergh to sort out the now-complicated situation and review the detailed plan for the entry of the reoccupying force into Singapore.

Christison, however, was concerned with what he felt were more pressing matters. Field Marshal William Joseph Slim, commander-in-chief of the Allied Land Forces, Southeast Asia had signalled him on the evening of 3 September with an intercepted Japanese message from the Japanese naval fleet in Singapore to Tokyo. The intercepted message read:

> The impression received by our representative who made the negotiations with the British navy in PENANG (from 28 August to 2 September) was that the British are extremely worried about our unrestricted movements and specially fear our special attack boats on the occasion of their occupation of Singapore. Since the primary objective of the agreement reached by the supreme army and navy commanders at Singapore and the British navy is to guarantee the safety of the above it would seem best to comply with this agreement. I believe that unreasonable demands such as that of today to the effect that all Japanese forces on Singapore (I)sland evacuate the island by 5 September are a reaction to the permission to wear swords granted by the above commanders [16].

Slim wanted to know if Christison had asked for swords to be handed-in and the present status of negotiations. Holland's signal to the Japanese on 30 August called for the evacuation of Japanese troops by 5 September and Vice Admiral Walker had asked for Japanese swords to be handed-in during the negotiations at Penang earlier in the week. Christison had not been involved in any of these instructions and was unaware that such instructions had been issued. He was now upset that he had to respond to Slim's query on the present status, which was not of his doing. It was obvious that Christison and Holland were at odds and each was unhappy with the unilateral actions of the other.

However, the most crucial part of the signal was the Japanese reference to the British fear of special attack boats. Although the signal indicated that the Japanese navy would not use them against the British fleet in Singapore, this did not mean that the TIDERACE fleet would not receive a rude shock from rogue naval elements when they moved into the outer Singapore roads the next day.

At about 9.00am on 4 September, Holland, Mansergh and Christison, all aboard the *Sussex*, arrived at the rendezvous point just outside Keppel Harbour and were met by Admiral Arthur Power, commander-in-chief of the British East Indies Fleet, who had arrived on the scene aboard the *HMS Cleopatra*. This was a fortuitous turn of events for Holland as it meant he would have support from his superior in determining who would hold the negotiations with the Japanese. In the end, however, Power convinced Holland to go along with Christison and hold the negotiations. In his own report, Power did not mention the disagreement but was at pains to portray the meeting among the commanders as cordial and that, "TIDERACE appeared to be running smoothly"[17]. Power left the *Sussex* just as the Japanese delegates were being escorted from their vessel.

The next few hours would determine whether the British takeover would be smooth or whether resistance would break out. Just after 8.00am, liaison officers on the *Sussex* reported that General Seishiro Itagaki and Vice Admiral Shigeru Fukudome were waiting to come aboard. This was a good sign. With the two top commanders coming aboard, it was unlikely that an attack was imminent. Nonetheless, all ships remained on alert.

The Japanese ships were kept waiting until about 10.00am when they were signalled over:

> General ITAGAKI and Vice Admiral FUKUDOME were brought on board at 1013 (hours), and were met by Captain A.F. de Salis (Captain of *HMS Sussex*)...and an armed officer escort...
>
> ... They were taken to a cabin (Major General Ralph Hone's cabin), where they left their swords, and were then brought into the Admiral's Dining Cabin. Here the British representatives were seated to receive the Japanese envoys, who were instructed to sit down facing them. They were given the terms to read...[18]

The terms of surrender were comprehensive[19] (see "Appendix F: Part I"). The Japanese forces on Singapore island and in Malaya were to be treated as "surrendered personnel" rather than as prisoners of war. In an order to his commanders, Mountbatten had made it explicit that it would be at his discretion whether Japanese forces would be made POWs or Surrendered Enemy Personnel. The reasons, he noted, were two-fold:

Major General EC Mansergh: Commander of the 5th Indian Division, he would later become commander-in-chief of British Land Forces.

a) It avoids any claim by the Japanese to the standard of treatment and privileges which should be accorded to P.W. (prisoners of war) under the Geneva Convention.

b) It saves us from the embarrassment of having to deal with a large number of P.W. immediately capitulation (*sic*) takes place, and with which we have neither the forces nor the material resources to deal[20].

The Allied commanders also ordered that 100 large staff cars in "high-class condition" be made available for the use of the occupying forces. A further 500 lorries, with drivers, were to assemble in the dock area, and another 100 at the Kallang airfield on the day of occupation.

A curfew from sunset to sunrise was also imposed until further notice. Orders were also issued for all stocks of spirits and liquor shops to be sealed and guarded, and reports were also required of all epidemics or infectious diseases, the location of hospitals and laboratories, together with that of all Allied sick and wounded men. The Singapore Military Hospital (at Alexandra) would be emptied of all Japanese patients except those who were too ill to be moved. It would then be cleaned and made ready for use by the Allied medical services. In addition, interpreters and guides were to be available to help the landing forces[21] (see "Appendix F: Part II").

A Japanese general was selected to report twice daily to Mansergh for orders and this would be the only official line of communication. The 28 Japanese generals who remained in Singapore were left housed in Raffles College on Upper Bukit Timah Road[22].

The two Japanese representatives took six hours to consider and negotiate the terms with the Allied representatives. They raised many points but in the end agreed to most of the instructions. At 6.05pm, Itagaki and Fukudome signed the Singapore Surrender document.

Holland noted that the agreement would not have been signed had it not been for the tough position taken by the Allied generals:

> In dealing with the Japanese, firmness pays. He will endeavour to spin out negotiations as long as possible, in order to save face, and will take advantage of any loophole to twist out of his obligations. A little determination will quickly get the Japanese down, but he has great resilience and will bounce up again if not held in his place. Many Japanese Naval Officers (like Fukudome) understand and speak English well, but they will not at first admit it[23].

Sixty years on, the original Surrender of Singapore and Surrender of Penang documents cannot be located at the National Archives in London, nor in files of the former Colonial, War or Foreign Offices. Although copies of the various texts have been found, the original with Itagaki and Fukudome's signatures and stamps are no longer part of the collection of files in which they should be located. The documents are believed to have been forwarded to SEAC Headquarters and then to the War and Colonial Offices but there the trail ends. No trace remains of who were the last officials in Whitehall to see these original surrender documents. The documents could have been removed so that they would not detract from the historical impact of the formal Japanese surrender on 12 September, or simply 'misplaced' in the last days of the war. However, the creation of these documents and the events they cover can no longer be hidden. Sixty years after the war, the secret surrenders have now come to light but the original documents that represent it have been lost in time. It will remain one of the last mysteries of the end of the war.

Although the surrender on board the *Sussex* was covered by the international press, most of Singapore was unaware of the momentous events happening in the seas off Singapore . As international publications and radio transmissions were prohibited within the country, much of the population of Singapore remained blissfully ignorant of the British return until their ships docked at Keppel Harbour. As the liberated newspapers would only begin publishing four days later (with most of the local journalists liberated only days before from internment camps and clearly not up to speed on what was going on) the first edition of *The Straits Times* made no mention of the Japanese surrender of Singapore aboard the *Sussex*. Even British newspapers with correspondents on board the *Sussex* did not report the event beyond a brief mention of British troops reoccupying the region[24]. The only item in *The Times* was a one-paragraph report on Power meeting Holland off Singapore. As a result, most of the people in Malaya and Singapore who lived through the war remember the 12 September ceremony as the official Japanese surrender of Singapore.

Although the 12 September ceremony is considered the only Japanese surrender of Singapore and Southeast Asia, this becomes problematic as Mountbatten, by his own account, admitted that the Rangoon Conference on 28 August was the effective surrender of Japanese forces in Southeast Asia, not in name but in action. Thus, all agreements following this would be local surrenders. Count Terauchi in Saigon and his field commanders throughout the region were well aware of the Rangoon agreement and the Japanese responsibility to adhere to the terms of the agreement. This is what followed in Penang on 2 September, when the garrison surrendered to the British followed by the Surrender Agreement signed aboard the *Sussex* on 4 September. With the signing of the document and the reoccupation of Singapore by the 5th Indian Division on 5 September, the communal violence in Singapore and Malaya, which had caused the deaths of so many, came effectively to an end[25]. Less than a day after the 4 September surrender, 35,000 Japanese troops were also evacuated from Singapore to prison camps in Johor[26]. With the ZIPPER landings begun on 9 September and the major cities and towns in Malaya under effective—but not 'official'—British military control by 11 September, the ceremony on 12 September was nothing more than just an additional floorshow.

Mountbatten had already shown with the reoccupation of Singapore on 5 September and the Malayan mainland on 9 September that the Allied forces had retaken Malaya with a superior force. It was clear to all Japanese military commanders that they would have to surrender and accept British military rule. Moreover, General Itagaki had signed the Singapore Surrender Agreement on 4 September on instructions from Count Terauchi. He then reprised that same role on 12 September. As a result, Mountbatten was only taking a purely ceremonial surrender of the Japanese forces in Southeast Asia on 12 September. The effective surrenders of Japanese forces had occurred in Rangoon on 28 August, when Terauchi's representative signed the terms of the Japanese Southern Army's instructions for surrender, and in Singapore on 4 September, when Terauchi's military commanders signed the surrender of Singapore, ending communal violence in most of Malaya and with the detention of 35,000 Japanese troops within a day of the surrender.

By the evening of 4 September, most of the TIDERACE convoy had arrived in the waters off Singapore with a patrol of military launches established around the *Sussex* and its convoy from dusk until dawn.

It was a night filled with great tension and expectation as the huge naval fleet stood on the eve of liberating Singapore after three years of Japanese military occupation. Troops were placed on the highest degree of alert in case of any last ditch attempts by the Japanese to resist.

Just before dawn on 5 September 1945, the *Sussex* headed to the convoy waiting position in the Singapore Straits as the *HMS Attacker* carried out an air tactical reconnaissance at the request of the 5th Division. The Japanese minesweepers had been ordered to complete sweeping the channel to Singapore by 10.00am but as the Japanese vessels "proved slow and useless, they were told to keep clear"[27].

As the first British ships approached Raffles Lighthouse, six landing craft were lowered from the RFA Dewdale and troops boarded from *HMS Devonshire*. Embarkation was slow as the Indian troops had had only little practice in land mock-ups. Eventually, the group was ready and passed the *Sussex* at about 8.45am.

Mansergh, who was on the deck of the *Sussex*, addressed the troops through a loudhailer in fluent Urdu, wishing them good luck in the landings. The initial assault group was led by *HMIS Godavari* and *HMS Rotherham*, with four military launches on each wing and the *Sussex* in the rear giving gun support and acting as the headquarters ship of the assault commanders.

The 5th Division's diary recorded the landings in detail[28]:

> Full war precautions were taken. At seven o'clock on the 5 September, the landing craft, many of which had taken part in combined operations in North Africa and Europe, came alongside, and boatload-by-boatload the troops scrambled down the nets into them. By 8.30am the craft were ready in battle formation. On board, everyone felt a thrill of expectancy. How would the Japanese take the surrender? Would there be treachery?

On landing at Keppel Harbour, Brigadier Denholm-Young, 5th Indian Division being met by a Japanese interpreter on General Itagaki's staff.

The first troops of the division ashore were 'D' company of the 2/1st Punjab, under Major Niaz Mohammed Arbad.

Units of the 5th Indian Division landing at Keppel Harbour.

The first flight, which steamed in from a distance of some 25 miles, was composed of, on the left, the 3/9th Gurkha Rifles, and on the right, the 2/1st Punjab. (The) 123(rd) Brigade Headquarters travelled with the latter. And the 1/17th Dogras moved off to secure possession of certain islands—Pulau Brani, (Pulau) Blakang (*sic*) Mati, and Pulau Hantu, two miles south of Singapore harbour. These were occupied without incident at 10.30am. The rest of the convoy passed a series of these small islands, striking by their greenness, many of them only two hundred yards or so in length, with sandy beaches and palm trees, and a few white houses.

Then, Singapore itself appeared, no longer hidden from view by these islands that cover(ed) the approaches. Suddenly, the scene opened up, and the water line became visible in its wide semicircle, a mass of buildings along the front showing clearly against a dull and thundery sky. Soon after 11.00am (*sic*) the landing craft, in single file and with pennants gaily fluttering, passed *H.M.S. Sussex*, lying with her guns trained upon the city, and entered the harbour to berth, alongside the main wharfs.

In the dock area there were only a few civilians. But a small number of dockers and coolies gave a cheer and a wave of greeting, and several Chinese shouted from the roof of the customs sheds.

The first troops of the Division ashore were 'D' Company of the 2/1st Punjab, under Major Niaz Mohammed Arbad. The battalion was met by two senior Japanese officers who wore ceremonial swords and highly polished jackboots. All were standing rigidly to attention, at the salute. Behind them again was

> parked a line of glittering civilian cars, each with a booted chauffeur. On the main wharf, Brigadier Eric John Denholm-Young, Commanding Officer of the 123rd Indian Brigade, was met by one Major General Shimura who was staff officer to General Itagaki. And soon after midday, Denholm-Young held a conference with a number of senior Japanese officers, who showed themselves most helpful. All went as had been planned during the voyage, and no opposition was met.
>
> The battalions moved out fanwise from the docks and according to pre-arranged instructions occupied such key positions as arsenals, installations, airfields, the railway station, and camps. The Japanese officers, assisted by interpreters and by maps, showed our officers the dispositions of all enemy guards in Singapore itself.
>
> Meanwhile, 161(st) Brigade had landed at the West Wharf, near the Power Station, and were (*sic*) greeted by a lone Chinese boy, full of smiles. Led by the 4/7th Rajputs, they moved straight through northwards across Singapore Island to the naval base and causeway at Johor Bahru[29].

By dark, all personnel ships had been anchored in the Singapore roads and unloaded by a ferry service of military launches. *Sussex* and the nine other main ships of the force were berthed at Keppel, including *LCI 104*, the press ship, which brought the first Allied media into liberated Singapore.

That night, looting began to occur on the jetty and the captain of the *Sussex* responded by landing about 80 men to guard important stores that had been offloaded in the dock area. In the meantime, *HMS Rotherham* had begun disarming all Japanese military vessels in the harbour and its vicinity.

To boost morale, SEAC broadcast a special message from King George VI to the people of Singapore on all radio frequencies:

> Now that final victory over the forces of aggression has been achieved, I send to my peoples, and to the peoples under my protection in the Far East who have suffered the horrors of Japanese aggression, a message of real sympathy and heartfelt thanksgiving on their delivery.
>
> The thoughts of the Queen and myself have been constantly with you during your years of suffering so bravely borne, and with the dawn of the day of liberation we rejoice with you that the ties which unite my people everywhere will now be fully restored. I know full well that these ties of loyalty and affection between myself and my Far Eastern peoples have never been broken; that they have been maintained in darkness and suffering. The time has now come when their strength and permanence will again be displayed in calm before the whole world.

> The traces of a cruel and ruthless oppression cannot be wiped out in a day, and the work of restoration will be long and heavy, but it is a work in which we should be united in pride and in confidence, sure in the faith that security and happiness will, with God's help, be fully restored[30].

By midnight, Malayan time had once again been established in Singapore. The island was now an hour behind of Tokyo time, to which watches and clocks in Singapore and Malaya had been set to for the last three-and-a-half years.

On 6 September, day two of the reoccupation, Holland ordered the *Rotherham* and two military launches to retake the naval base in the northern part of the island while Japanese officers came on board the *Sussex* with plans to evacuate all Japanese naval personnel to Johor.

The reoccupation of Singapore was going according to plan. However, the chaotic conditions faced by the returning Allies would take months, if not years, to sort out. Three-and-a-half years of Japanese occupation had taken its toll and stepping ashore on recently occupied enemy territory, the British would now face much more than they had bargained for.

Endnotes

1 *From: F.O. Force 'N', 30 August 1945, WO203/2307.* London: The National Archives.

2 *Letter of Proceedings – Operation TIDERACE, 18 September 1945, ADM116/5562.* London: The National Archives. 2.

3 *Singapore Broadcast 31 1130 IST, GSI (s)/1, 31 August 1945, WO203/2435.* London: The National Archives.

4 *From: Lt. Gen. Numata T.O.O. 271115, 27 August 1945, WO203/2435.* London: The National Archives.

5 *JURIST Signal, 28 August 1945, WO203/4917.* London: The National Archives.

6 Kirby, Major General S. Woodburn. *The War Against Japan: The Surrender of Japan*, vol. 5. London: HMSO, 1969. 266.

7 *Proceedings of Operation JURIST, V.A.E.I.F. NO.737/743D, 13 September 1945, WO203/4675.* London: The National Archives.

8 Ibid.

9 Ibid.

10 Gough, Richard. *The Jungle was Red.* Singapore: SNP Panpac, 2003. 154.

11 *58108SIGS. Unclassified for S.O.inC., 2 September 1945, WO203/2435.* London: The National Archives.

12 *From TAC HQ 15 Ind Div, 28 August 1945, WO203/2308.* London: The National Archives.

13 *Letter of Proceedings – Operation TIDERACE, 18 September 1945, ADM116/5562.* London: The National Archives. 2.

14 *Letter of Proceedings, 18 September 1945, ADM116/5562.* London: The National Archives. p. 1.

15 *From: S.O. Force 'N', 3 September 1945, WO203/493.* London: The National Archives.

16 *1889 Int Secret Chritison from Slim, 3 September 1945.* London: The National Archives.

17 *Report of Proceedings—Commander-in-Chief, East Indies Station's letter, No.3001/E.I.15002/45, 17 September 1945, ADM199/168.* London: The National Archives. 5.

18 *Letter of Proceedings—Operation TIDERACE, 18 September 1945, ADM116/5562.* London: The National Archives. 3.

19 *Instructions to the Japanese Forces under Command or Control of Japanese Commanders Singapore Area, 4 September 1945, ADM116/5562.* London: The National Archives. 1, Appendices A, B, C, D.

20 *C.S.300.4/M, 25 August 1945, WO203/4922.* London: The National Archives.

21 *Order of the Commander Occupying Force to the Japanese Commander of Singapore, 31 August 1945, WO203/2308.* London: The National Archives. 1–2.

22 Ibid.

23 *Letter of Proceedings, 18 September 1945, ADM116/5562.* London: The National Archives. 2.

24 "Surrender Ships from Singapore Met". *The Times*, 5 September 1945.

25 Chin Peng. *My Side of History.* Singapore: Media Masters, 2003. 128.

26 *Letter of Proceedings – Operation TIDERACE, 18 September 1945, ADM116/5562.* London: The National Archives. 3.

27 Ibid.

28 Brett-James, 1951.

29 Ibid.

30 "Message from the King". *The Times*, 6 September 1945.

Chapter 6

Reoccupation

The reoccupation of Singapore meant different things to different people. For liberators like Catherine Baker, her role in the historic reoccupation of Singapore came from out of the blue. A nurse based with the contingent of s nurses (QARANC) in Bihar, India, looking after the wounded from Burma[1], Baker suddenly received top-secret orders:

> We were given orders... pack up your belongings and be ready to move to an unknown destination within 24 hours. Take what you can carry and the rest of the luggage will follow later...
>
> ... We were then transported to Calcutta by train and stayed in a transit camp before embarking on a hospital ship (with no patient) where we slept and ate in the wards. At Rangoon, we waited for three days (no shore leave) for orders to go to our final destination.
>
> We then sailed in a convoy of about 10 ships (ours the last one) in a dead-straight line down a narrow channel which had been mine-swept. We wore our life jackets as we watched the naval frigates acting like sheepdogs to ensure that there was no deviation from the narrow lane.
>
> We docked at Singapore, I think on 31 August (*sic*), as darkness fell and saw a desolate, ruined, unlit city. On the quayside were what appeared to be skeletal ragged and barefoot coolies: they were in fact our own prisoners of war.
>
> We disembarked the following day, to be taken by truck through deserted streets to our hospital 49 B.G.H. (49 British General Hospital, also known

as the Singapore General Hospital) in which had been the civilian one. It was insect-ridden, filthy, ill-equipped and overrun by monkeys. There we prepared to receive wounded, diseased and emaciated patients from Changi and other jails.

By the time Japan had surrendered on 15 August, Southeast Asia Command (SEAC) realised it was no longer a matter of recovering prisoners and internees over a period of time as operations progressed, but of getting them evacuated simultaneously from all camps in the region. Estimates in the Official History listed close to 70,000 prisoners of war (POWs) in the Southeast Asia theatre with another 55,000 in Java, spread over 250 known camps[2].

By 12 August, Force 136 had carried out extensive clandestine reconnaissance in Malaya and provided SEAC with an initial breakdown of POWs in the various camps[3]:

SINGAPORE: There are numerous camps scattered all over the island of Singapore and the total number of POWs is estimated as:

UK	2,700
Aust.	6,600
Ind.	5,600
Total	14,900

JOHORE:

MUAR	300 unknown POWs.
KLUANG	500 Ind. POWs.
ENDAU	? Unknown POWs.
JOHORE BAHRU	500 Aust. POWs.
BATU PAHAT	? Unknown POWs.

SELANGOR:

KUALA LUMPUR	2,500 Ind. POWs.

NEGRI SEMBILAN:

PORT DICKSON	1,000 Unknown POWs.

More recent information indicates the possibility of an unknown number of white POWs, believed Aust., in KUALA LUMPUR.

There is also information, ungraded, that there are 1,000 Gurkha POWs at TANJONG RAMBUTAN, PERAK.

Liberated Prisoners of War at Changi: The clothes they are wearing were provided by returning forces so that the first pictures of POWs would not cause morale problems.

As information like this began filtering in to SEAC headquarters, it was unclear how many POWs would have to be evacuated and what state they would be in. Thus the first phase of the rescue and evacuation operation, codenamed BIRDCAGE, was:

> The dropping by air of leaflets giving notice of the surrender of Japan to guards at POW camps, to the local population and to prisoners and internees. Leaflets in Japanese and the local language were to be dropped first on all known camps, main towns and concentrations of Japanese troops, followed about an hour later by leaflets in English giving instructions to prisoners and internees to stay in their camps until contacted so that food and medical supplies could be dropped to them, In the second phase (Operation MASTIFF), which was to follow as soon as possible after the leaflets had been dropped, food and medical supplies were to be dropped and medical and Red Cross relief teams with wireless sets and operators parachuted into known camps as quickly as possible[4].

While this was happening, Force 136 officers and 'E' parties (evacuation) that were operating in Malaya were to also contact the camps[5].

As soon as the initial drops had been completed, the RAF was tasked with keeping these camps resupplied by dropping special food, medical supplies, clothing and Red Cross stores:

> Liberator squadrons with experience of special duty (clandestine) operations were to be used for the long-range tasks since many of the camps were likely to be difficult to find. The short-range tasks were to be carried out by Thunderbolt, Dakota and Lysander squadrons as operationally convenient. The squadrons covering Malaya and Sumatra were to work from airfields in Ceylon and the Cocos islands, those covering western Siam from airfields around Rangoon, and those covering eastern Siam and French Indochina from airfields around Jessore (the original base for special-duty squadrons some 60 miles northeast of Calcutta)[6].

Despite the airlift, it was a desperate scene that greeted Baker and the relieving forces of the 5th Indian Division as they reoccupied Singapore on 5 September 1945.

> ... They (POWs) evinced no feelings of joy at being released after three-and-a-half years of starvation and misery. Just a quiet acceptance of the change of events.
>
> One patient, a merchant seaman, with stick-like legs and arms but an enormous pot belly due to beriberi, was given a drip of plasma for his dehydration but unfortunately the body could not take this life-saving fluid and he died. The ward was engulfed in misery. The patients knew he had fought to survive, giving encouragement to others, and now his life was ended when aid was at hand but to no avail...
>
> ... The following Sunday, a few of us were asked to open a ward in the third-class block in readiness to receive patients who were being flown in from Sumatra and were due to arrive in the afternoon. The ward had not been used by the Japs; the beds and mattresses were there, but little else. The filth was indescribable, and the mattresses alive with bugs and creepy crawlies. The kitchen was empty except for a refrigerator with the innards hanging out, and monkeys chattering and furious at being disturbed and ousted.
>
> It was hard work scrounging around for equipment. Chairs, lockers, kitchen utensils, anything we could lay our hands on, cleaning as best we could, and then putting sheets on infested mattresses. We were exhausted (and dirty!) when the men arrived. Half were stretcher cases; all weighed no more than 5 stone (32kg). I shall never forget their expressions when they came in. Wonderment, disbelief as they looked at the clean sheets (hiding the bugs!! And us nurses, sweaty and filthy in our khaki outfits). There was a stillness among them, but it was soon made evident that there was trouble brewing. There was a mixture of British POWs and Dutch Indonesian soldiers and there was resentment between them. Luckily, we managed to divide them

> by putting one lot in the beds on the veranda. We guessed the reason why there was this strong feeling between them but nothing was said.
>
> We had to be very careful with the food we gave them. Small amounts at a time. M and V (meat and vegetables) was the staple food and biscuits (no bread) but it was supplemented by Australian Red Cross parcels of tomotao (*sic*) juice, asparagus tips, and tinned fruit of all kinds with condensed milk and cream. Vitamins were given out three times a day, the 'brown smell' of them I remember so well that it brings back memories whenever I take them.
>
> We had to cope with men, after years of deprivation, cut off from news of family and home, suffering from malnutrition and the effects of cruelty, who now had to adjust to a normal way of living. Some hid their food in their lockers, in case. Some wept uncontrollably at times and some wanted to stand at attention if spoken to. Letters brought misery to some. Parents had died and, in one case, a wife had deserted him. It was a noiseless ward and not really happy as if the patients could not express their thoughts of release. They had obviously thought so much about the end of hostilities that it was almost an anticlimax, and their spirits had been deadened by all their sufferings.
>
> Amongst the patients was one of our staff who sat at the table for his dinner with six other patients. He left a piece of gristle on his plate. Without a word being said, this gristle was divided equally among the six. And woe betide if the food was not always equally divided. Two potatoes on one plate and only one on another could almost cause a riot. Everything, literally everything had to be equal, including time spent talking to a patient. The men did not talk about their experiences but neither did they ask any questions about events of the last three-and-a-half years. It was as if they had fought so long to survive and seeing their friends die from starvation that they just wanted both their bodies and brains to rest before they tackled their thoughts of home... and victory[7].

For the international press accompanying the TIDERACE convoy, covering these momentous events proved a formidable challenge. Douglas James Mackie, Traffic Manager for Cable and Wireless Ltd Singapore in 1941, and a team of eight technical staff were put in charge of helping the press contingent transmit their stories.

SEAC provided the journalists with a press ship, installed with a mobile cable office. Stories and photographs were to be filed and transmitted to Colombo, from where they would be retransmitted to the rest of the world. From the start, noted Mackie, the press faced numerous constraints:

The vessel chose(n) for the Press ships (*sic*) was an LCI (L) (Landing Craft Infantry, Large), tonnage 300 and, of course, quite unsuited for the purpose. Out of this flat-bottomed reinforced biscuit tin, which was designed to transport troops for a maximum period of 36 hours, the R.N. 'Dockies' at Colombo made a reasonably comfortable floating wireless telegraph branch complete with cabin, mess-wardroom, instrument room, engine room, transmitter room, salt-water showers and the inevitable 'heads'.

... Space was my biggest headache, as the original passenger list showed 36 bodies. The sleeping-cum-baggage flat was 22-feet-by-26-feet, tapering to practically zero at the sharp end. Kit had, therefore, to be restricted to one kit bag per person.

As planned, the Ceylon Force, the Rangoon Force, and the LCI Force joined at a point off Penang Island. En route down the Malacca Straits, I had a signal sent to the Flagship asking that the Press ship be berthed remote from other vessels for technical reasons. I suggested Telok Ayer Basin.

As anticipated, I received a rocket from the Flagship asking me "not to send unnecessary signals" but I was not unduly disturbed by this reply.

After many hours of movement outside Singapore while the fleet of over 100 vessels manoeuvred into position, we steamed majestically, line ahead with the Flagship leading into the Outer Roads. As we approached, our ship was signalled to leave convoy and proceed to berth three cable lengths off Telok Basin mole—a quick dividend to my signal. The value of this berth was that it is (*sic*) the nearest sea frontage to our C.T.O. (Central Telegraph Office) and about a quarter of a mile from it. We were anchored by 3.00pm, considerably in advance of the main fleet. After arranging for the hoisting of our Cable and Wireless flag, I asked the skipper to lower the dinghy and, with a SEAC Press observer, rowed ashore.

As we steamed in, our transmitter was run up and Colombo was warned to stand by for heavy filing. Duties had been arranged and the operators were at their posts in the receiving Room (*sic*) below decks. By 6.30pm, the Navy, using ML's (*sic*) (military launches), had cleared away the jumble of Japanese tugs, fishing vessels, etc., from the mole to permit us to tie alongside.

Then came the flood from the P.R.O. (Press Receiving Office). Placidity was replaced by intensity. Eight bodies stripped to the waist, sweating mightily in an atmosphere comparable to a steam room of a Turkish bath, could not cope. All staff were called on and the mess tables used for counting and preparing traffic.

> With one senior on the auto and control, the other three and myself could barely keep abreast of the counting, which in the best of conditions is slow work, with Press badly-typed on any old flimsy and plastered with inked-in amendments...
>
> ... My view, which was shared by the Assistant Director of Public Relations, was that it was better to limit the takes to 250 words per correspondent (there were about 80 of them) per day which would be duly delivered to the agencies and editors in time for going to press, rather than a few long takes to be delivered to some agencies to the indignation of the rest of the editors[8].

At a rate of 2,000 words an hour in the first four days of landings, more than 161,000 words were transmitted and the staff also radioed pictures of the landings to London[9]. Mackie made a trip to the old Cable and Wireless offices at Robinson Road to gather reinforcements but as the Associated Press reported, he faced the enemy head on:

> Mackie made a sortie to his old office and found a Japanese colonel sitting in his old office chair. With typical Scots brevity, he jerked a thumb and said, "Oot!" and the colonel 'ooted' at great speed. Then he called his old Sikh watchman and ordered him muster as many of the old Cable and Wireless staff who could be found. To his surprise and delight, 90 out of his 100 employees turned up. He said "No money, no food. Do you want to work?" The response was unanimous. So these loyal Chinese operators were installed in the Press Ship and started operating, telling the story of Singapore[10].

However, for local journalists, most of whom had been interned, freedom would have to come first before they could begin work. For Harry Miller, the pre-war chief reporter at *The Straits Times* and a civilian internee at Sime Road, the arrival of Allied troops on 5 September was a historic event:

> The troops, carrying arms strange to Singaporeans and wearing odd-looking camouflaged uniforms, climbed aboard innumerable trucks at the docks and began journeys to strategic points around the island. Those laughing, rifle-waving British, Indian and Ghurkha troops provided the exclamation point to the termination for Singapore of 1,328 days of Japanese occupation and terror.
>
> Neither the conquering heroes nor the people who welcomed them took the slightest notice of Japanese troops, who under British orders, stood on traffic control at important road junctions, a humiliating role for those men of *Bushido*.

> But for me and about 3,000 British civilian men, women and children who had been Japanese prisoners of the lowest calibre, and of the many more thousands of British military prisoners of war in vast camps around Singapore, that was our personal 'freedom day'.
>
> In Sime Road, our camp a few miles inland, bronzed but emaciated men, women and children, many wearing rags, gathered at midday round a specially erected flagpole near the entrance and watched a Union Jack hoisted over our few acres of once-Japanese land. It was a profound, intense and passionate moment and few attempted to hold back.
>
> It was with broken voices and choked throats that we tried to sing the national anthem. But the loudest voices in praise were from the women who, three-and-a-half years before had, with faces held high and shoulders firmly back, marched into Changi singing, "There'll Always Be An England". Now they were singing victoriously[11].

For Miller, it was suddenly back to work again. The call came for all released journalists and printers of *The Straits Times* to head for the offices in Cecil Street and augment the local staff. Robert Burns, the managing editor and now ex-internee, wanted the newspaper to be born again, but fast. It appeared on 7 September 1945, the paper's centenary year[12].

The hospital and medical conditions in Singapore were appalling. Although the new British Military Administration (BMA) in Malaya (announced by Mountbatten on 15 August but who only arrived with TIDERACE on 5 September) attempted to improve medical facilities, the main aim was to evacuate as many POWs as possible and only treat those who were in critical condition. Mountbatten's wife, Lady Edwina, as superintendent-in-chief, Nursing Corps and Divisions, St. Johns Ambulance Brigade, provided much support and visited numerous POW camps in the region. However, hospital conditions would take months to improve, as Baker noted:

> When we sisters first arrived at the hospital, we were given the old nurse's quarters, no beds, no furniture and no water except for a filthy trickle. But we did have rats galore. Our camping gear had been shipped with us and the canvas bed, bucket and wobbly bath were put into use. The water was undrinkable, pink and yellow tablets had to be put in jugs and it was still undrinkable! We managed to cadge pineapples to eat with our K rations. Our ration of cigarettes was used as money for we ate pineapples till our tongues were sore. We still only had our one suitcase with one change

of clothes... We found that in our room of four sisters we had an Amah allocated to us and when we came off duty on the first day all our dirty clothes had been washed, ironed and mended. JOY! But the next day, she had disappeared. These conquerors had no money and away she went! As there was no money for a while, we bartered with our drink ration and ciggies for fruit.

After the surrender, Tragedy (*sic*), as wood alcohol was being sold in popular cafes. First, one patient was admitted who dies and he was followed by others. If they survived, the optic nerve was damaged, resulting in blindness. Warning posters with thick black lettering were shown everywhere, but sailors off the ships and others did not heed them. As far as I can remember, it was never discovered where the drink came from but there were many casualties. And then it suddenly stopped[13].

By the end of September, close to 53,700 POWs and internees had been evacuated from Southeast Asia to India, Australia and the United Kingdom, with numbers increasing to almost 71,000 by October 1945. The majority were moved by sea from Singapore. By May 1946, 96,575 POWs and internees had been evacuated but, owing to the political situation in Java, it was believed that some 30,000 Dutch internees were still there[14].

Although the POWs and European civilian internees were being taken care of, the general population in Singapore, which had suffered just as badly through the occupation, was in desperate need of food and supplies.

The main shopping areas were Chinese, and in the shops excited crowds of waving, cheering Chinese, particularly children, watched our troops arrive. Union Jacks were flying from buildings or being waved. The streets were empty of buses, trams and *tongas,* and the sole means of transport seemed to be a few rickshaws. So few were the Malays and Indians by comparison with the Chinese inhabitants that you might have thought yourself in China[15].

It was obvious to returning soldiers like Richard Munby that the local Chinese population had suffered terribly at the hands of the Japanese and that many wanted revenge[16]:

For the past three or four years, the Chinese in particular have lived a life of inconceivable hardship and intense humility, many having been tortured into submission, and thousands have never lived to see the day of their city's liberation. Their joyous faces, their national flags which they sported

> on every possible occasion, their spotlessly clean clothes which they wore as if saved for the great day, the scorn and derisive laughter with which they greeted the hundreds of Japanese prisoners (under Indian guards—how they hate the Indians) who, as if planted there to be publicly jeered at, were filling in the trenches and taking down the barbed wire in the great open space in front of the Municipal Building (in preparation for the surrender ceremony at the Padang on 12 September 1945)—all these pointed without any doubt whatsoever to the fact that the Japs were despicable creatures, ill-behaved in every respect...
>
> ... we saw hundreds of Japs being marched under Indian guards to the green open space in front of the Y.M.C.A., and there made to fill in air raid trenches and clear debris under the eyes of a mocking crowd. The Japs passed within three feet of where I was standing and it was interesting to note the expressions on their face. Some showed signs of great humiliation and were probably unwilling tools forced to carry out their Government's orders; others were arrogant, brutal creatures to whom the catcalls and derision of the crowd meant not a thing. These are the men, if they can be sifted out, who should be made to pay for their country's merciless inhumanity. Each party of prisoners was under a Jap Major but orders were issued by a British Major to the Jap Major, who then carried on as "foreman first class". According to an intellectual Chinaman to whom I spoke, the Japs had made countless hundreds of his countrymen, men and women, including himself lie on this selfsame small open space for three days on end without food or water, herded together as cattle, and left exposed to the blazing tropical sun, hardly able to turn over. No wonder that hundreds of them wished to die, and had their wishes granted; no wonder that the spectators... were fierce in their hostility towards these defeated, though in many cases, unbroken, Japs.
>
> The Y.M.C.A. (Young Men's Christian Association), centre of goodwill and Christian relaxation before the war, was converted by the Japs into the vilest of *kempei* or *Gestapo* headquarters. Any one entering the walls of this building for interrogation—with one known exception, the Bishop of Singapore—never lived to see Liberation Day. Many were the heads, arms, legs and bodies strewn throughout the streets as warning to the citizens not to feed and succour our prisoners of war.

However, it was clear that as the end drew near, many of these torturers realised they would have to face Allied justice. For other Japanese officers, their warrior code, the *Bushido*, would not allow surrender. For these men, capitulation was not an option:

> Later, we had a walk along the seafront and in the luxurious lounge of the great Raffles Hotel, known to almost every traveller in the east, we disposed of a glass of iced water—all the beaming waiters had to offer in the way of food or drink. Only a few days before, according to the waiters, 300 Japanese officers had committed *hari kiri* in that very lounge when General (Seishiro) Itagaki had told them he was surrendering under orders from the Emperor. They held a farewell party at which a good deal of *saki* (*sic*) was drunk, then, leaning on their short swords, they hastily returned to their ancestors. A whole platoon of officers later blew themselves up with hand grenades[17].

Two days after the return of the British, the local population was in for another rude shock. After three-and-a-half years of occupation and rule by the Japanese, on Friday, 7 September, the BMA issued a Currency Proclamation declaring that:

> ... apart from $1,000 and $10,000 dollar notes, which had to be handed in and accounted for, all pre-war Malayan and Straits Settlements currency notes and coins would be legal tender. But it also gave the chief civil affairs officer discretion to authorise acceptance of other currencies. This proclamation was published in *The Straits Times* and also in the official *Malayan Times* newssheet, but the latter went on to explain this meant Japanese military 'banana' money was now worthless. Since this was virtually the only currency in circulation, the news threw the population into a panic. On Saturday, black market prices soared. Beef, which could previously be bought for 20 cents a *kati* (605g) or 150 Japanese Dollars on the black market, went up to $1,000 Japanese Dollars. The next day, when the full implication of the news had sunk in, no one would accept Japanese Dollars. By Monday (10 September) every shop, food stall and market was closed, and even people with Malayan currency could find nothing to buy...
>
> ... The BMA reacted quickly to the crisis. The chief civil affairs officer assured reporters that large quantities of Straits Dollar notes were available, everyone would be paid salary advances, and Allied servicemen were already spending their local dollars, so that soon there would be plenty of legal currency in circulation. At the same time, the first free rations of rice, sugar and salt were being distributed[18].

The reoccupation of Singapore and Malaya was clearly not going to be easy. It would take many months before some semblance of normalcy would return to the economy and for the next nine months, the BMA would provide the colony with its main lifeline. Now, the next major objective for SEAC troops was the reoccupation of the rest of Malaya. Operation ZIPPER was scheduled for 9 September and SEAC planners felt this final operation would be just as easy. Their overconfidence would ultimately lead to much confusion on the Malayan peninsula.

Endnotes

1 Baker, Catherine M.S. *Personal Papers, 96/34/11*. London: Imperial War Museum, 1996.

2 Kirby, Major General S. Woodburn. *The War Against Japan: The Surrender of Japan*, vol. 5. London: HMSO, 1969. 245.

3 *E Group/Force 136 Plan for Immediate Assistance to PWs in Malaya, T.W. 1460/E Gp., 12 August 1945, HS1/328*. London: The National Archives.

4 Kirby, 1969. 246.

5 *E Group/Force 136 Plan for Immediate Assistance to PWs in Malaya, T.W. 1460/E Gp., 12 August 1945, HS1/328*. London: The National Archives.

6 Kirby, 1969. 247.

7 Baker, 1996.

8 Stewart, Athole. "How History was Written at Singapore". *The Zodiac*, December 1945. 208.

9 "'Oot!' said Mackie and the Jap Colonel Fled". *The Zodiac*, November 1945.

10 Ibid.

11 Miller, H. "An End to 1,318 Days of Terror". *The Daily Telegraph*, 12 August 1985. 12.

12 Ibid.

13 Baker, 1996.

14 Kirby, 1969. 249.

15 Brett-James, Anthony. *Ball of Fire: 5th Indian Division in World War II*. Aldershot: Gale and Polden, 1951.

16 Munby, Richard. *SACSEA Surrender Mission to Singapore, 87/34/1*. London: The Imperial War Museum. 7.

17 Ibid. 8.

18 Turnbull, Mary. *Dateline Singapore: 150 Years of the Straits Times*. Singapore: Singapore Press Holdings, 1995. 136.

Chapter 7

Operation ZIPPER

In May 1945, Vice Admiral Lord Louis Mountbatten issued orders that set in motion the formulation of a plan for the invasion of Malaya, and instructed Lieutenant General Ouvry Lindfield Roberts, General Officer Commanding (GOC), XXIV Indian Corps, Rear Admiral BCS Martin (Flag Officer, Force 'W') and Air Vice Marshall Sir Percy Ronald Gardner (224th Group RAF), the Earl of Bandon, to execute the operation.

By 15 May, the Joint Planning Staff at Southeast Asia Command (SEAC) had come up with a plan for the recapture of Malaya and subsequently Singapore. The plan would call for an invasion of Malaya, codenamed Operation ZIPPER, which was scheduled for 9 September 1945, and the eventual recapture of Singapore, codenamed Operation MAILFIST, with seven divisions and three armoured brigades:

> In examining the advance on Singapore, the Force Commanders decided that, since stress had been laid on capturing the port and dock facilities at Singapore intact, the defeat of the Japanese army was merely incidental to the task and could be left to the stage subsequent to the capture of the island. In the operations leading up to the capture of Singapore, every effort should therefore be made to prevent the enemy from concentrating his forces on the island. Once a landing had been made in Malaya, it would be evident that the ultimate Allied objective was Singapore, which meant that surprise could only be achieved by the speed and method of advance. Since it might be possible to persuade the Japanese that the intention was merely to secure

> a bridgehead of sufficient size to cut their communications between north and south Malaya with a view to a relatively slow build-up and subsequent advance on Singapore, any action taken until the advance began should appear to support this intention but, once the advance did begin, it should be carried out at speed, full use being made of amphibious operations[1].

The plan would also call for the capture of advanced naval and air bases on Phuket island in Thailand (Operation ROGER) and Penang island in Malaya (Operation JURIST) before ZIPPER would be activated. The invasion of Singapore (MAILFIST) could occur immediately after ZIPPER was launched.

The recapture of Rangoon in May 1945 and the decision by Mountbatten to advance directly to Malaya, instead of first seizing Phuket, made it unnecessary to implement ROGER or to wait for forces from Europe to create the seven divisions needed. Mountbatten decided to launch ZIPPER from India with resources held by SEAC.

On 24 July, Mountbatten had just landed in Cairo, on his way to a meeting with British Prime Minister Sir Winston S. Churchill, when a telegram from the prime minister instructed him to fly directly to Berlin so that he could also meet with American President Harry E Truman and his chiefs of staff[2].

That afternoon, he arrived in Berlin and went into a meeting with the combined chiefs of staff. After the meeting, the American chief of staff, General George C Marshall, revealed to Mountbatten the top-secret plan to drop the atomic bomb on Japan. That evening, when Mountbatten dined alone with the prime minister, Churchill told him that in view of the imminent Japanese surrender, he should take all necessary steps to be prepared[3].

After dinner, Mountbatten sent an urgent signal to his deputy, Lieutenant General Raymond A Wheeler, and his chief of staff, Lieutenant General (later Sir) Frederick Arthur Montague Browning, saying that there were strong reasons for thinking that Japan would surrender by mid August and that the prime minister wanted SEAC to have a plan ready for occupying Singapore, either direct, or through Port Swettenham and Port Dickson, the moment that Japan capitulated[4].

This new development meant that ZIPPER would no longer have the Singapore (MAILFIST) component. A new top-secret plan for the emergency capture of Singapore would have to be drawn up, giving birth to TIDERACE on 4 August 1945.

As for ZIPPER, Mountbatten noted that it would go on as planned on 9 September but as Japan was expected to surrender, there was no longer a need to assault-load Force W. This meant that ZIPPER would no longer be an invasion force but a reoccupation force.

With the completion of JURIST and TIDERACE on 2 September and 4 September respectively, ZIPPER was given the all-clear. The ZIPPER convoys set out from various ports in India for their landing beaches in the Port Swettenham-Port Dickson area. As the official history noted:

> During the voyage, the formations were given detailed orders regarding their areas of occupation and the procedure to be adopted towards Japanese who surrendered. The landings were to be carried out as rehearsed, except that there was to be no covering fire and a Japanese envoy would be at the Morib rest house with an officer of Force 136 at 6.30am to meet the commander of the 25th Division (Major General G.N. Wood) and the Brigadier General Staff of XXXIV Corps. The first landings were to be made on 9 September by 25th Division on the Morib beaches, 18 miles south of Port Swettenham, and by 37th Brigade of 23rd Division on the beaches west of Sepang, eight miles northwest of Port Dickson. Their immediate objectives were Kelanang airfield (on which 11th and 17th Spitfire Squadrons RAF were to be based) and the Sepang road junction respectively, both of which were a few miles inland from the beaches. After occupying the road junction, 37th Brigade was to move south to Port Dickson where the rest of the 23rd Division (Major General D.C. Hawthorn) was to land over the beaches south of the town on the 12th. Escorted by the battleships *(HMS) Nelson* and *(HMS) Richelieu,* the cruisers *(HMS) Nigeria, (HMS) Cleopatra* and *(HMS) Ceylon*, a carrier force consisting of the cruiser *(HMS) Royalist* and six escort carriers *((HMS) Hunter, (HMS) Stalker, (HMS) Archer, (HMS) Khedive, (HMS) Emperor* and *(HMS) Pursuer)*, with a screen of fifteen destroyers, the D-day convoys arrived off their respective beaches at daylight on 9 September, and the first flights of landing craft moved into their appointed beaches on time[5].

However, at this point things started to go wrong. By the first week of September 1945, the India Mission of the Special Operations Executive (SOE) had signalled the operational details for ZIPPER to its field units. Force 136 was left out of TIDERACE completely and so was not involved in the reoccupation of Singapore. 'P' Department at SEAC ordered Davis and his colleagues to the ZIPPER landing beaches.

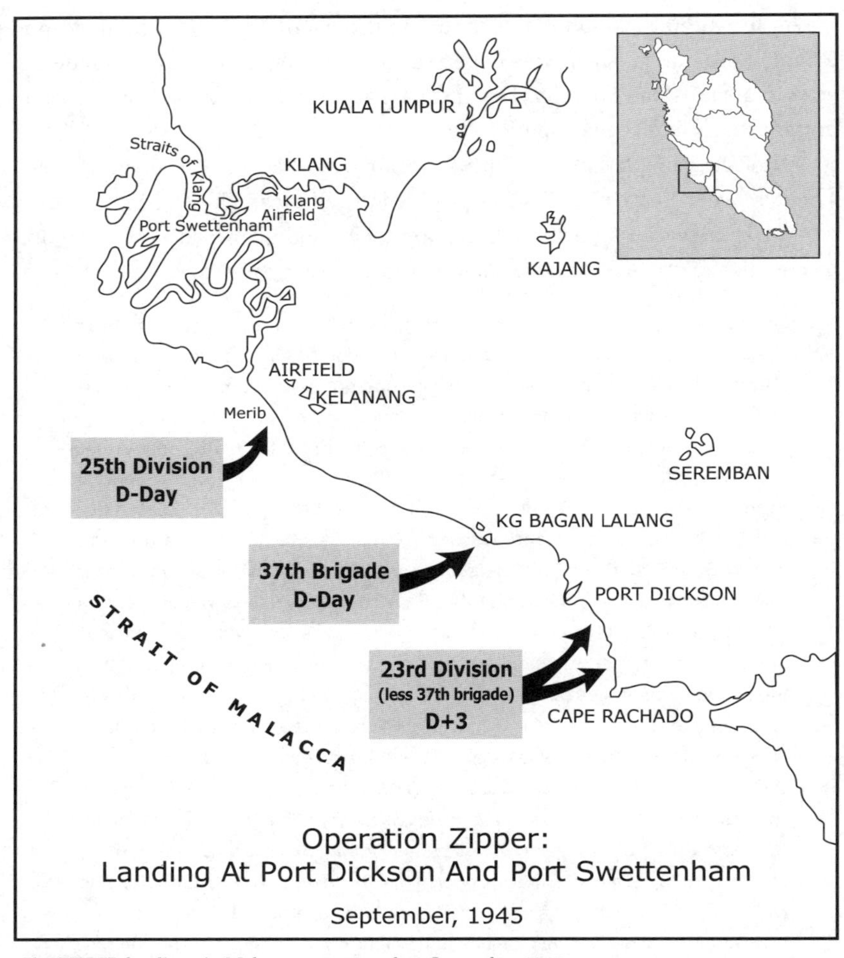

The ZIPPER landings in Malaya on 9, 10 and 11 September 1945.

Davis, along with Chin Peng (whom he had invited to view the landings), moved to Telok Datok, close to Morib Beach. This was a beach Davis knew well from pre-war holidays to the west coast. Dawn was still over the horizon. It was dark, the air warm and the beach was at its tropical best. There were neither Japanese defences nor troops, only broken-down trenches.

> Somewhere out at sea, in the darkness, we heard the sound of marine engines, then at first light we saw the fleet. The horizon was filled with ships, large and small, all shapes and sizes. Then, low-flying fighter aircraft swept over the empty beach waggling wings in a greeting, but the crew of a naval launch close to the beach looked them over and ignored us[6].

Later, on the road alongside the beach they saw the first landing craft, ahead of the main flotilla, surge towards the empty beach. As the boats drew close, Davis and Broadhurst (who had come over from northern Selangor) walked across the beach to meet the newcomers. One of the first men down the ramp was the beach master. Minutes later, a flotilla of landing craft hit the beaches, dropped their ramps and disgorged hundreds of Indian troops, jeeps, lorries and small amphibious DUKWs (an acronym derived from manufacturer General Motors Corporation's codes: 'D' for model year 1942, 'U' for amphibian, 'K' for all-wheel drive and 'W' for tandem axles). Immediately, the tranquil beach was transformed into chaos.

The invasion force was operating on Ceylon time and not on Malayan time, so it arrived an hour late on a receding tide. This left four large vehicles carrying DUKWs and smaller vessels stranded. In the growing disorder, the landing craft carrying bulldozers and heavy plant equipment beached at low tide, forcing vehicles to drive off ramps into the water to struggle ashore. Some became stranded and were towed up the beach past lorries stuck in the soft sand. Beyond the beach, tanks became trapped in ditches and those that did get off the landing area churned up and broke the roads. If it had been an opposed landing, observers at the landing noted, the initial wave would have been pinned down until reinforcements and higher tides freed them from their muddy traps[7].

The after-action reports for ZIPPER catalogued the problems:

> The three LSTs (Landing Ship Tanks) beached on ITEM sector at 8.30am to swim off DUKWS and to dry out. Although MUCK-A-MUCK roadway had been provided in LST, the Army Beach Group decided not to use it, as they

> considered the beach firm enough to take the traffic. As soon as vehicles drove off, however, the under-surface of the beach collapsed and vehicles bogged down on their axles. This meant that MUCK-A-MUCK had to be carried ashore to bridge the worst patches, and in the end, only 46 vehicles, exclusive of amphibians, were got ashore. It was impossible to clear four of these before the tide came up, and they were drowned.
>
> As soon as the treacherous nature of the beaches was discovered, unloading of LST's (sic) 280 and 1021 was stopped, as it was clear that to continue would result in the loss of many more vehicles[8].

To add to the farcical landing, the Japanese officer with the maps, who was supposed to turn up in the early morning, did not arrive until the afternoon. Eventually, a table was set out on the beach for the Japanese delegation to lay their maps and report the disposition of their troops.

At Port Dickson, a second invasion beach some miles down the coast, Captain GP Brownie headed the Force 136 reception committee:

> Seremban had emptied and the roads were choked with people, either walking or packed in bullock carts, old wood-burning lorries and cars. All full of families. It was a circus atmosphere, a carnival with roadside food stalls, puppet shows and entertainers.
>
> We were well behind the lines, using a five-figure code to keep the fleet informed of Japanese reactions. If things went wrong and the Japanese changed their minds, we would pinpoint targets for the big guns and aircraft. I understand the landing was a bit of a mess and the Japanese had to be called out to tow landing craft off the beaches[9].

The biggest embarrassment ensued when a message had to be passed to the local Force 136 officer telling them to break cover, find the local Japanese commander and borrow his transport to get the landing party out of trouble. Although the official account noted that, "despite the chaos on the beaches, there is little doubt that had it been necessary to take Malaya by force of arms, Operation Zipper would eventually have achieved its object,"[10] it also outlined the great challenge that would be faced had there been actual opposition[11]:

> It is equally true that... the invasion forces would have been very roughly handled and at least pinned to the beaches for some time. It is even possible that the troops landed on the Morib beaches might have had to be withdrawn[12].

Upon landing, the infantry, however, did not face such problems, and by 4.30pm, Port Swettenham and Klang had been occupied by troops moving by way of Telok Datok. A hundred Japanese guards handed Kelanang airfield over to the troops. After spending the night on the beaches of Morib without their equipment, the 25th Division moved to Klang on 10 September. However, it was still bedlam on the beach:

> Conditions on the beaches were chaotic, vehicles drowned in scores as there was no decent exit from the beaches, and roads became choked with ditched tanks which tore up the road surfaces and grass verges... A lack of vehicles ashore made movement of stores an impossible undertaking[13].

On 10 September, Port Dickson was occupied and Major General Douglas Cyril Hawthorn, GOC, 23rd Indian Division, landed and met with Force 136 members. The next day, Mountbatten, Roberts and the commander-in-chief of the Allied Land Forces, Southeast Asia, Field Marshal William Slim, visited the 25th Division in Klang before it moved inland to Kuala Lumpur, where XXXIV Indian Corps planned a ceremonial entry on 13 September. Reconnaissance of beaches south of Port Dickson showed a few south of Cape Rachado that were suitable for landing men and vehicles and the leading troops of the rest of the 23rd Division began to land there on 12 September.

Although ZIPPER finally managed to reoccupy Malaya, the lack of effective planning and alternative arrangements did not reflect well on a force that was trying to impress the enemy with overwhelming strength and superiority:

> Although it was realised that the information about the beaches might not be accurate, a risk was accepted that might have proved unjustifiable had the Japanese opposed the D-day landings with even a few battalions. There would in any case have had to be a quick and sound revision of the plan when it turned out that there was no possibility of the follow-up division being able to land at Morib as planned. Only good generalship could have avoided the delay that would have given the Japanese time to concentrate their available forces to oppose a breakout from the beachheads[14].

With the landing of ZIPPER, the British were once again in control of Malaya. However, that control would remain tenuous. The seeds of rebellion, which had been planted by the Malayan Communist Party (MCP) among the guerrilla forces during the occupation would now begin to blossom and the British would have a full-blown communist insurgency in their hands in less than three years after the end of the war. However, all this was still in the future. With the 'success' of ZIPPER, Mountbatten could now bask in the glory of the final Japanese surrender in Singapore that would occur on 12 September 1945.

Endnotes

1 Kirby, Major General S. Woodburn. *The War Against Japan: The Surrender of Japan*, vol. 5. London: HMSO, 1969. 69.

2 Kirby, 1969. 226.

3 Ibid.

4 Ibid.

5 Kirby, 1969. 268.

6 Gough, Richard. *The Jungle was Red.* Singapore: SNP Panpac, 2003. 157.

7 Ibid.

8 Sayer, Vice Admiral Sir Guy. *Operation ZIPPER, 311/13, 14 September 1945, P68.* London: The Imperial War Museum.

9 Ibid. 158.

10 Kirby, 1969. 270.

11 Stripp, Alan. *Codebreaker in the Far East.* Oxford: Oxford University Press, 1989. 176.

12 Ibid. 271.

13 Kirby, 1969. 269.

14 Ibid. 271.

Chapter 8

The Final Surrender in Singapore

On 9 September, Lieutenant General Sir Alexander Christison held a meeting with the army, navy and air force representatives to plan for the official Japanese surrender, which was to be held three days later at the Municipal Building in the heart of downtown Singapore.

Signals had already come in from units of the SEAC fleet that were arriving to participate in the ceremony on 12 September. Christison faced a major problem. The 5th Indian Division had no Caucasian British troops and so there would only be Indian faces at the moment of British triumph at the Padang. The planners felt that white faces were needed in order to boost the morale of the local population and to show that the British were still in charge. Accordingly, Rear (later Vice) Admiral Cedric Holland ordered shore leave to be given to the crew beginning on 8 September and by 12 September, more than 4,000 'British' libertymen were ashore for the surrender parade[1].

Although these libertymen were not involved in the actual liberation of Singapore and they did not face the same risk of death that each Indian soldier took on reoccupying Singapore, their presence at the parade was obviously aimed at taking the credit for the liberation. What clearly mattered was showing who was in charge. This myth of the White European as the ruler of the local populace needed to be propagated as it had been one of the key justifications for British colonial rule in Malaya and the special treatment and status accorded to the *Tuan*. On the resumption of British rule, a clear delineation had to again be drawn between the colonial masters and the subject races. It would be unacceptable if the local population began to believe that these Indian troops, similar in colour to them, were the actual liberators. This would obviously mean that the colonial masters were not as superior as they had claimed. As Holland later wrote:

> The 5th Indian Division had no British troops to show the flag, therefore libertymen were landed on the fourth day after entry, and on 12 September, 4,000 men were ashore for the Surrender Parade. This had an excellent effect upon the civilian population and helped CAS (M) (Civilian Administration Service Malaya) authorities to restore order[2].

By this time, instructions had already been relayed to the Japanese on preparations to house Mountbatten and his staff for the upcoming ceremony. In signals to SEAC on 31 August, the Japanese high command noted its preparations:

> Your msg No. 26 instructing us to make the SINGAPORE Government House ready for occupation by 5 Sept has duly been received here in SHONAN. Incidentally, we might add that we already started making the necessary preparations as laid down in your msg no. 24 prior to receiving this[3].

Richard Munby was a Sergeant in the Royal Signals attached to Mountbatten's personal staff. As part of the SACSEA's advance party, Munby and Mountbatten's personal staff landed at the Seletar Sea Plane Base on 9 September[4]:

> During the 10-mile drive to Singapore, we were greeted joyously by the crowds who had assembled to line the route; most houses and shops permanently displayed either the Chinese National Emblem or the Union Jack and many of the menfolk jumped to attention as we passed and saluted us, whilst the women and girls smiled charmingly, momentarily forgetful of their natural eastern modesty.
>
> Proceeding through the magestic (*sic*) gates and up the winding drive to Government House, we were soon confronted with one of the most beautiful and stately buildings imaginable. Outwardly at least, the Japs had treated Government House with due respect even to the extent of keeping the lawns and gardens in good condition. This of course was purely for their own convenience and advantage.

> Ascending the carpeted steps and entering the big reception hall, we were greeted by beaming, smartly dressed Chinese waiters, each carrying a tray containing glasses of most refreshing sherry. We were then taken up in a lift—lifts are very few and far between in the east—and whilst walking along the passages to our rooms we saw, and saw into, a number of stately chambers with cards on the door indicating that they were earmarked for our fellow guests, which included the Supremo, Generals Slim, Stopford, Christison, Dempsey, Carton de Wiart, Wheeler (USA), Leclerc (France), Feng Yee (China), Air Vice Marshal Cole (Australia), Air Chief Marshal Sir Keith Park, Admiral Sir Arthur Power; War Correspondents Tom Driberg, M.P., Alan Humphries, and the Marquis of Donegal, etc.
>
> We learnt that General Itagaki, the so-called "Tiger of Singapore" and commander of the Japanese forces in Malaya, had only vacated this palatial building with his staff three days previous to our arrival. Even so, not a vestige of Japanese occupation was visible, except that some of the annexes, including the Governor's library, had been pillaged, and that a number of third-rate Japanese cigarettes were found in the bedrooms, which the servants refused to smoke. I tried one and it proved rather American in flavour. In the library, searching amongst the remains, we found several most interesting and highly confidential documents, one or two of which had the signature of Queen Victoria and King Edward VII appended.

Mountbatten arrived on 11 September in preparation for the surrender ceremonies in the city. However, food remained a significant problem and even the supreme allied commander had to rely on military rations:

> There was no standing on ceremony. We all mixed freely with one another, equally sharing the discomforts of an acute shortage of water—one of the main reasons for the British collapse in Singapore in 1942—and ate of the same meagre ration. It was rather amusing to watch the Supremo and Lady Louis—when she arrived—eating the same hard, butterless, dog biscuits about which the troops on exercise back in England used to grumble so incessantly[5].

Preparations for the ceremony were going into overdrive as a skeleton rehearsal was held on the Padang on the afternoon of 11 September to ensure there were no glitches during the event the following day.

However, as Munby relates, not everything for the supreme allied commander had gone according to plan:

The reality: Joyous scenes as the local populace welcome their liberators—not the British but MPAJA and Chinese nationalist resistance fighters, riding on lorries through downtown Singapore. Note the Chinese nationalist flag at the top left hand corner of the picture.

The fiction: Posed propaganda stills like these were taken to show the warm welcome the British received upon their return. Although the majority were happy to have the British back, the smiles would soon turn to sneers and looks of fear as the communist insurgency took hold of Malaya and Singapore less than three years after the end of the war.

> ...Lord Louis apparently had been looking over his white Admiral's uniform which he intended wearing for the Surrender Ceremony on the following day and found his medals and ribbons missing. He rushed up to our bedroom where he found his batman enjoying forty winks. On being hastily roused, the confused man explained rather haltingly that he had forgotten to pack the ribbons before leaving Kandy. The Supremo, I thought as I lay on my bed pretending to be asleep, retained an amazing degree of composure, merely mentioning that he would have a plane fly immediately back to Kandy for the ribbons and that meanwhile the batman would have to design a makeshift set from those he was wearing with his K.D. (khaki dress) uniform. Needless to say, the batman worked on the ribbons well into early morning, but the special plane just arrived in time back from Kandy, and the improvised set did not have to be worn for the ceremony[6].

The Japanese also faced similar problems. At about 4.30pm, Vice Admiral Yaichiro Shibata[7], commander-in-chief of the Japanese 2nd Southern Area Expeditionary Fleet, who was flying in for the surrender ceremony, landed at the wrong airfield, where he was met by the Special Correspondent from *The Sunday Despatch*, who then escorted him to his quarters.

By the evening of 11 September, Mansergh had arranged for more than 22,000 Japanese naval personnel to be transported in former enemy ships to holding camps around the Batu Pahat area in Johor. However, the shift was not easy. Japanese officers were trying to take with them much of what they had looted from Singapore prior to the Allied liberation. This enraged Mansergh so much that he instructed his men to ensure that all Japanese officers, regardless of rank, would from then on have the same baggage allowance as non-commissioned officers and that all bags were to be thoroughly searched before they were loaded onto the vessels[8].

All Japanese personal effects were thoroughly examined and the retained loot was thrown open to Allied prisoners of war (POWs). This, Holland noted in his report, fulfilled two requirements. It showed the POWs the Japanese were only being allowed to take strict service kit with them and it allowed the POWs to replenish their non-existent wardrobes.

The other challenge was evacuating as many POWs as possible from the island. Due to the lack of maritime transport, merchant navy ships had to be drafted in to help evacuate as many POWs as possible.

As dawn broke on 12 September 1945, there was a great sense of excitement in Singapore city. Streams of people began making their way to the Padang on foot, bicycles, rickshaws and wood-burning lorries. British Royal Marines lined the streets as the crowds filled the Padang, which was now level, the trenches having been filled in the day before by hundreds of Japanese surrendered personnel, who had worked double-time to complete the task in a day.

By about 10.00am, the Padang was packed, except for the square space in front of the Municipal Building where the Guard of Honour was drawn up. All vantage points had large groups of spectators. Any roof within sight of the Padang was packed with Chinese, Malay, Indian and Eurasian observers who were determined to see the historic event unfold before them.

In the bay, the Allied fleet consisted of the capital ships *HMS Sussex*, *HMS Nelson*, *HMS Richelieu* and numerous warships, which filled the harbour and inner roads. All the ships were gaily decorated in pennants and flags to mark the events taking place on the Padang. Fighter planes and bombers zoomed overhead as the troops began forming up for the event.

The sky was overcast as the guards of honour took to the Padang. The sun appeared only briefly through the clouds but the threatening rain held off.

The guards of honour comprised detachments from the 5th Indian Divison, commandos, gurkhas, Punjabis, Australian paratroops, detachments from the *Sussex* and other vessels of the Royal Navy as well as a British battalion of West Yorks. Flanking the steps of the Municipal Building were Royal Marines from *HMS Cleopatra* and just inside the building was a double file of men from the MPAJA, under the command of a British officer. "Slick and determined looking, they carried tommy and sten guns and with their khaki uniforms wore the peaked khaki caps bearing the three red stars"[9].

Harry Miller had a place inside the surrender chamber from which to cover the proceedings. Editor of *The Straits Times*, George Peet, who had also been interned, gave Miller the honour of covering the event. Breaking away from his straight, factual reporting style, Miller's report (although without a byline) in the special four-page issue described the scene thus[10]:

> The scene was set. Newsreel men and photographers from all over the world got ready. Commanders-in-Chief of the British Navy, Army and Air Force in South East Asia, the men who would have led their forces into action against the Japanese arrived.

General Seishiro Itagaki and his fellow generals are led to the Municipal offices as the gathered crowds jeer at their former rulers.

Cheering from the direction of Stamford Road told us that the Supreme Allied Commander himself was approaching.

Ex-prisoners of war and ex-internees watching the spectacle—thus completing the cycle of the last three-and-a-half years—gave him a special cheer. He turned and saluted them.

"Present Arms" rang out, and then the Royal Salute. A high-ranking naval officer, standing next to me, muttered, "Good!" when the parade clicked to a man. The National Anthem was played by the band of the Royal Marines. Various aircraft was (*sic*) heard. Then the bugles.

That was a great moment indeed—to hear British bugles sounding again on the Padang, scene of so many historic events in the history of Singapore. "Order Arms!". Once again, the parade clicked to a man and the high-ranking officer again muttered "Good!". The polish and smartness of the parade was good to see. Lord Louis Mountbatten inspected the parade. He did it leisurely, stopping here and there to talk to a British Marine, a Dogra, a Punjabi, a Commando, a British soldier, a French soldier and so on until he reached a long line of British sailors. We had another thrill. 'Mosquito bombers' flew over in salute. Then there were cheers from the crowd as the big Sunderland flying boats, used on long-range reconnaissance and bombing missions, droned over, and finally some Dakota transports.

> Before Lord Louis had finished his inspection, hoots and jeers from the local crowds by the Singapore Cricket Club told us that the seven Japanese representatives had arrived. Dust flew up on the Padang as the crowds rushed in the direction of the High Street to see the Japanese step out of their cars, each of which bore a white flag. These officers lined up, one behind the other, and then escorted by men from the British, Indian, Chinese, Australian and American Forces, walked down the road, looking neither to the right or left, faces pale and expressionless under their cloth caps. They wore no swords.

General Seishiro Itagaki was followed by Lieutenant General Tokazo Numata, General Hyotaro Kimura, Vice Admiral Shigeru Fukudome, Vice Admiral Shibata, Lieutenant General Akita Nakamura, Commander of the 18th Area Army (Siam), and Lieutenant General Bin Kinoshita, Commander of the 3rd Air Army (Singapore)[11]. Miller continued with his report[12]:

> It was a tense moment. The crowd watched them grimly, wondering what were the thoughts in those bowed heads. They walked up the steps into the building, and past the Chinese Resistance Army, whose exploits in the jungles of Malaya had demoralised Japanese forces, and were taken to a room to wait until they were summoned to sign their surrender.
>
> Lord Louis Mountbatten finished his inspection, came up the steps smiling and saluting, to the cheers of the spectators on the balconies of the Municipal Building and went into a room, where he waited until he was informed that the Japanese representatives were standing, waiting for him to enter the signature room and formally surrender South East Asia to him.
>
> Scene of so many important civic meetings which had produced decisions leading to the great development of Singapore in the old era, the Municipal Council Chamber yesterday became a stage for a drama of the most historical importance. The two great bronze chandeliers threw a soft light on the assemblage of representatives of Malayan communities. Government officers straight from the internment camps, officers and men of the British Dominions, Chinese, French and American forces, famous admirals, generals and air officers. Seated in the audience was the Sultan of Johore (*sic*), Sir Ibrahim, wearing a grey suit and a black Malay cap. His Highness told me afterwards, "I have never been so stirred. I have been glad to have been there to watch those fellows sign. I am proud to have had the honour of witnessing their formal surrender." Practically opposite him and in the front row of chairs situated immediately behind the table to be occupied by the Japanese was the Bishop of Singapore, The Right Rev. JL Wilson, a victim of imprisonment and torture by the Japanese Military Police.

The Official Surrender, 12 September 1945: The Japanese delegation stands at attention as Mountbatten arrives.

The Official Surrender: Mountbatten signs the Instrument of Surrender as the Japanese delegates look on impassively.

The Official Surrender: Mountbatten reads aloud the Instrument of Surrender as General William Slim, on Mountbatten's left, and Lieutenant General Raymond Wheeler (on Mountbatten's right), look on.

Also there was Mr L Rayman, former President of the Singapore Municipality, and Mr Justice N.A. Worley, another victim of the military police. There were other men who had been captives. Mr E.C.H. Charlwood, the only Eurpoean representative of the legislative Council. There were leaders of Malayan communities, Dr Lim Han Hoe, Dr Moonshi, Mr Ong, Mr Koek and many others.

The Commanders-in-Chief and other representatives took their seats at a long table covered in green baize. From the galleries hung the flags of Britain, France, Holland, China, the United States, Australia, the Straits Settlements and the Federated Malay states.

Standing at the bases of the buff-coloured marble pillars were representatives of the fighting forces: a Gurkha, a Sikh, an Australian, a British airman, an English corporal, a Dutchman, a Chinese, an American and a rep of the 5th Indian Division.

All is ready. We are told that the Japanese delegates are about to come in, but we hear a request, "Please remain seated." The buzz of conversation dies down. There is silence, except (for) the whirr of newsreel cameras, as a door opens and in file the seven men headed by General Itagaki, and flanked by their army escort, one to each Japanese. They take their places at a table in front of the Allied representatives and remain standing, looking straight ahead. Their heads appear to have been recently shaved. The lights glint on bald pates.

It is a very dramatic moment. They seat themselves amidst silence. Their escorts sit behind them. Lieutenant General Numata, Chief of Staff to Field Marshal Count Terauchi rises, opens a black dispatch case, extracts a document, walks to the front of General Itagaki, bows and puts it in front of him. It is General Itagaki's credentials as Count Terauchi's representative. It is time for the Supreme Allied Commander to enter. The audience and the Japanese stand. Lord Louis walks in and takes his seat between General Slim and Lieutenant General Wheeler.

Mountbatten, basking in the glory of the moment, reached for the document in front of him and read the opening statement that would go down in history[13]:

I have come here today to receive the formal surrender of all the Japanese forces within the Southeast Asia Command. I have received the following telegram from the Supreme Commander of the Japanese forces concerned, Field Marshal Count Terauchi:

"The most important occasion of the formal surrender signing at Singapore draws near, the significance of which is no less great to me than to your Excellency. It is extremely regretful that my ill-health prevents me from attending and signing it personally and that I am unable to pay homage to your Excellency. I hereby notify your Excellency that I have fully empowered General Itagaki, the highest senior general in Japanese armies, and send him on my behalf."

On hearing of Field Marshal Terauchi's illness, I sent my own doctor, Surgeon Captain Birt, Royal Navy, to examine him, and he certifies that the Field Marshal is suffering from the effects of a stroke. In the circumstances, I have decided to accept the surrender from General Itagaki today, but I have warned the Field Marshal that I shall expect him to make his personal surrender to me as soon as he is fit enough to do so.

In addition to our Naval, Military and Air Forces which we have present in Singapore today, a large fleet is anchored off Port Swettenham and Port Dixon (*sic*), and a large force started disembarking from them at daylight on 9 September. When I visited the force yesterday, there were 100,000 men ashore. This invasion would have taken place on 9 September whether the Japanese had resisted or not, and I wish to make it entirely clear to General Itagaki that he is surrendering to superior force here in Singapore. I now call upon General Itagaki to produce his credentials.

Miller noted the pin-drop silence in the room as Mountbatten made the last statement:

> He (Mountbatten) calls on General Itagaki to produce his credentials. These are handed to him. Lord Louis reads it out (See "Appendix F: Part III"). Then he says, "This is the Instrument of Surrender" He reads that out too (See "Appendix F: Part III").
>
> The Japanese remain immobile, except for one who twiddles his thumbs and twitches his feet. The others are impassive, looking straight ahead of them, three of them wearing horn-rimmed spectacles.
>
> The Supreme Allied Commander reads, "Any disobedience of, or delay or failure to comply with orders and instructions may be dealt with as the Supreme Allied Commander, South East Asia may decide".
>
> He finishes and Major General Penney places 11 copies of the instrument before General Itagaki. The Japanese officer takes his spectacles out of his pocket and puts them on. He reaches for the pen and dips it into the ink. He signs on behalf of the Supreme Commander, Japanese Expeditionary Forces, Southern Regions. The time is 11.10am.
>
> General Itagaki reaches in his pockets again, bringing out a large seal and a tablet of vermillion wax. It is the large square seal of the Japanese Army that he sets on the table. He reaches in his pockets for the third time and produces a little leather case from which he extracts his own personal seal. He 'chops' the instrument with both. Major General Penney takes it up and passes it to the Supreme Allied Commander who puts his signature on it. The 11 copies are signed. All the while, all the other Japanese delegates look straight ahead. They do not look at General Itagaki who is the only one showing movement except for that same Japanese delegate who continues to display nervousness by twiddling his fingers and twitching his feet behind the table.
>
> The instruments are all attested. Nine pens have been used by Lord Louis. He looks up at the Japanese and calls on them to withdraw. They stand, bow, and shuffle out. The signing has taken nine minutes. A signal is given, and all spectators move out to the balcony for the final ceremony of the morning. As we move out, we hear once again the jeers and catcalls of the crowd. It is the Japanese delegates departing.

However, Munby, who was on the steps of the Municipal Building, recalls the jeering differently[14]:

General Seishiro Itagaki signs the official surrender document, handing over Southeast Asia to the victorious Allies.

The Japanese delegation being led away to captivity after the surrender ceremony. Itagaki would be hanged as a war criminal in 1948.

> A very amusing incident occurred outside, as the Japs were marching away. Amongst the military detachments was one from Chiang Kai Shek's Chungking Army, and to one who is unaccustomed to seeing many troops of different nationalities massed together, the Jap uniform is not unlike the Chinese. Consequently, when the Japanese delegation moved off in the direction from which the Chinese Military Detachment had arrived, and the Chinese in the direction from which the Japs had arrived, a number of the local inhabitants were completely bamboozled. The Japs received tumultuous cheers, and the Chinese, loud, derisive laughter and boos.

Miller then observed Mountbatten heading towards the microphone at the head of the steps in front of the Municipal building where he[15]:

> ... announces to the parade that he has received the surrender of the Supreme Commander of the Japanese Forces. "I have accepted this surrender on behalf of all of you". When Lord Louis says that he has ordered Count Terauchi to report to him in person and that he does not intend to put up with "any evasion or trickery on the part of any defeated Japanese however important he may consider himself," the crowds cheer. He ends his address by telling the history of the Union Jack which is about to be hoisted.
>
> Another stirring moment arrives. The band strikes up the National Anthem, the flag slowly moves upwards and spreads out. We see that the colours have faded, but it is the Union Jack. It is a never-to-be-forgotten moment. Throats are choked and eyes are misted. The red emblem of Japan during the last three-and-a-half years has stood for so much oppression and persecution. But freedom, liberty and justice prevailed. The Union Jack says that. The band plays the anthems of the United States, China, Holland and France.
>
> Dakotas fly over, the ceremony is over. The Supreme Allied Commander and others leave to ringing cheers from the crowd and troops.

The crumpled Union Jack that now fluttered in the morning sun had 43 months earlier flown over Government House in Singapore. It had been pocketed by Malayan civil servant Mervyn Cecil Frank Sheppard (who later became Tan Sri Mubin Sheppard, a renowned historian and academic in Malaysia), a scholar-administrator, just as the Japanese were on the outskirts of Singapore city on 14 February 1942, and had remained in his possession throughout his captivity. "I put it inside my pillow. I wrapped a towel around it and there it remained for the rest of the Japanese Occupation"[16]. When the

Japanese ordered that the Union Jack and the white flag should be carried through the streets of Singapore, Sheppard told them that there were no flags available, as they had all been burnt. In Changi, Sheppard's flag was draped over every coffin, always in great secrecy away from prying eyes, and so had been used countless times in the camp. "Not only was it faded, but ragged and torn in places"[17].

Later, the Union Jack was again flown over Government House. One of Mountbatten's aides, Lieutenant Colonel Guy Armstrong, the last of the delegation to leave Government House, took the Union Jack with him for safekeeping and this flag was subsequently used to drape the coffin of Armstrong's father and that of Lord Louis Mountbatten after he was assassinated by the Irish Republican Army (IRA) in 1979. Armstrong was later ordained, and served as the Vicar of Bagshot and Ripley in the 1970s. In 1993, he was awarded an Order of the British Empire (OBE). He died in 2002, taking with him the fate of the liberation Union Jack[18].

At the same time that the ceremonies at the Municipal Building were taking place, a similarly hidden Australian flag was raised over Changi Prison. The flag, which is now framed and held at the Returned Services League in Canberra, is displayed with a plaque that reads, "This important artefact was concealed in Changi Prison by Captain Strawbridge MBE, from 1942–1945. It was raised over the gates of the prison, the day of formal liberation in September 1945". Several Australian flags were secretly made of scavenged pieces of cloth by Australian POWs in various enemy camps. Some of these flags are now held by the Australian War Memorial[19].

However, not everyone was pleased with the ceremony at the Municipal Building. Admiral Arthur Power, a believer in procedure and protocol, was upset with the way the Press had done their job:

> It is with regret that I must place on record that the behaviour of the Press and cameramen during the parade was disgraceful, and marred the conduct of the proceedings. Subsequently, in the signing hall, the sides and galleries resembled batteries of searchlights. There was a great number of correspondents armed with cameras and sited in favourable positions for using them. As an example of their unseemly behaviour, one of these creatures came up to the signing table behind the Supreme Allied Commander and, from a range of a few feet, 'shot' him... I informed Rear Admiral Holland and, through him, Major General Kimmins of SACSEA's

> staff, that I hoped the Press, whilst being given good facilities, would not be allowed to make the scene resemble a football match. I much regret that no success attended my efforts, and many distinguished spectators have expressed to me their disgust[20].

On 13 September, another surrender ceremony was held in Kuala Lumpur. This time, it was to officially surrender the Japanese army in Malaya. Crowds had already gathered outside the Victoria Institution school in the early afternoon as the Japanese military officers were driven in with a few interpreters and a guard of Indian soldiers. The crowd jeered and booed on seeing the Japanese, who maintained a calm and unperturbed demeanour[21].

Lieutenant General Ouvry Lindfield Roberts, who had previously commanded the 23rd Indian Division in Burma and was now General Officer Commanding (GOC) of the 34th Indian Corps in Malaya, would take the formal surrender. He arrived with Captain ET Cooper of the Royal Navy; the Earl of Bandon, Air Vice Marshal Sir Percy Ronald Gardner; and several other military representatives.

The Guard of Honour, comprising men of the 2nd Punjab regiment, was drawn up just outside the front entrance. After inspecting the guard, Roberts waited in a classroom near the hall as the Japanese officers entered the hall, bowing low to the Union Jack at the entrance. Two rows of tables had been arranged for the two groups of representatives. The Japanese were handed a copy of the surrender document and the interpreters explained the contents to them. The main fact was that this was an unconditional surrender. The Japanese nodded in agreement. At this point, Roberts and his fellow commanders entered the room and took their places at the other table, facing the Japanese.

> Lieutenant General Teizo Ishiguro, Commander in Chief of the Japanese 29th Army, Major General Naoichi Kawahara, Chief of Staff and staff officer Colonel G. Oguri faced the SEAC representatives. General Ishiguro used a brush to sign the document, followed by Roberts who inked it with his pen. The surrender was completed in 20 minutes and by 2.30pm, the event was over[22].

Outside the school, the crowd had become restless but a large group of British, Punjabi, Baluchi and Gurkha troops maintained order. Loud cheers greeted the British staff cars as they were driven out of the school premises onto Shaw Road (now Jalan Hang Tuah). The Japanese had to put up with loud jeering and jibes hurled at them by the local population[23].

General Roberts then proceeded to the Selangor Padang (now Dataran Merdeka) where at 3.00pm he took the salute at a Victory Parade and march-past in which Allied forces and units of the Malayan People's Anti-Japanese Army (MPAJA) took part. Taking the salute with him were Force 136 members Spencer and Davis, who by then had already moved from the jungle and set up their headquarters in Kuala Lumpur more than three weeks past.

These were followed by a ceremony for the surrender of swords and firearms, which had not taken place earlier due to Japanese refusal when the signing of the Singapore surrender took place on the *Sussex* on 4 September.

The surrender of swords ceremony for the Japanese troops in Kuala Lumpur eventually took place at the old airport at Sungei Besi on the outskirts of Kuala Lumpur on 14 September 1945. Finally on 22 February 1946, General Itagaki along with his chief of staff and 14 other Japanese generals were brought up from Singapore to Kuala Lumpur and representing all Japanese troops in Malaya, surrendered their swords to Lieutenant General Sir Frank Walter Messervy, GOC, Malaya Command, at another ceremony held in Victoria Institution[24].

So Japanese dominance in Southeast Asia came to an end, 1,374 days after the first bombs fell over Singapore in the early hours of 8 February 1942, marking the beginning of the war in the Pacific. However, the end of the war did not mean the end of the challenges and problems faced by the peoples of Malaya and Singapore. The end of the war marked only the beginning of the struggles for independence that would mark the next two decades in the region.

From Mountbatten's remarks in the chamber and the way the ceremony played itself out at the Padang, it appeared obvious the surrender ceremony at the Municipal Building was being staged to save British face and pride. The loss of Singapore had been a devastating blow to British pride. Now was the time to erase memories of that ignominious defeat on 15 February 1942 when Lieutenant General Arthur E Percival surrendered close to 100,000 British and Commonwealth troops to the 35,000-strong advancing Japanese army. Thus, the 12 September surrender ceremony was significant purely as a tool to restore British pride and status among the local population.

Just as Holland had insisted on having white faces at the parade, the 12 September surrender was meant to show the superiority of the British empire in race and force within the region. However, this had already been achieved with the effective surrender of Japanese troops in Singapore and the end of the communal violence with the signing of the Surrender Agreement on board the *Sussex* on 4 September. The landing of ZIPPER forces with the unofficial recapture of the key towns and cities in Malaya meant the British were back in control. As such, the 12 September ceremony had little, or only ceremonial, impact on the subject races. Peace had been restored in Singapore by 5 September and in most of Malaya by 11 September.

If it was hoped that the surrender ceremony would restore a pre-war acceptance of complete British superiority in Malaya, this was all but dashed less than a year later when plans for the Colonial Office's Malayan Union faltered, and was replaced with a federation. Within the next three years, the beginnings of a 12-year communist insurgency to overthrow British rule in Malaya took shape.

Endnotes

1 *Letter of Proceedings, 18 September 1945, ADM116/5562.* London: The National Archives. 3.

2 Ibid. 2.

3 *Singapore Broadcast 31 1130 IST, GSI (s)/1, 31 August 1945, WO203/2435.* London: The National Archives.

4 Munby, R. *SACSEA Surrender Mission to Singapore, 87/34/1.* London: The Imperial War Museum.

5 Ibid.

6 Ibid. 9.

7 *Ammentorp, Steen. "Biography of Yaichiro Shibata, Imperial Japanese Navy". The Generals of WWII.* [Internet]. Accessed 4 February 2005. Available from: <http://homepage2.nifty.com/nishidah/e/index.htm>.

8 *Letter of Proceedings—Operation TIDERACE, 18 September 1945, ADM116/5562.* The National Archives, London. 8.

9 "Japanese in Malaya Surrender in Singapore". *The Straits Times*, 13 September 1945. 1.

10 Ibid.

11 "Smooth Reoccupation of Singapore". *The Times*, 8 September 1945. 4.

12 Ibid.

13 *Instrument of Surrender of Japanese Forces in Southeast Asia, COS (45)229, 26 September 1945, CAB122/494*. London: The National Archives. Appendix A.

14 Munby, R. *SACSEA Surrender Mission to Singapore, 87/34/1*. London: The Imperial War Museum.

15 "Japanese in Malaya Surrender in Singapore". *The Straits Times*, 13 September 1945. 1.

16 Keay, John. *Last Post: The End of Empire in the Far East*. London: John Murray, 1997. 214.

17 Baker, C.M.S. *Personal Papers, 96/34/11*. London: Imperial War Museum, 1996.

18 "Obituary: The Rev. Guy Armstrong". *Daily Telegraph*, 15 January 2003.

19 Australian National Flag Association. "Timeline". *Australian National Flag Association*. [Internet]. Accessed 14 August 2004. Available from: <http://www.australianflag.org.au/timeline.php>.

20 *Report of Proceedings—Commander-in-Chief, East Indies Station's letter, No.3001/E.I.15002/45, 17 September 1945, ADM199/168*. London: The National Archives. 15.

21 Chung, Chee Min. "The Japanese Surrendered at the V.I.—TWICE!". *The Victoria Institution Web Page*. [Internet]. Accessed 14 August 2004. Available from: <http://www.viweb.freehosting.net/japsurr.htm>.

22 Ibid.

23 Ibid.

24 Ibid.

Chapter 9

Locations

The previous chapters in this book have dealt with the events surrounding the end of the war in Malaya and Singapore. This chapter deals with the locations in Singapore where many of these events occurred; locations that have become inextricably linked to our collective memory of that period and time.

The sites of these surrender events are sacred to many in the region and beyond. Although some are used for new purposes and others abandoned to time and decay, these locations remain crucial in telling the story of the end of the Second World War in Singapore. There exist many more locations, from the beaches at Morib and Port Dickson, to Victoria Institution in Kuala Lumpur, that are significant in marking the end of the war in the region. However, the stories of those locations will be told at another time. The ones that are mentioned here will focus on sites in Singapore, the crown colony that was the location of the final ceremonial Japanese surrender, and the effective centre of the Japanese forces in the Southern Region[1].

City Hall

The site where Lord Louis Mountbatten accepted the Japanese surrender of Southeast Asia, the Municipal Building in Singapore (later renamed City Hall upon independence), has long been associated with historic events on the island. Built in the 1920s on the site of the Europa Hotel, the Municipal Building was home to the Singapore municipality. The council chambers in

The City Hall: The backdrop to most civic events in the city, City Hall remains an iconic symbol of colonial Singapore. Used as municipal offices by the British and the Japanese, the buildings is most remembered as the background for the Japanese ceremonial surrender on 12 September 1945.

the middle of the building first hosted the council and later the legislative meetings of the colony. At the onset of the Second World War, the Padang, or field, in front of the building was the site of many Singapore Volunteer Corp parades and training sessions. On 16 February 1942, a day after Singapore fell, the new Japanese rulers ordered all European civilians in Singapore to gather on the Padang. After waiting there for several hours in the burning sun, they were force-marched into captivity at Changi. It was a desperate sight as women and children, many of whom were injured, struggled to keep up with the other civilians during the march. The Padang marked the beginning of internment for the European population in Singapore.

During the occupation, the Japanese municipality, or Syonan Tokubetsu, took over the building and the Padang was used by the Japanese military to punish locals. The Padang was also the site of an Indian national army parade to mark the arrival of Subhas Chandra Bose in July 1943 as the new leader of the Indian independence movement in Southeast Asia. The Indian independence movement held several mass rallies at the Padang and another major INA parade was held when Japanese Prime Minister Hideki Tojo visited Singapore later that month. By the end of the war, the Japanese had forced locals to dig numerous trenches all over the field as air raid precautions, with barbed wire fences set up on the field. In the post-war period, the Padang became the centre of civic events, where in 1959, Singapore's first prime minister, Lee Kuan Yew, and the nation's Yang Di-Pertuan Negara, Yusof Bin Ishak, proclaimed the creation of the State of Singapore. The same field would in 1966 bear witness to the first National Day Parade, marking the birth of the Republic of Singapore a year earlier. Today, City Hall and the Padang remain bold reminders of the country's colonial past and of its more recent role in the independence of the republic.

Kranji War Memorial

The top of Kranji Hill in northwest Singapore was the site of a British military field hospital during the last weeks of the battle for southern Johor and Singapore. A cemetery was established by the British here as the main Christian cemetery was far away and there was no manpower to transport the bodies for burial at the Bidadari Christian Cemetery in Aljunied. During the occupation, the hospital was used as a prisoner of war (POW) camp and more bodies were added to the cemetery. At the end of the war, it was decided that Kranji would be turned into the main Allied cemetery on the island. The Commonwealth War Graves Commission (CWGC) redeveloped the site and today the Kranji War Cemetery is the final resting place of more than 4,000 Allied soldiers who gave their lives in the Second World War.

The Kranji War Memorial lies in the northern part of Singapore island, overlooking the Straits of Johor, also known as the Straits of Tebrau. It consists of war and military graves, memorials and a state cemetery. Although the cemetery is closed, a few plots remain for veterans who, having fought during the Malayan Campaign and/or survived the Japanese occupation, want to be buried with their comrades.

The main feature of the Kranji War Cemetery is the Singapore Memorial. The memorial was constructed as a tribute to the men and women of the armed forces of the British commonwealth and empire who have no

> known grave. One of the memorials is dedicated to 789 British Indian army soldiers who died during the Malayan Campaign and were cremated. Others remembered here are those who also perished during the Malayan Campaign and in Indonesia as well as in subsequent captivity. These include a large number who died during the building of the Siam-Burma Death Railway, and also many who died at sea while being transported from Malaya into prison camps elsewhere. The memorial also pays tribute to men of the Commonwealth air forces who died during operations across Southeast Asia. This includes those who retreated from northern to southern Malaya, then to Sumatra and finally to Java, as well as those who helped liberate Burma[2].

The central avenue of the cemetery is built on a hill and slopes gently from the Stone of Remembrance near the entrance up to the Cross of Sacrifice, beyond which a short flight of steps lead to the terrace on top of the hill, on which the Singapore Memorial stands.

The Singapore Memorial has a flat roof that is supported by 12 columns, which are inscribed with names of the war dead. A great 80-foot pylon crowned by a star rises above the central axis of the roof. On a curved panel at the foot of this pylon are displayed these words[3]:

> On the walls of this memorial are recorded the names of twenty-four thousand soldiers and airmen of many races united in service to the British Crown who gave their lives in Malaya and neighbouring lands and seas and in the air over Southern and Eastern Asia and the Pacific but to whom the fortune of war denied the customary rites accorded to their comrades in death.

An additional inscription, "They Died for All Free Men", is engraved in Hindi, Urdu, Gurmukhi, Chinese and Malay.

At one end of the Singapore Memorial is a small, separate memorial to the 107 men who died in captivity and are buried in a single grave on the grounds of the Singapore General Hospital. At the other end, a similar memorial bears the names of 255 men buried in isolated places in Malaya, where their graves cannot be maintained.

Also buried at Kranji are the remains of Lieutenant Colonel Ivan Lyon, the daring leader of Force 136's Operation JAYWICK, which saw the destruction of more than 50,000 tons of Japanese shipping in Singapore harbour in 1943.

A similar operation in 1944, codenamed RIMAU, ended in the death of Lyon and his team, five of whom were missing in action until 1994, when the remains of two were found. A solemn ceremony was held at Kranji two years later to inter Sub Lieutenant Gregor Riggs and Sergeant Colin Cameron, with their fallen SOE comrades. The remains of the three men of Lyon's team still listed as missing in action, Lieutenant BP Reymond, Corporal CM Craft and Able Seaman FWL Marsh, have yet to be found.

To the west of the main War Cemetery lie the remains of Commonwealth troops and their dependants who were buried in the Ulu Pandan and Pasir Panjang Military Cemeteries. When the British pulled out of Singapore in 1971, the lands on which these cemeteries were located were handed back to the Singapore Government. As the government needed the land for future development, the CWGC decided to accept all the graves for reburial at Kranji. This was done with the exception of the graves of stillborn babies, belonging mainly to those of the Gurkha troops in Singapore. These graves would be combined into a single mass grave at Kranji. This mass grave then ended up reinterred with those remains from Ulu Pandan and Pasir Panjang that could not be identified. In a note to the Foreign Office in 1972, the CWGC was amenable to the shifting of the remains:

> The spare ground at Kranji on the west side above the Caretaker's Quarters slopes away to the west and it would seem that a very satisfactory cemetery could be established here with entry from an un-made up road coming in from the south west behind the new State Cemetery. This roadway already runs over part of the Commission's land on its route to a rather ramshackle house just outside the SW corner of the Commission's boundary.
>
> Fencing and provisions of suitable gates and the siting of the Celtic Cross feature, now in Pasir Panjang, should not prove difficult and there is already a fence (with a small service gate), with a hedge inside, running along the war cemetery side[4].

Today, the Singapore State Cemetery sits next to the War Cemetery. The republic's first president, Yusof Ishak, and his successor, Benjamin Henry Sheares, are buried here. Groups of school children are often brought up to the Kranji War Cemetery, to show them what the previous generations had given up for future Singaporeans. On 15 February (Fall of Singapore),

Kranji War Cemetery: Most of the remains of the Allied War dead were centralised at the Kranji War Memorial by 1946 with the Commonwealth War Graves Commission building a large complex to house the remains. Today, Singapore's State Cemetery is located next to the War Cemetery.

Changi Prison: Prisoners marched into the compound behind these walls during the Second World War faced unimaginable hardship. Those liberated during the reoccupation were often extremely thin and malnourished.

25 April (ANZAC Day) and 11 November (Armistice Day) every year, memorial services are held at the cemetery to remember the sacrifices made by the few for the many.

Changi Prison

A trip to the Changi Prison complex is crucial for anyone who visits Singapore and wants to have an understanding of what happened to the colonial masters and parts of the civilian population during the Japanese occupation.

The story of Changi would fill several thick volumes. It was earmarked in 1927 to become a base for the Royal Artillery batteries, covering the eastern approaches to the Straits of Johor as part of the British defensive strategy for Singapore. However, the whole Changi area went through stops and starts in development from 1927 to 1941 as a result of political indecision and budget cuts at Whitehall.

With the fall of Singapore on 15 February 1942, the Japanese decided to turn the Changi complex into a huge POW camp.

Many do not realise that the prison, which has come to symbolise Changi, had not initially been used to hold POWs. Built in 1936, the new prison in Changi was meant to house 800 civilian prisoners. Shortly after the Japanese conquest of Singapore, the European community was gathered on the Padang and force-marched to Changi. The prison became home to mainly white, civilian internees—3,000 men, and 400 women and children. For two years, they endured the brutality of their captors within the prison's stone walls. It was not until May 1944 that they were ordered out to make way for POWs.

Allied POWs had been located in various barracks throughout Changi, forcing close to 20,000 troops to live in abject squalor and hunger. As there was not enough space, crude tents and huts were fashioned to house this defeated army. Beginning early 1944, thousands more prisoners returned to the Changi area following the completion of the Siam-Burma railway.

The civilians were moved out of Changi Prison into an internment camp at Sime Road and 5,000 POWs were moved into the vacated cells, which were filthy and foul-smelling. Each cell had a concrete block in the centre that served as a bed for one prisoner. Two more prisoners slept on the floor on either side. One small window gave a little light while a hole in the floor served as a toilet. A further 12,000 POWs were concentrated in the surrounding area of the prison, living in camps made up of *attap* huts and rough accommodation. The Outram Road Jail was used as a punishment camp[5].

In addition to building the Siam-Burma Railway, many POWs from Changi were also forced to labour for two years to build the Changi airstrip for the Japanese, whose planes first started using the airstrip in 1944. It was very hard work in the searing heat as the men flattened mangrove swamps and built a rudimentary tarmac made of earth. Working 10 to 12 hours a day, suffering from starvation and disease, many died building the precursor to today's Changi International Airport.

By early August 1945, it was clear that the Japanese were losing as secret radios in the camps relayed news of Allied victories in the Western and Pacific theatres.

When Japan announced its unconditional surrender on 15 August 1945, POW work parties began returning to Singapore from other destinations, eager to return home. By early September, more than 17,000 men were congregated in and around the Changi prison compound. At about the same time, medicines and medics were parachuted in to assist the suffering men.

Changi continues to be a very significant reminder of man's inhumanity toward man. Although the main prison will be torn down by the end of 2005, the entry gate through which thousands of Second World War prisoners

The Japanese Cemetery: This cemetery at Chuan Hoe Avenue holds the ashes of almost all Japanese troops who died during and after the end of the war.

SHRINE TO OUR WAR HEROES IN SYONAN-TO

Commemoration Of Battle For Singapore

(Domei)

CONSTRUCTION work has been started on the Syonan Shrine which will serve as a commemoration of the fall of Singapore into Nipponese hands.

It is also learned that a memorial dedicated to those Nipponese soldiers who sacrificed their lives in the battle for Singapore is also being constructed as well as other landmarks where our forces made successful crossings over the Johore Straits.

The Japanese Cemetery: The remains of Field Marshal Count Terauchi were buried beneath this tombstone, in a remote corner of the cemetery. It remains well tended close to 60 years after his death. On the right is a newspaper article published in the Syonan Shimbun marking the erection of the two shrines in Syonan (Singapore) and another on Johor Bahru's esplanade facing Singapore.

The Syonan Chureito: The Japanese built a shrine on Bukit Batok to commemorate those who fell during the fierce fighting in Bukit Timah in the battle for Singapore. Allied POWs built a Cross behind the Japanese shrine to mark their dead as well. On reoccupation, the Allied forces blew up the shrine and the Syonan Jinjya shrine at MacRitchie, consolidating all Japanese remains at the cemetery in Chuan Hoe Avenue.

marched into Changi, never again to leave, will be preserved as a reminder of the grim days of the occupation.

The Japanese Cemetery

The Japanese Cemetery along Chuan Hoe Avenue was founded in 1891 as a burial ground that, until 1947, was exclusively Japanese. Almost 1,000 of early Singapore's Japanese community leaders and members are buried at the Shakkyozan Nihonji[6].

During the Japanese occupation, the cemetery continued to be used for civilian Japanese burials while the Japanese military administration built two shrines, the Syonan Jinjya near MacRitchie Reservoir and the Syonan Chureito on Bukit Batok, to hold the ashes of Japanese soldiers who died in the Malayan Campaign and the battle for Singapore.

At the Chureito on Bukit Batok, a large pillar was erected with a shrine dedicated to the war dead. The Japanese also gave permission to British POWs to build a small wooden cross behind the pillar to pay tribute to the British and Allied troops who died in the Malayan Campaign and the fall of Singapore. When the British recaptured Singapore, sappers blew up the two shrines and the consolidated ashes were dumped at the Japanese cemetery.

The question subsequently arose as to who would be responsible for the remains of Japanese soldiers who died during the war and the remains of Japanese surrendered personnel who died before they could be repatriated to Japan. There was also concern over what would happen to the ashes of Japanese war criminals who were to be executed.

In a flurry of letters between the British Foreign Office, Commonwealth Office and War Office, no one could decide what to do with the remains or who would pay for the maintenance of the remains. The Foreign Office was of the view that the Japanese Government would have to bear the full cost:

> The limit of British responsibility in respect of any Japanese 'war graves' would appear to be physical maintenance, which would presumably be at the expense of the Japanese Government. Such maintenance, I suppose, would be on a scale commensurate with the amount of money which the Japanese were prepared to pay. If, to take the extreme case, the Japanese Government declared that they had no interest in the graves at all, and were not prepared to pay anything, we should no longer be under any moral

> obligation to see that the "graves... were treated with respect and suitably maintained".
>
> At the present moment the Japanese Government are not, I think, in a position to give us any foreign currency in exchange for services in respect of the graves. By the time the Peace Treaty is signed, there will presumably be some arrears to collect. I do not know whether this will amount to anything substantial.
>
> If it is desired to recover the expenses in question, it would seem to be desirable to ensure, as soon as possible, that the Japanese are aware that a claim will be made. This could, of course, be notified to them through the Supreme Commander for the Allied Powers in Tokyo. It is just possible that it might be thought worth covering the question in the Peace Treaty, by some general clause making it clear that the Japanese Government must be responsible for all past and future expenses in connexion (sic) with the maintenance of graves of J.S.P. (Japanese Surrendered Personnel) in Allied territory; and the same considerations presumably apply to the graves of Japanese who died during the occupation. I presume whichever Department undertakes the immediate responsibility of paying the caretakers would undertake to make suggestions for any such clause in the Peace Treaty which they might deem necessary[7].

As a result of this indecision at Whitehall and the inability to get the Japanese Government to commit funds, the local Japanese community along with the Singapore municipal authorities contributed funds for a very simple mass grave at the Japanese Cemetery. It was then that the ashes of more than 10,000 Japanese war dead from MacRitchie and Bukit Batok were deposited under two markers at the Japanese cemetery. Also interred there were the remains of 200 Japanese war criminals tried and executed in Singapore between 1946 and 1948. The Japanese Association in Singapore later contributed funds to landscape and build granite pillars over the tombs.

As mentioned in the previous chapter, Field Marshal Count Hsiaichi Terauchi, commander-in-chief of the Japanese Southern Army, had suffered a stroke just before the Japanese surrender and was unable to sign the surrender document in Singapore on 12 September 1945 due to his weakened state. Although he did finally surrender himself and his two swords to Lord Louis Mountbatten in November 1945, Terauchi did not live very long after. When he died in 1946, his cremated remains were buried in a separate shrine at the Japanese Cemetery, where it is one of the most well-known graves.

The cemetery became a memorial park in 1987 and is currently maintained by the Singapore Japanese Association with donations from the Japanese community.

The Civilian Monument

Known affectionately as the "Chopsticks" monument due to its long, pillar-like structures, the Civilian Monument in downtown Singapore was built only in 1967. However, the history behind the setting up of the monument is tied to the end of the war and to Singapore's rocky road to independence.

In the late 1950s and early 1960s, as Singapore began redeveloping its land to meet the needs of its population and industry, contractors and workmen began finding huge mass graves all over the island. The mass graves were filled with the bodies of Chinese civilians who were killed by the Japanese in the opening days of the occupation. In what was known as the *Sook Ching* Operation, thousands of Chinese who were believed to have collaborated with the British before the war and those who appeared 'educated' or likely to put up a struggle against Japanese rule were rounded up at concentration points throughout the island. They were then taken in trucks to remote spots on the island where they were made to dig and stand in their own graves while the Japanese troops bayoneted or shot them where they stood.

The discovery of numerous mass graves created an enormous outcry among the Chinese community in Singapore and Malaya who demanded that the Japanese compensate them for the 'blood debt' that was owed to the peoples in the region. However, by this time, the Japanese Government had already signed a treaty with the Allied powers specifying that a full and complete compensation had been made. Consequently, in 1963, the Japanese Government took the position that no other compensation could be considered.

In and of itself, the issue could have been resolved quickly as, privately, the Japanese Government was willing to pay a certain amount of compensation. However, the Chinese Chamber of Commerce felt that any offer by the Japanese would have to match the 'donation' of 50 million Straits Settlement dollars that the Chinese community in Singapore had been forced to make to the Japanese during the occupation.

The Civilian Memorial: This memorial has come to symbolise the suffering of the general populace in Singapore during the Occupation. Its creation helped to repay a 'blood debt' that was demanded from the Japanese in compensation for the sufferings of a generation.

To complicate matters, the Japanese consul general in Singapore, Tanaka, did not appear to have the authority to settle the dispute on behalf of his government. However, the biggest complication was the fact that, in 1963, Singapore was supposed to merge with peninsular Malaya, Sabah and Sarawak (British Borneo) as well as Brunei to become an independent and sovereign state in the Malaysian federation.

The day of merger, Malaysia Day, was, by the agreement of all parties involved, to fall on 31 August 1963. However, the Malaysian prime minister, Tunku Abdul Rahman, after meeting with the Indonesian and Philippine presidents between 30 July and 5 August, had agreed to postpone Malaysia Day to 16 September in order to give the United Nations time to ascertain the popular will in the Borneo territories on the proposition to join the Malaysian federation. The then prime minister of Singapore Lee Kuan Yew and chief ministers designate of Sabah and Sarawak were not consulted on this decision and as a result all three called on the Tunku to set up Malaysia on 31 August. Regardless, the Malaysian prime minister decided that Malaysia Day would be postponed to 16 September 1963[8].

Thus, Lee, who was in the midst of a political struggle with the Malayan Communist Party (MCP) for control of the hearts and minds of the populace and to garner support for the upcoming merger with Malaysia, declared Singapore's *de facto* independence on 31 August 1963. He said the PAP government would hold Singapore in trust until the formation of Malaysia. Lee called for unity and pledged the state's loyalty to the central Malaysian government[9]. In the same speech, Lee decided to turn the heat on the Japanese by announcing that as the Japanese had yet to settle the issue of the blood debt, the Singapore Government would now also take on the foreign relations portfolio of the state until Malaysia Day in an attempt to resolve the blood debt issue[10].

A day before Lee's speech, he had written to the British Colonial Secretary, saying that:

> ... one of the steps towards independence which he wishes to announce at a mass rally on 31 August is that Her Majesty's Government have delegated to the Government of Singapore complete powers in the matter of foreign relations "to the extent and in order that the Government of Singapore can between 31 August and 16 September settle the question of the nature and substance of the Japanese gesture of atonement for atrocities"[11].

The British Commissioner General for Southeast Asia, and later High Commissioner to Singapore, Sir George Nigel Douglas-Hamilton, the Lord Selkirk, cabled Whitehall that Lee's request would have a disastrous effect on British relations with Japan:

> If Lee attempts to turn the heat on, the Japanese will refuse to negotiate under pressure and will simply stand on the legal position under the Peace Treaty until things cool down. There would be no prospect of the early settlement which would be in everyone's interest.
>
> ... The fallacy in Lee's request lies of course in the fact that he has already for some time been exercising the powers he now suggests we should delegate as from 31 August, and indeed in his speech on 25 August gave some account of the way he had been doing so...
>
> ... If our position were distorted in any way by Lee in public utterances suggesting that he had received new powers, we would feel obliged to issue the statement ourselves to clear the record[12].

Three days later, Lord Selkirk submitted his report to London to explain the strategy adopted by the Singapore Government in negotiations with the Japanese:

> The Singapore claim against the Japanese for atrocities committed during the period of occupation is naturally getting a great deal of public support and whilst the leaders are all prepared to say privately they want a settlement, they are clearly not going to take a strong line advocating a limit to the amount which should be considered reasonable for Japan to pay.
>
> Lee is playing a very equivocable game and I am not surprised to learn that the Japanese view him with suspicion. The truth is that he wants to gain political kudos for himself by making a favourable settlement with the Japanese whilst he knows anything he agrees to will be denounced by his political opponents as totally inadequate. I believe he is genuinely out to get a settlement within this political setting.
>
> In the meantime, Lee has been very inaccessible to the Japanese Consul-General, Tanaka, and I have had the utmost difficulty in seeing him myself. He has been discourteous in public to the Japanese Consul-General. Although the communists may be trying to exploit the situation, the feeling among the Chinese is widespread; indeed hardly a family cannot recall a relative who disappeared...
>
> ... I have explained to the Singapore Ministers that there is no chance of blackmailing the Japanese Government. If they do not make a sufficient effort, they may find themselves with a continuing disagreement without any compensation. Lee is anxious to settle this himself with the Japanese Government; so far we have given him every chance to do so. I would not advocate our taking an open part in any negotiations. I believe that would complicate, rather than facilitate, matters but I have got to say that I think it is going to be very difficult to make a quick settlement below the figure of about $(Malayan) 50,000,000. This was the amount of the forced loan which the Japanese raised from the Chinese Chamber of Commerce during the occupation[13].

Speaking to one of the Japanese Consuls in Singapore, Lord Selkirk underlined the difficult position faced by the Singapore Government:

> We told the Consul that in our view it seemed increasingly unlikely that the Japanese Government would be able to achieve a settlement within the figure of $5 million; that however projects might be dressed up, they would be bound to be evaluated in monetary terms by the Chinese Chamber of Commerce; and that in the end they would have to be prepared to bargain seriously over the Chamber of Commerce figure of $50 Million[14].

However, more importantly, the Singapore Government had upped the ante on 3 September by asking the British legation to inform all visa-issuing authorities (until the merger occurred, visas for Singapore were supposed to be issued by British diplomatic posts around the world) that all Japanese visa applications were to be referred to Singapore. Lord Selkirk noted that from 16 September 1963 onwards, immigration would be a matter for the federal government in Kuala Lumpur but it was likely "to be some months before the federal government assumes control in Singapore. Until that time the status quo will be maintained and visa applications will continue in practice to be a matter for the Singapore Government"[15].

Pressure on Lee and the PAP government was also mounting, not only on the issue of Japanese reparations but also on whether Singapore would actually become a part of Malaysia. The PAP government was poised to hold local elections in Singapore five days after Malaysia Day[16]. The United Malay National Organisation (UMNO), the main political party in the Alliance coalition that made up the federal government in Kuala Lumpur, clearly wanted to break the PAP's control over the island. The communal parties in the Alliance, the Malaysian Indian Congress (MIC) and the Malaysian Chinese Association (MCA), had formed Singaporean versions of the mainland coalition to contest in the elections and UMNO clearly wanted their communal cousins to win. Although Lee had pledged Singapore's loyalty to the federal government in public, Lord Selkirk noted that he was actually willing to unilaterally declare Singapore's independence in September 1963:

> I saw Lee Kuan Yew this morning when he showed considerable intellectual arrogance, repeatedly referring to the stupidity (reference deleted) and of the Japanese Consul-General Tanaka...
>
> ... He still professes to be very anxious and determined to set up Malaysia but is worried whether it will hold together and insists on agreement being reached on the remaining conditions of Singapore's entry, which are now being discussed in Kuala Lumpur. If he does not get this settled by 12 September (nomination day for the Singapore elections), he will fight the election on programme for Singapore's independence and immediately ask for recognition by a number of countries as from 16 September. I did not discuss all that was involved in a declaration of independence but called on his co-operation (*sic*) in arriving at agreement with the Federation on the outstanding points. This he was willing to do and suggested that Goh Keng Swee should conduct these negotiations when he came back from Bangkok on 6 September instead of himself.
>
> He also promised to hold off anything which might damage relations during the period until 12 September but will attack the Malays wholeheartedly

> thereafter. He claims that if he does not get the points he has in mind, it will be because of the Malay intention to crush Singapore and he would be ashamed to accept the responsibility of entering Malaysia on these terms[17].

Lord Selkirk noted that Lee was fighting a battle for reparations and a larger battle for merger, both of which had a great impact on the way Singaporeans would vote in the coming elections. In dealing with reparations, it was clear that Lee was frustrated:

> In the course of my conversation with Lee Kuan Yew this morning, he referred to the Japanese problem and said he had done his utmost to lay it down for 15 months. But there was so little response from the Japanese that he had had to put himself at the head of the movement. He complained of some reference he said emanated from Japan that this matter would more easily be settled after Malaysia. The result of this has been that all parts of Malaysia have started agitating for Japanese compensation.
>
> I warned him of the danger of antagonising Japan which might lose (*sic*) their support for Malaysia at the United Nations and also of the danger of the communists getting hold of the whole movement, to which he agreed.
>
> He clearly found it very difficult to get on with the present Japanese Consul-General Tanaka, and I would strongly recommend that the Japanese Government should be encouraged to send someone here of stronger personality and with a better command of English if these negotiations are to be brought to fruition. At the present time, I do not judge the Prime Minister considers it worthwhile giving Tanaka a proper chance to do his job[18].

In the end, Singapore did join the federation on Malaysia Day, only to become an independent country two years later on 9 August 1965. As for the issue of reparations, Japan sent a new ambassador to Singapore but the negotiations continued long after the 16 September deadline Lee had set. It was not until 1966 that Japan and Singapore finally resolved the issue with a significant contribution made by the Japanese that resulted in the creation of the Civilian Monument. The monument was inaugurated on 15 February 1967, 25 years to the day that Singapore fell to the Japanese.

Even then, there was still controversy. The famous Chinese poet Pan Shou had been asked to write an epitaph for the Civilian Monument. The epitaph, written in Mandarin (translated into English and reproduced below), was scathing in its attack on the Japanese but clearly represented the feelings of the local Chinese community. However, the epitaph never saw the light of day and has long been forgotten, relegated as a curiosity in academic journals and books. Nonetheless, it remains a strong and poignant summation of the horrors that faced the Chinese community in Singapore and the desire for future generations to learn from it. Perhaps it will one day be installed at the location for which it was written[19]:

> THIS MEMORIAL MARKS AN UNPRECEDENTED TRAGEDY IN THE HISTORY OF SINGAPORE
>
> The occupation of Singapore by the Japanese Army between 15 February 1942 and18 August 1945 was a dark and tragic epoch.
>
> The people of Singapore were subjected to lashing, humiliation, enslavement and extortion. Under the pretext of "mass screening" (*Sook Ching*), the Japanese Army massacred tens of thousands of non-combatants in secrecy. God was ridiculed. Civilisation was buried, and the dignity of mankind trampled. Everywhere, tears flowed. Everywhere, blood splattered. And everywhere, terror reigned.
>
> In January 1962, some of the remains of the civilian victims were first unearthed. This led to the setting-up of a committee by the Singapore Chinese Chamber of Commerce for conducting further investigation, for exhumation, as well as for the planning of the construction of a mass grave and a memorial for the remains. In July the same year, a permit for exhumation was obtained from the Authority. In March 1963, the Singapore Government allotted a four acre plot of land for the site of this Memorial Park. During the last four years, more and more remains of these victims were exhumed. In the meantime, as a result of the widespread response received from the public and the encouragement from the government who contributed to the Memorial Building Fund on the basis of a-dollar-to-a-dollar from the public, this memorial is (*sic*) eventually completed.
>
> Now this memorial stands towering over the Equator, gazing at the ever-changing scenes of Southeast Asia and the world at large.
>
> Now this memorial stands aloft at this hub of communication between the Eastern and the Western Hemispheres, beckoning friendly day and night to the passers-by of Southeast Asia and the world.
>
> No one knows the exact number of our compatriots of the different races massacred during the dark days of the Occupation. Although countless

sets of bones are already buried under the podium, it is most probable that they might represent only a fraction of the civilian victims massacred, whose number might be five or ten times greater. No one can list all our multiracial compatriots who were killed in the massacre. They deserve to be posthumously honoured as loyal, brave, virtuous and righteous men who have sacrificed their lives long before the independence of Singapore and should thus be enshrined in the spiritual foundation of the country.

The four towering columns of this memorial symbolise loyalty, bravery, virtue and righteousness, traits of which are reflected in the traditional harmony and solidarity of the multiracial, multicultural and multi-religious society of Singapore.

This memorial stands to prove that the people of Singapore were able to hold their own together in adversity and it also signifies their ever-readiness to share the common prosperity of the country in future.

Let this memorial echo the voice of the people of Singapore.

War is evil. Peace is sacred. The big and the strong nations want to live, so do the small and weak ones. The big and strong ones who oppress the small and weak ones will never escape condemnation and punishment on the final judgement of history. However, the best policy is to redress grievances amicably and not to generate enmity. The people of Singapore are always with the peoples of the world, including the people of Japan, who are peace-loving and who oppose aggression, imperialism and colonialism.

May the souls of the civilian victims of the Japanese Occupation rest in eternal peace and accept this epitaph dedicated to them by the people of Singapore.

"Tears stained flower crimson like
And blood tainted the blue ocean
Ye wandering souls who rise with the tide
Shall guard this young emerging nation."

The INA Monument

Set up by exiled Indian patriots with the help of the Indian community in Southeast Asia and support from the Japanese army, the Indian National Army (INA) was part of the Indian independence movement in Southeast Asia. The independence struggle against the British in India led many in the Indian diaspora to look for ways and means to liberate their country.

Before the start of the war, the Japanese were already encouraging Indian nationalism. During the Malayan Campaign, they recruited former British soldier Captain Mohan Singh to become commander of the newly created INA. Although the INA was received warmly by the Indian community in Malaya, political infighting between Rash Behari Bose, an exiled Indian patriot in Japan, and Singh, as well as the Japanese demand to control the INA led to the dissolution of the first INA and Singh's detention.

The INA was resurrected under Subhas Chandra Bose, a staunch Indian nationalist and former president of the Indian National Congress. Bose had been in exile in Germany, where he had set up an Indian liberation army (Azad Hind Fauj) to fight alongside the Germans. After he grew disillusioned with German führer Adolf Hitler, Bose joined up with the Japanese in 1943, taking on the mantle of the Supreme Commander of the INA. Addressed as *Netaji*, or "Leader", Bose arrived in Singapore in July 1943 and within a month, had mobilised thousands of Indians in the region to fight for the freedom of their motherland. Through the Indian Independence League, Bose began to create a base of support and funds for the INA. On 21 October 1943, in the cinema hall at the Cathay Building, Bose declared the creation of the Free India Provisional Government (FIPG). With this act, Bose created a government and army in exile that would take over the running of India once the British were ousted by the Japanese.

Early Japanese successes meant that Bose could raise the tricolour Indian flag over Port Blair in the Andaman islands, the first Indian territory to come under the rule of the government-in-exile. However, this turned out to be just a symbol as the Japanese were the ones who wielded the real power. Not satisfied with such small wins, Bose wanted the INA to spearhead the fight against the British in Burma and to be the first ones to reach Indian soil. Although the Japanese did manage to capture Manipur and the INA did raise their flag on Indian territory, these successes were short-lived as the British managed to rout the Japanese forces, forcing them to begin their retreat in late 1944. By early 1945, it was clear that the Japanese had lost the battle for Burma and the Japanese army was in retreat. Many INA soldiers died in the retreat, even though most had served in the rear, because of the confusion and chaos that reigned.

Reports of these losses meant that Bose needed to boost the morale of Indians in Malaya and Singapore. Using funds the Indian Independence League had begun to raise in late 1944, the INA Memorial was built.

On 8 July 1945, Bose laid the foundation stone for the Memorial to the Unknown Soldier of the INA, located on the Esplanade in Singapore, a

The INA Memorial: Built by public contribution, the memorial located on the Esplanade, was unveiled by Subhas Chandra Bose on 8 July 1945. It came to symbolise the sacrifices made by the Indian populace for the Indian Independence movement. On the return of the Allies, it was blown up. These are some of the very few photographs which exist of the memorial. A sketch of the memorial has been etched on a bronze plaque, near the Lim Bo Seng memorial, which commemorates the building of the INA memorial.

few feet from the British Cenotaph dedicated to the war dead in the First World War.

The memorial consisted of three joined pillars, inscribed in Urdu with the words *Ittefaq* (Unity), *Itmad* (Faith) and *Kurbani* (Sacrifice). At the ceremony, Bose spoke passionately to the assembled troops:

> The future generations of Indians who will be born, not as slaves but as freemen, because of your colossal sacrifice, will bless your names and proudly proclaim to the world that you, their forebears, fought and suffered reverses in the battle of Manipur, Assam and Burma, but through temporary failure you paved the way to ultimate success and glory[20].

However, on the return of the Allies, the memorial was destroyed by sappers from the 5th Indian Division. In its place, the British Military Administration built a memorial to Lim Bo Seng. The INA Memorial was forgotten for close to 50 years before the Singapore Information and the Arts Ministry began installing plaques marking important Second World War sites in Singapore in 1992. Although the plaque for the INA Memorial does not list the location of the memorial, it provides recognition of the sacrifices made by the Indian community in Southeast Asia for the cause of freedom in India.

The Cathay Building

Prior to the Second World War, the Cathay building was the tallest structure in Singapore. It was home to rich tycoons and provided office space to big businesses in Singapore and Malaya. The Cathay was one of the only air-conditioned buildings in Singapore and had a state-of-the-art cinema at its base. The Malayan Broadcasting Corporation had one of its studios in the building while the British military occupied some of its suites as a wireless transmitting station.

During the Malayan Campaign, the building also housed the offices of the British Ministry of Information. As the battle for Singapore drew nearer, a top-secret radar unit was set up in the building to help coordinate radar traffic from air bases around the island and filter it to the Gun Operations Room at the Battlebox in Fort Canning.

On 15 February 1942, as one of the preconditions of surrender to the Japanese, the British were instructed to raise a Japanese flag and a white flag above the Cathay Building for 10 minutes to signal British acceptance of the surrender terms. When the flag was raised, it was shot at by British units, forcing it to be pulled down quickly.

With the fall of Singapore, the Japanese began using the Cathay Building for their propaganda units and broadcasting station. On 21 October 1943, Subhas Chandra Bose proclaimed the creation of the Free India Provisional Government (FIPG) in the cinema auditorium of the building. The very same auditorium was also the scene of frenzied discussions, following which the FIPG declared war on the United States of America and the United Kingdom.

Upon the reoccupation of Singapore by the British in September 1945, the Cathay Building was taken over as the headquarters of the supreme allied commander, Southeast Asia (SACSEA). Reverting to its owners in the late 1940s, the Cathay was refurbished and became an important location for post-war businesses in Singapore.

Today, the cinema and office buildings have been torn down and all that remains is the façade. Nonetheless, the site of the Cathay Building will always remain an important reminder of Singapore's not-so-distant wartime past.

Endnotes

1 Although the 29th Japanese Army had shifted its headquarters to Taiping in early 1945 in preparation for the expected Allied assault on Malaya, Itagaki as Commander of the 7th Area Army, which included the 29th Army, remained in Singapore.

2 Commonwealth War Graves Commission, The. "The Singapore Memorial: Introduction to the Register". *The War Dead of the British Commonwealth and Empire; The Register of the Names of Those who Fell in the 1939–1945 War and have No Known Grave*. London: The Commonwealth War Graves Commission, 1957. 17.

3 Ibid.

4 *DFE's Visit to Eastern and Pacific Regions (Delhi, Singapore, Melbourne) April 1972—Singapore 11 April, 22 May 1972, FCO24/1291*. London: The National Archives.

5 Cooper, Carol. "South East Asia Under Japanese Occupation: The Story of Changi". *The Children (& Families) of the Far East Prisoners of War (COFEPOW)*. [Internet]. Accessed 13 February 2005. Available from: <http://www.cofepow.org.uk/pages/asia_singapore_changi_story.htm>.

6 Lam, Pin Foo. "Japanese Settlers were Here Before the War". *The Straits Times: Life*, 25 February 1998. 2.

7 *F13687/13687/23, 17 October 1947, FO371/63826*. London: The National Archives.

8 Lau, Albert. *A Moment of Anguish: Singapore in Malaysia and the Politics of Disengagement*. Singapore: Times Academic Press, 1998. 17.

9 Ibid.17.

10 *The Straits Times*, 3 September 1963.

11 *Colonial Secretary to Lord Selkirk. Signal No. 560, 30 August 1963, PREM11/4325*. London: The National Archives.

12 *Selkirk to Colonial Secretary. Signal No. 2540, 30 August 1963, PREM11/4325*. London: The National Archives.

13 *Selkirk to Colonial Secretary. Signal No. 632, 2 September 1963, PREM11/4325*. London: The National Archives.

14 *Selkirk to Colonial Secretary. Signal No. 636, 3 September 1963, PREM11/4325*. London: The National Archives.

15 Ibid.

16 Lau, 1998. 21.

17 *Selkirk to Colonial Secretary. Signal No. 641, 4 September 1963, PREM11/4325*. London: The National Archives.

18 *Selkirk to Colonial Secretary. Signal No. 642, 4 September 1963, PREM11/4325*. London: The National Archives.

19 National Heritage Board, National Archives of Singapore. *The Japanese Occupation 1942–1945: A Pictorial Record of Singapore During the War*. Singapore: Times Editions, 1996.

20 *Syonan Shimbun*, 9 July 1945.

Chapter 10

Postscript

The end of the war marked a new beginning for the region but it was one that would be filled with bloodshed and violent clashes as the former colonial subjects began their clamour for independence.

With the ceremonial end to the Far Eastern War on 12 September 1945, the British objective of recapturing and reoccupying their former colonies and possessions in Southeast Asia was met. From the beginning, the British had been under tremendous pressure to settle the situation in the Far East quickly. In March 1945, the Joint Intelligence Committee (JIC) had estimated that it would take at least another 12 months to force a Japanese collapse in the region. Moreover, the chiefs of Imperial General Staff agreed that the only way Britain could take part in the American-led CORONET and OLYMPIC operations to invade the Japanese home islands would be with the quick recapture first of Singapore and then Malaya. The British knew the Americans would not help in the reoccupation of their colonies because of their distaste for the British brand of colonialism. So the reoccupation of Malaya and Singapore would be a purely British affair and would tax British resources to the fullest. However, Britain was also keen to be seen as a key American partner in the invasion of Japan as this would give them a seat at the surrender table, reinforce the special relationship they shared with the US and ensure significant influence in any post-war settlement[1]. Thus, Japan's early surrender meant that British forces would not be forced to fight their way down the Malayan peninsula in order to retake Singapore and they could now take part in the occupation of the Japanese home islands.

However, Singapore had figured prominently on the minds of SEAC planners in Colombo for other reasons. The island fortress had been the symbol of British might in the region and its loss in 1942 was a severe blow to British pride and morale. The Japanese then used Singapore as their headquarters with the 7th Area Army based on the island. As such, it was imperative to British pride and strategy to capture Singapore as quickly as possible. Its recapture would symbolise to the Japanese the destruction of the heart of their southern forces and at the same time restore Britain's prestige in the region. The initial plan to recapture Singapore (prior to the Japanese surrender on 15 August) through ZIPPER meant a prolonged fight down the Malayan peninsula before Allied troops reached Singapore. The Japanese were aware of the British strategy and were in the midst of boosting their defences on Malaya's west coast when the war ended.

Now, it appeared even more imperative for SEAC to reoccupy Singapore quickly. The British wanted to ensure a total Japanese surrender and the fastest way to accomplish that was to capture the various Japanese headquarters in the region. Rangoon had fallen in July 1945 and the Japanese Burma army was now effectively destroyed. However, the forces in Malaya were still armed and fresh, a potential threat should Field Marshal Count Terauchi decide to continue the struggle in Southeast Asia.

However, the geopolitical necessity to have the Japanese government surrender first was clearly paramount to any other smaller surrender. Once the documents on board the *USS Missouri* were signed and sealed at Tokyo Bay, all other ancillary surrenders could take place. Although this delay was crucial to the last act of a world war, its repercussions for the people in Malaya and Singapore were tremendous. There was a span of three weeks between Emperor Hirohito's surrender announcement on Japanese Radio on 15 August and the eventual landing of the 5th Indian Division at Singapore's Keppel Harbour on 5 September. In the meantime, a state of virtual chaos had reigned in numerous towns and villages as well as in the Malayan countryside.

SEAC planners were taken aback when the phoney surrender period erupted into communal violence. Some violence would not have been unusual but the large number of revenge killings and lawlessness throughout the country was unexpected. Vice Admiral Lord Louis Mountbatten, keenly aware that the power vacuum had to be quickly filled, wanted Singapore recaptured at the earliest possible date. Once British power had been restored in Singapore, all other parts of Malaya would fall in line. Singapore remained a symbol of power in the peninsula and Mountbatten planned to use it as such.

Although the British had infiltrated clandestine outfits like Force 136 into the Malayan jungles, their main role was in working with resistance groups to destabilise Japanese rule and in providing ground intelligence for the returning British forces. Despite having very loyal support from local agents who risked their lives running spy networks, like Lim Bo Seng who gave his life for Force 136, these heroes were given only minimal recognition and that, more than three years after the war ended. Lim's network was supposed to be the foundation of spy rings in towns and villages throughout Malaya but the destruction of the network left Force 136 with no external source of information except the Malayan People's Anti-Japanese Army (MPAJA). By the end of the war, more groups were sent in to build jungle resistance forces. Restoring order and filling in a power vacuum were neither part of Force 136's mandate nor scope of operations. As such, Force 136 officers and men could only stand by and watch as much of the revenge killings by groups of the MPAJA and other resistance fighters took place. It was not until the first troops landed in Singapore on 5 September 1945 that the communal violence and killings of collaborators ended.

Moreover, the overriding priority for SEAC was not in restoring order in these towns or among the resistance groups but in reoccupying Malaya at a rapid pace. Greater focus was given to getting British troops into Malaya urgently and then leaving it to the field commanders to restore the peace in villages and towns throughout the peninsula.

The impact of the phoney surrender was far reaching. In taking over towns and villages throughout Malaya and exacting revenge on collaborators and ethnic groups during the three weeks of violence, the Malayan Communist Party (MCP) and the MPAJA were given a taste of real power and control. By setting up People's Committees and Central Committees in the open, the MCP had created a *de facto* government in the peninsula and became, in the eyes of many in the Chinese community, the true liberators of Malaya. This reputation would hold the MCP in very good stead when it began its armed struggle three years later as the goodwill among local Chinese leaders ensured the rebuilding of the MCP's secret army. Had there not been a phoney surrender period, the MPAJA would have remained in their jungle camps and would not have had that taste of self-government. It is unlikely that this would have prevented the MCP's eventual armed insurrection in 1948 but it could possibly have delayed the MCP's bid for power.

In reoccupying Malaya, Mountbatten needed to ensure that, in order for the official surrender ceremonies of 12 September to take place, the British had effective and almost total control of Malaya. This meant the reoccupation of Singapore by 5 September and the effective, though not official, reoccupation of Malaya by 11 September 1945.

Thus, the surrender of Singapore on 4 September came to play a much more crucial role in ending the war for the people of Malaya than the events of 12 September.

General Seishiro Itagaki's surrender agreement on board the *HMS Sussex* was effectively the Japanese surrender of Singapore. Within 24 hours of the signing, 35,000 Japanese troops had been moved across the causeway and had started building accommodation in concentration areas as outlined in the surrender orders. The removal of 35,000 frontline troops within a day clearly indicated the seriousness with which the Japanese took the agreement signed on board the *Sussex*. Therefore, the *Sussex* surrender marked the return of the British to Singapore and the Japanese handover of power. More importantly for the people of Singapore and Malaya, the disembarkation of the 5th Indian Division on 5 September as a result of the *Sussex* surrender put an immediate stop to the communal violence on the island and parts of the peninsula. Although most had not heard of the surrender ceremony, news of the British arrival in force spread quickly and this had the effect of immediately stopping the ongoing ethnic clashes. The populace believed that the British would now be the adjudicators of the numerous disputes and troubles plaguing the people.

From the outset, Lieutenant General Sir Alexander Christison and his fellow generals were concerned that the Japanese would not surrender. The TIDERACE force of one division, which had not been assault-loaded, was in no shape to carry out an invasion should Itagaki have decided to carry on fighting. If negotiations failed and fighting broke out, Christison and Rear (later Vice) Admiral Cedric Holland were under instructions not to engage the enemy but to retreat and hold back until they joined the ZIPPER forces which would land in central Malaya on 9 September. Until the *Sussex* surrender, SEAC was unsure as to whether the Japanese troops in Malaya would abide by the emperor's declaration and the Tokyo Bay Agreement. Thus, the *Sussex* surrender ensured, for SEAC, the unopposed ZIPPER landings five days later. Although ZIPPER forces far outnumbered Japanese troops in Malaya, the fact that they were also not fully assault-loaded meant that there would have been significant Allied losses and civilian casualties if the Japanese had resisted.

However, that is not to say the 12 September ceremonies were unimportant or insignificant. The events at the Municipal Building were crucial to closing the final chapter of a global conflict. It was important to have representatives of the various Allied powers accept the surrender from the commanders of the Japanese military in Southeast Asia. On the world's stage, it clearly signalled the complete and total victory of the Allied forces and provided a happy ending to close four years of warfare in the Pacific.

Photographs and newsreel footage of Mountbatten's acceptance of the Japanese surrender and pictures of the Supreme Commander Southeast Asia Command holding aloft his admiral's peaked cap as the crowds thronging the Padang cheered him on provided signal proof that the British had been restored to their rightful place and that the defeats early in the war were now a thing of the past and could now safely recede into memory.

However, to the people of Malaya, the ceremony was of little significance. Of greater concern was how to feed one's family now that Japanese 'banana' money was worthless and how to get life back to normal now that the British had finally returned. Although SEAC invited members of the MPAJA to take part in the 12 September ceremony and even awarded an OBE to the future Secretary General of the MCP, Chin Peng, in an attempt to appease and recognise the contributions of the communists, the MCP had other ideas and would begin brewing trouble less than a month after the war was over. The first communist-led dockworker's strike began on 21 October 1945 when 7,000 wharf labourers refused to work on ships in the Tanjong Pagar docklands. The situation was only resolved when the British Military Administration (BMA) began using Japanese surrendered personnel and a few British units as wharf labourers[2].

On the Japanese side, the emperor's announcement on 15 August 1945 came as a complete shock. The first reaction by Japanese Southern Army commanders was denial but as emissaries of the emperor met with Count Terauchi, General Kimura and General Itagaki, it became clear that the war was over. Generals like Itagaki found it hard to accept the surrender but, under orders from Terauchi, had finally agreed to comply. It was also not easy for Itagaki's commanders to accept that they had lost the war. Many of these officers subsequently committed suicide rather than surrender to the enemy.

During the three weeks of the phoney surrender period, Japanese commanders began to lose control of their men and the areas they were in charge of. The demoralisation that comes with being a member of a vanquished force meant the Japanese were hardly in a position to remain in command. Defeat made strange bedfellows as close to 200 Japanese soldiers decided to join the communist guerrillas whom they were fighting just days before, in a bid to continue the fight against the British. It was only when they found out that the MPAJA did not plan to fight the returning British that many Japanese soldiers returned to their units. Nonetheless, some stayed hidden in the jungles with the communists and when Chin Peng and the remnants of the MCP ended their struggle in 1989, two former Japanese soldiers emerged from the jungles with the communists[3].

At the end of the war, the Japanese were keen to develop nationalistic groups that would be a thorn in the side of the returning British. Their decision to help ally Malay nationalists with Indonesian freedom fighters like Sukarno was aimed at creating groups within Malaya that would fight against the return of the British. Although the majority of these groups disintegrated on the return of the British, the idea of Malay independence had begun to take root. When the colonial authorities introduced the idea of the Malayan Union, giving the Chinese rights of citizenship and reducing the power of the Malay Sultans, political parties like the United Malay National Organisation (UMNO) were formed in a bid to fight for Malay rights and independence.

Nonetheless, the Japanese were nothing if not thorough in ensuring their part in the surrender took place quickly and effectively. The Japanese had detailed evacuation plans drawn up within a day after the *Sussex* surrender and provided further plans for the evacuation of remaining Japanese personnel to prisoner camps on the islands off Indonesia. However, altruism had nothing to do with these moves. From the very beginning, Itagaki and Fukudome realised that the surrendered Japanese would face retribution from the local population, especially the resistance groups, and they wanted to ensure that their men would be repatriated to Japan alive. In order to do this, they would have to build camps and segregate themselves in remote areas far away from towns and villages. This was what Itagaki had proposed in the very first meeting with Holland and Christison on the *Sussex*. In the end, a vast majority of Japanese were relocated to these types of camps and from there, eventually to Japan.

Although many of the Japanese commanders and men were tried for war crimes, the majority of men who served in the region were released to go on with rebuilding their decimated country. However, the legacy of its occupation in Malaya would continue to haunt the Japanese government despite the signing of a peace treaty and war reparations to the Allied powers. The discovery of mass graves in Singapore and Malaya in the late 1950s and early 1960s led to a demand for compensation and accountability for the wartime atrocities committed in the region. Although the Japanese Government eventually made contributions to settle the 'blood debt', the issue became entangled in the politics of the proposed merger between Singapore and Malaysia, as well as the fledgling People's Action Party (PAP) and Lee Kuan Yew's bid to continue governing Singapore. Today, the blood debt still remains a very sensitive issue among Chinese communities in Malaysia and Singapore.

For the MCP, the end of the war marked the beginnings of its plans for an armed insurgency. In December 1943, the Secretary General of the MCP, Lai Teck, accompanied by his Perak state political commissar, Chin Peng, negotiated a treaty with Force 136 leaders Richard Broome, John Davis, Spencer Chapman and Lim Bo Seng for the MPAJA to work hand in hand with SEAC towards the restoration of British rule in Malaya. Lai Teck, who was a triple agent working for the British, Japanese and Chinese communists, agreed to plans for the MPAJA to create a resistance army with which to fight the Japanese. This army would be supplied with weapons, training and stores by SEAC, who would airdrop the supplies needed. Unbeknownst to the Force 136 members, Chin Peng revealed (in an interview in 1999) that the MCP had created two armies:

> We made an agreement with the British, to cooperate with them. But we must be prepared that, if the allied forces landed, we had to act on our own, to occupy as wide as possible an area and the towns... In order to have our freedom of manoeuvring, we must set up ourselves when the time comes to receive British arms. One day they would airdrop the arms, so our army must be divided into two forces, one called the 'Open Army'— that is to receive British arms and to cooperate with the British. The other portion, we called the 'Secret Army'. The Secret Army must not be known to the British. When the time came, and the British started to drop arms, we would pretend as if we were poorly armed. All the best weapons, automatic weapons, we would try our best to transfer to our Secret Army. And our best cadres, experienced fighters, would all be transferred to the Secret Army, to prepare for future fighting. In the Open Army we only keep a skeleton of experienced cadres to be the backbone of the Army...It seemed this was the only way to deal with the British. We cooperate with them on the one hand, to receive their aid, their military supplies, and on the other hand we still preserve our main force, under our control[4].

By August 1945, the MCP had established numerous MPAJA units throughout Malaya and provided the only real large-scale anti-Japanese resistance force on the peninsula. Although communist leaders wanted to take an "enhanced military posture" against the Japanese, Lai Teck insisted that the MCP concentrate more on organising labour. As a triple agent, he had to ensure that the Japanese were protected while he organised labour to serve the interests of the Chinese Communist Party and, at the same time, keep the MPAJA from beginning an armed struggle against his British handlers [5]. So it came to pass that by the end of the war, the MCP controlled labour unions throughout Malaya and Singapore.

However, once the Japanese surrender was announced, MPAJA regiments that did not receive directives on Lai Teck's new change of tack began occupying towns and villages throughout the country. This gave the MCP leaders their first taste of governing and ruling. Following the September surrender, the MPAJA disbanded its open army, while burying much of the war material supplied by Force 136, to be dug up and used later. By 1947, Lai Teck found his position untenable and fled with the coffers of the MCP. He was subsequently killed in Bangkok and Chin Peng took over as the new leader of the party.

However, Chin Peng was to claim later that he had not initially pushed for an armed struggle but that he had instead "resolved, along with my fellow Politburo members and the Central Committee, merely to enhance the political format we were following. As I saw it, the requirement was for subtle readjustments"[6].

Chin Peng also claimed that the Malayan Emergency did not start in June 1948 with the killing of three British planters in Sungei Siput. He argues that it began on 21 October 1945 when British troops were called in to disperse a huge labour demonstration in Sungei Siput, Ipoh and Batu Gajah. He noted that in Sungei Siput and Ipoh, the troops were ordered to fire directly into the crowds. He claimed that 10 demonstrators were shot dead in Sungei Siput and three more in Ipoh. "In Batu Gajah, the emotions were so high that the British civil affairs officer was cornered in the court house and surrounded by 500 furious demonstrators. Troops were ordered to rescue him," he said[7].

The British Government had by then begun enacting ordinances to close down the MCP-controlled unions and had developed plans for a Malayan Union. The proposal was made in 1946 with the intention to create a union of Malaya, composed of all the former federated and unfederated states, including Penang. Singapore would be left out of this mix and become a crown colony, due in part to the large Chinese population on the island. If Singapore were to have been included in the union, the population of immigrant Chinese would then clearly outnumber the Malays, leading to increased friction over the racial ratio. The union also proposed equal voting rights for all races and citizenship for the Chinese.

After numerous riots and strikes, colonial authorities abandoned the plan for the union. By 1948, a compromise federation was set up in Malaya. The MCP, however, remained dissatisfied, as it believed the citizenship rights did not go far enough. Moreover, it was constantly being attacked by colonial authorities who had attempted to close down the MCP's offices. In March 1948, the decision was made at the MCP's Singapore party offices at Queen Street to begin an armed struggle. As Chin Peng noted, "Finally, we came to the conclusion that the Lai Teck policy, stopping the armed struggle, and only struggling for self-government, was wrong". The precipitating factor for armed insurrection was the planned introduction of the Trade Union Ordinance Amendment of 31 May 1948, which would ban the MCP's trade unions:

> ... So, in that case how do we respond? We consider that as a full-scale attack. If they ban our trade union, or in some other way paralyse our trade union or perhaps they openly banned our party and arrested us. Then, how to respond? In the last resort, we have to launch armed struggle[8].

By June 1948, the Malayan Emergency had begun, as the secret army began remobilising their forces and digging up the hidden arms and weapons. A general plan of attack throughout the peninsula was launched in 1949[9]. The Emergency would last 12 years with more than 25,000 casualties on both sides[10].

Thus, the end of the war clearly signalled the beginning of independence movements throughout Southeast Asia. In the Dutch-controlled East Indies, Sukarno and Hatta declared an independent Indonesia shortly before the end of the war. After four years of Nazi occupation, the Dutch were in the midst of rebuilding their cities and were in no position to recover their colonies as quickly as the British. As a result, the Netherlands East Indies was administered by a British military governor for more than a year before the Dutch were able to resume control of their colonies. The British military administration in Indonesia witnessed the beginnings of the bloody fight for independence with several hundred troops killed in violent clashes with Indonesian nationalists. In 1946, the British handed power back to the Dutch colonial authorities, having received a huge black eye for their efforts at recolonising the country.

Although the British did manage to regain their colonies and start reestablishing their power, it was obvious that the days of colonial rule were numbered. Although both countries faced differing scenarios and struggles in their path to independence, the experiences in Indonesia and particularly in Malaya would plague the British for the next two decades, with insurgencies, confrontations and independence struggles eventually leading to the independent nations of Indonesia, Malaysia and Singapore.

The impact of the end of the war and its repercussions still resonate today; in the form of architectural artefacts as well as in how societies in the region were impacted and changed by British reoccupation policy, clandestine groups, the communal violence and the eventual surrenders that purportedly ended the war but which really marked the beginning of more violence to come. Such elements obviously shaped post-war attitudes towards the British and some of the nationalist groups fighting for the hearts and minds of the local populace. Today, countries like Singapore, Malaysia and Indonesia appear very far removed from those war-torn ruins of 60 years ago. However, many issues like race relations, Malay rights and the place of the Chinese community in these countries still continue to be informed by the events of those times. Nonetheless, the return of the British in 1945 and their rule in Malaya till the early 1960s meant that stability and progress had also returned, a model that has been modified extensively by each country but adhered to in principle by present-day governments in Malaysia and Singapore. That these countries today were able to have the freedom over the last 60 years to evolve in their own ways and forms remains a testament to those who gave their lives and those who persevered in the belief that victory, liberty and independence would surely come.

Endnotes

1 Baxter, Christopher. "In Pursuit of a Pacific Strategy: British Planning for the Defeat of Japan, 1943–45". *Diplomacy & Statecraft*, vol. 15, no. 2, June 2004. 258.

2 Chin, Peng. *My Side of History*. Singapore: Media Masters, 2003. 141.

3 Hack, Karl & Chin, C.C. (eds). *Dialogues with Chin Peng: New Light on the Malayan Communist Party*. Singapore: Singapore University Press, 2004. 95.

4 Ibid. 106.

5 Chin, 2003. 162.

6 Ibid. 193.

7 Ibid. 142.

8 Hack & Chin, 2004. 135.

9 Ibid. 144.

10 Hagan, Max. "Open Letter to My Daughters". *National Malaya & Borneo Veterans Association UK*. [Internet]. Accessed 10 December 2004. Available from: <http://www.nmbva.co.uk/paddy%20articles.htm>.

Appendices

Appendix A: Chronology of Events, August – September 1945

4 August	The deputy to Vice Admiral Lord Louis Mountbatten, Supreme Allied Commander, Southeast Asia (SACSEA), Lieutenant General Raymond Wheeler, orders planners at Southeast Asia Command (SEAC) to devise an emergency plan to recapture Singapore quickly.
8 August	Operation TIDERACE is born.
15 August	Emperor Hirohito of Japan announces in a radio broadcast the end of hostilities and Japan's surrender.
18 August	General Seishiro Itagaki, Commander-in-Chief of the 7th Area Army in Singapore, flies to Saigon to meet with Field Marshal Count Hisaichi Terauchi, Commander-in-Chief of the Southern Army, to discuss the surrender order. Terauchi orders him to comply. Mountbatten declares the institution of a British Military Administration (BMA) in Malaya led by Major General Ralph Hone. However, the BMA does not begin operations in Malaya till the landings on 5 September.
19 August	SEAC Staff Signal Officer, Captain Frank O'Shanohun, parachutes into Singapore's racecourse to discuss Itagaki's surrender.
	Japanese delegates leave Tokyo for the Manila headquarters of General Douglas MacArthur, Supreme Allied Commander, South West Pacific Command. Japanese delegates also meet with General Heitaro Kimura, Commander-in-Chief of the Burma Area Army, ordering him to surrender.
20 August	Itagaki meets O'Shanohun and signals SEAC that he will abide by the surrender terms. In a signal sent in the clear, Mountbatten orders Terauchi to send representatives to surrender talks in Rangoon on 23 August. Terauchi signals Mountbatten that he is unable to send his staff due to lack of transport and preparation time and both sides eventually set the date for 26 August.
21 August	Newspapers in Singapore are finally allowed to print the Emperor's surrender message.
	X-Day for Operation TIDERACE.
22 August	More than 300 Japanese officers and men in Singapore commit suicide rather than face surrender to the Allies.
26 August	Terauchi's delegates, led by his Chief of Staff Lieutenant General Takazo Numata, arrive in Rangoon for surrender talks.
27 August	Surrender talks take place in Rangoon with Japanese representatives initially arguing about the terms for surrender.

28 August	Japanese delegates finally sign the surrender agreement at 1.00am in the Throne Room, Government House, Rangoon. Vice Admiral Harold Walker arrives in the waters off Penang Island and begins negotiations with the Japanese to surrender the island and get more details on enemy dispositions in Malaya.
2 September	General Douglas MacArthur accepts the formal Japanese surrender on board the *USS Missouri* in Tokyo Bay, Japan. At 9.15pm, the Japanese garrison commander in Penang, Rear Admiral Jisaku Uozumi, surrenders to Vice Admiral Walker on board *HMS Nelson*.
4 September	General Seishiro Itagaki and Vice Admiral Shigeru Fukudome sign surrender terms on board *HMS Sussex* in Keppel Harbour, handing over Singapore to SACSEA's naval and military representatives, Rear (later Vice) Admiral Cedric Holland, Naval Fleet Commander and Lieutenant General Sir Alexander Christison, GOC, 15th Indian Corps.
5 September	Major General Eric Mansergh, Commander of the 5th Indian Division, and his troops land at Singapore's Keppel docks and assume control of Singapore. Communal violence in most parts of Malaya ceases as a result.
9 September	Operation ZIPPER is carried out as the 34th Indian Corps begin landing on Morib Beach.
10 September	Remaining ZIPPER forces land in the Port Dickson area.
12 September	Mountbatten accepts the formal Japanese surrender at a nine-minute ceremony in the Municipal Hall in Singapore, followed by a flag-raising and parade at the Padang. Itagaki represents Terauchi, who is too ill to attend.
13 September	ZIPPER forces, led by the 25th Indian Division march into Kuala Lumpur with Lieutenant General Ouvry Roberts, GOC, 34th Indian Corps, accepting the Japanese surrender from Lieutenant General Teizo Ishiguro, Commander of the Japanese 29th Army, at Victoria Institution.

Appendix B: List of Operations

CARPENTER/MINT
Force 136 blind landing three miles off Tanjong Balau, on the east coast of Johor on 5 October 1944 to contact, arm and train any local resistance. Two weeks later, MINT, a joint SOE/Inter-Services Liaison Department (SIS) operation to spy on the naval base in Singapore, landed at the same location.

CORONET
Plan for the invasion of the Japanese island of Kyushu, led by American forces with the participation of the British.

CULVERIN
A British military operation with the objective of capturing north Sumatra that was never put into action.

DRACULA
A British military operation, involving an amphibious landing at Rangoon, to recapture Japanese-occupied Burma.

FUNNEL
Force 136 airdrop of supplies and trained Malay resistance fighters close to the Tapah/Bidor Road on 25 February 1945.

GUSTAVUS I, II, III, IV and V
British Special Operations Executive Force 136 operations to infiltrate Malaya and set up clandestine resistance networks (beginning with Perak) during the Japanese Occupation.

JAYWICK
An operation undertaken by Force 'Z' under Lieutenant Colonel Ivan Lyon to sneak into Keppel Harbour in Japanese-occupied Singapore and destroy enemy shipping.

JURIST
A British military plan to capture advanced naval and air bases on the island of Penang in Malaysia. Initially part of ZIPPER, it was eventually implemented under TIDERACE.

MAILFIST
A British assault plan to retake Singapore as part of ZIPPER. This was later replaced by TIDERACE.

MARKET GARDEN
A combined airborne and ground offensive launched by Allied forces in Holland that, had it succeeded, would have ended the Second World War by Christmas 1944.

MODIFIED DRACULA
A scaled-down version of Operation DRACULA, successfully executed, with the British arriving in Rangoon in May 1945.

OLYMPIC
Plan for the invasion of the Japanese island of Honshu led by the American forces but in which the British participated.

RIMAU
Another operation, similar to JAYWICK, in which Force 'Z' destroyed enemy shipping in Singapore Harbour.

ROGER
A British military plan to capture advanced naval and air bases on the island of Phuket in Thailand as part of ZIPPER that was never implemented. A modified version of ROGER was used to minesweep the Andaman Sea and as a feint for TIDERACE.

TIDERACE
An emergency reoccupation plan for the recapture of Singapore and Penang ahead of Operation ZIPPER.

TROPIC
Contingency British naval operation with the objective of recapturing Singapore and Penang that was never implemented.

ZIPPER
A British amphibious assault plan for the west coast of Malaya.

Appendix C: Operation ZIPPER, Order of Battle [1]

Headquarters 14th Army

Headquarters XXXIV Corps

Corps Troops:

11th Cavalry

25th Dragoons

18th Field Regiment Royal Artillery

208th Field Regiment Royal Artillery

6th Medium Regiment Royal Artillery

86th Medium Regiment Royal Artillery

1st Indian Medium Regiment

8th Sikh Light Anti-Aircraft Regiment

9th Rajput Light Anti-Aircraft Regiment

1st Heavy Anti-Aircraft Regiment, Hong Kong & Singapore Regiment Royal Artillery

Formations:

5th Indian Division

23rd Indian Division

25th Indian Division

26th Indian Division

50th Indian Tank Brigade

3rd Commando Brigade

5th Parachute Brigade

Endnotes

1 "Operation Zipper: The Invasion of Malaya, August 1945, Order of Battle". *Orbat.com* [Internet] Available from: <http://orbat.com/site/history/historical/malaysia/operationzipper.html>.

Appendix D: Ships Anchored in Singapore Roads During the Ceremony of Surrender, 12 September 1945 [1]

CLEOPATRA (Commander-in-Chief's vessel)

Battleships:

NELSON (Vice Admiral, East Indies Station)

RICHELIEU

Cruisers:

SUSSEX (Flag Officer, Force 'N')
CUMBERLAND
ROYALIST
CEYLON

Headquarters and Depot Ships:

KEDAH (Flag Officer, Malaya)
BULOLO (Flag Officer, Force 'W')
SANSOVINO
BARRACUDA, HMIS
MULL OF GALLOWAY (Captain, Coastal Forces, East Indies Station)

Destroyers:

TARTAR
SAUMAREZ
MYNGS
FARNDALE
RELENTLESS
PALADIN
BLACKMORE
VERULAM

Escort Vessels:

GORLESTON (Captain, East Indies Escort Force)
LOCH SCAVAIG
LOCH LOMOND
DART
CAUVERY, HMIS
GODAVARI, HMIS
KALE
AWE

Submarines:

SIBYL

Surveyor Ship:

CHALLENGER

Landing Ships & Craft:

Landing Ships, Tank, 11, 165, 199, 302, 321 and 324

Six landing craft from Force 'W'

Royal Fleet Auxiliary Ships:

DEWDALE
ORANGELEAF
CROMWELL

Hospital Ships:

ORANJE
MANUNDA
KARAPARA

Merchant Ships:

RAJULA
DERBYSHIRE
DEVONSHIRE
CHESHIRE
HIGHLAND BRIGADE
THALMA
PASHA
PAKHOI
CITY OF DERBY
JALAVEIRA
ITAURA
MORETON BAY
MANELLA

Minesweepers:

PELORUS (Captain, Minesweepers, Forward Areas)
FRIENDSHIP
VIRILE
GOZO
LENNOX
PERSIAN
POSTILION
MELITA
IMERSAY
LINGAY
PICKLE
RECRUIT

RIFLEMAN
CHAMELEON
PINCHER
PLUCKY
DECCAN, HMIS
PUNJAB, HMIS
BIHAR, HMIS
ROHILKHAND, HMIS
KUMAON, HMIS

Endnotes

1 *Report of Proceedings—Commander-in-Chief, East Indies Station's Letter, No.3001/E.I.15002/45, 17 September 1945, ADM199/168.* London: The National Archives. Enclosure No. 1.

Appendix E: List of Notable Personalities

THE ALLIES

The British

Armstrong, Lieutenant Colonel Guy Lionel Walter
Born in 1918, Armstrong served as staff officer in the Imphal campaign and was posted to Southeast Asia Command (SEAC) Headquarters (HQ) in Ceylon. He moved with Vice Admiral Lord Louis Mountbatten to Singapore after the Japanese surrender and retired as Second-in-Command of the 16th Parachute Brigade in 1960. Ordained in 1961, he served as Vicar of Bagshot and Ripley. He died on 14 December 2002.

Attlee, Clement Richard
Born in 1883, Atlee swept into power in the 1945 British General Election, giving the Labour Party its largest victory at the polls. He was prime minister of Britain (1945–1951) for six years and led the Labour Party until 1955, remaining active in the House of Lords until his death in 1967.

Auchinleck, Field Marshal Sir Claude John Eyre
Born in 1884, Auchinleck was Commander-in-Chief (CinC), India (1940–1941), before serving as CinC, Middle East Command (1941–1942), and then as temporary General Officer Commanding (GOC), 8th Army in North Africa (1942), before reprising his role as CinC, India (1943–1947), becoming Supreme Commander in India and Pakistan in 1947. Auchinleck died in 1981.

Brooke, Field Marshal Sir Alan
Born on 23 July 1883, he joined the British army and served in Ireland and India before going to France in 1914. In June 1940 Brooke played a leading role in the evacuation of British troops at Dunkirk. Alan Brooke was appointed Chief of Imperial Staff in December

1941. Promoted to Field Marshal in January 1944, he was created Baron Alanbrooke of Brookeborough in September 1945. He died on 17 June 1963.

Browning, General Sir Frederick Arthur Montague
Born in 1896, Browning served in North Africa and Northwest Europe (1941–1945) before being appointed SEAC Chief of Staff (CoS) (1945–1946). He later served as Military Secretary in the War Office (1946–1948) before retiring in 1948. He died in 1965.

Christison, Lieutenant General Sir Alexander Frank Philip
Born on 17 November 1893, Christison had served in the First World War and rose to the rank of Brigadier in 1941. He served as the GOC, 33rd Indian Corps, in Burma (1942–1943) before taking over as GOC, 15th Indian Corps (1943–1945). Christison was then appointed temporary GOC, 14th Army in Burma (1945), before taking over as CinC, Allied Land Forces Southeast Asia (1945). After concluding his role in TIDERACE, Christison became Allied Commander of the Dutch East Indies (1945–1946) and General Officer Commander-in-Chief, Northern Command (GOCinC) (1946–1947), and appointed Aide-de-Camp to the King (1947–1949) before retiring in 1949. Christison died on 21 December 1993.

Churchill, Winston Leonard Spencer
Born in 1874, Churchill is considered one of the greatest of British statesmen. A soldier and a journalist before he entered politics, he was elected twice as the prime minister of Britain (1940–1945, 1951–1955). Churchill received the Nobel Prize for literature in 1953 and was knighted in the same year by Queen Elizabeth II. He died on 24 January 1965.

Eden, Sir Anthony Robert
Born in 1897, Eden won the Military Cross at the Battle of the Somme in 1916. He became Under-Secretary for Foreign Affairs (1931–1934) and served as Foreign Secretary (1935–1938) until he resigned in 1938. He then served again as Foreign Secretary under Churchill (1940–1945) and became deputy leader of the opposition until 1951 when he again served as Foreign Secretary. Eden disagreed with Prime Minister Neville Chamberlain about the way to deal with fascism in Europe and in 1938 he resigned from office. When Churchill took over from Chamberlain in 1940, Eden was reappointed as Foreign Secretary. After the Labour Party victory in the 1945 General Election, Eden became deputy leader of the opposition. The 1951 General Election saw the return of a Conservative government and once more Eden became Foreign Secretary. He later replaced Winston Churchill as prime minister (1955–1957). Created Earl of Avon in 1961, he died in 1977.

Gardner, Air Vice Marshal Sir Percy Ronald, the Earl of Bandon
Born on 30 August 1904, Gardner became a Squadron Leader in 1936 and served as Air Officer Commanding, No 244 Squadron, in 1944. He was involved in the air invasion plans for ZIPPER and, after serving in various theatres, was promoted to Air Marshal in 1957 before taking over as CinC, Far East Air Force. In 1959, he was promoted to Air Chief Marshal and became Commander, Allied Air Forces Central Europe (1961), before retiring in 1964. He died on 8 February 1979.

Harcourt, Admiral Sir Cecil Halliday Jephson
Born in 1892, Harcourt served in the First World War before becoming Director of Admiralty's Operations Division (1939–1941). He then commanded the *HMS Duke of York* and was Flag Captain of the Home Fleet (1941–1942), later becoming the Flag Officer Commanding the 10th, 12th and 15th Cruiser Squadrons in North Africa and Italy (1942–1944). He was then appointed Naval Secretary to the First Lord of the Admiralty (1944–1945) before becoming Flag Officer Commanding, 11th Aircraft Carrier Squadron, on board *HMS Venerable* (1945).

Upon the Japanese surrender, he was put in charge of the force which accepted the Japanese surrender of Hong Kong on 30 August 1945. He was later appointed CinC and Head of Military Administration Hong Kong (1945–1946), becoming Flag Officer (Air) and Second-in-Command, Mediterranean Fleet (1947–1948), and Second Sea Lord (1948–1950) and was promoted to the rank of Admiral in 1949 before being appointed Commander-in-Chief, The Nore (1950–1952). Harcourt retired in 1953 and died on 19 December 1959.

Holland, Vice Admiral Cedric Swinton
Born in 1889, Holland served in the First World War with the Grand Fleet at Scapa Flow. Naval Attache for France, Holland, Belgium, Spain and Portugal (1938–1940), Holland took command of the aircraft carrier *HMS Ark Royal* in May 1940 (1940–1941). He later played the role of chief negotiator in discussions with the French during the Mers el Kebir affair (1940). He was subsequently appointed Director of Naval Communications (1942–1943), during which he was promoted to the rank of Rear Admiral. Attached to SEAC HQ (1943–1945), he was promoted to Vice Admiral in 1945 before being appointed as Naval Force Commander for TIDERACE and SEAC's naval representative at the Singapore surrender on board his flagship, the *HMS Susser*, on 4 September 1945. Holland retired from active service in 1946 and died on 11 May 1950.

Hone, Major General Sir Herbert Ralph
Born in 1896, Hone was Attorney-General of Uganda (1937–1940) and Commandant of the Ugandan Defence Force (1940) before serving as Chief Political Officer in the Middle East and the War Office. Following his appointment as Chief Civil Affairs Officer, Malaya (1945–1946), Hone took on the responsibility of developing plans for the British Military Administration (BMA) in the country and the eventual restoration of a civil administration in the peninsula. Hone arrived in Singapore with TIDERACE and took over as head of the BMA. On handing over power to the civilian government, he was appointed Secretary-General to the Governor-General of Malaya (1946–1948) before being made Governor and CinC of North Borneo (1949–1954). He was then appointed as the head of the Legal Division at the Commonwealth Office (1954–1961) and continued to serve in this role for five more years after his retirement in 1956. Hone died in 1992.

Leese, Lieutenant General Sir Oliver William Hargreaves
Born in 1894, Leese served as Deputy Chief of Staff (DCoS) to the British Expeditionary Force in France in 1940 and was made GOC of the 15th Division in 1941. He also served as GOC for the Guards Armoured Division (1941–1942) and 30th Corps in North Africa (1942–1943) and the 8th Army in Italy (1943–1944) before being appointed CinC, Allied Land Forces South-East Asia (1944–1945), where he was partly involved in preparations for ZIPPER and the Burma campaigns. He took over as GOCinC, Eastern Command in 1945, retiring in 1946. Leese died in 1978.

Mansergh, General Sir Eric Carden Robert
Born in 1900, Mansergh was appointed Commander of the Royal Artillery 5th Indian Division (1943–1944) and served in Burma where he was made GOC, 11th East African Division (1945). He was later appointed GOC, 5th Indian Division (1945–1946), during which time he led the 5th Division in the reoccupation of Singapore on 5 September 1945. Mansergh was then appointed CinC, Dutch East Indies (1946–1947), before returning to the War Office where he was later appointed Military Secretary to the Secretary of State for War (1948–1949). Mansergh then served as CinC, Hong Kong (1949–1951), before becoming CinC, Allied Powers Forces Northern Europe (1953–1956). He was later made CinC, British Land Forces (1956–1959), a post he held until his retirement in 1959. Mansergh died in 1970.

Martin, Vice Admiral Sir Benjamin Charles Stanley
Born in 1891, Martin had served in the Somali Campaign in 1908 and in the First World War. He was Captain of *HMS Dorsetshire* (1939–1941) during the Second World War and was involved in the sinking of the German battleship *Bismarck*. Martin then served as Commodore in charge of Naval Establishments in Durban (1942–1943) before retiring in 1944. Called back into service, he was attached to SEAC HQ. He was later appointed Flag Officer Force 'W' on board *HMS Bulolo*, as part of MODIFIED DRACULA. As Commanding Officer (CO) of the close-covering group, he was involved in the Rangoon landings off Ramree Island in February 1945. Martin was also involved in developing plans for ZIPPER. He was promoted to the rank of Vice Admiral (Retd.) in 1948. Martin died on 3 June 1957.

Messervy, General Sir Frank Walter
Born in 1893, Messervy served in the military as an Instructor at the Staff College in Camberley (1932–1936) before being stationed in East and North Africa. He become Acting Chief of Staff, Middle East Command, in 1942 and subsequently served as GOC of the 43rd Armoured Indian Division (1942–1943), the 7th Indian Division (1943–1944) and the 4th Indian Corps in Burma (1944–1945). He assumed the role of GOC, Malaya, in 1945. He later served as GOCinC, India (1946–1947), and as CinC, Pakistan army (1947–1948), before retiring in 1948. Messervy died in 1974.

Mountbatten, Admiral Lord Louis Francis Albert Victor Nicholas
Born on 25 June 1900, Mountbatten was the younger son of Admiral of the Fleet, the 1st Marquess of Milford Haven and Princess Victoria (daughter of Louis IV, Grand Duke of Hesse, KG, and Princess Alice, Queen Victoria's Daughter). He was known as Prince Louis Francis of Battenberg until 1917 when his father relinquished the German title and assumed the surname of Mountbatten. CO of the *HMS Illustrious* in 1939, he was appointed Commodore, Combined Operations (1941–1942), before becoming Chief of Combined Operations. He then became a member of the British Chiefs of Staff Committee (1942–1943) before being appointed Supreme Allied Commander Southeast Asia Command (SACSEA) (1943–1946). After the war, he was made Viscount Mountbatten of Burma (1946) for his role in Southeast Asia and a year later became Viceroy, and subsequently Governor General, of India. For his services in India, he was made 1st Earl Mountbatten of Burma (1947) and served in various capacities in the Admiralty, being promoted to Admiral of the Fleet in 1956. Upon retirement, Mountbatten assumed the post of First Sea Lord and Chief of Naval Staff (1955–1959). He then served as Chief of the UK Defence Staff and Chairman of Chiefs of Staff Committee (1959–1965). He was killed on his boat on 27 August 1979 in Donegal Bay, Ireland, by a bomb planted by the Irish Republican Army (IRA).

Penney, Major General Sir William Ronald Campbell
Born in 1896, Penney served as Deputy Director of Military Intelligence at the War Office (1939–1940) and as CO of the 3rd Brigade (1940–1941) before serving as Chief Signal Officer in the Middle East and for the 18th Army Group (1941–1943). He then served as GOC, 1st Division, in North Africa and Italy (1943–1944) before becoming Director of Military Intelligence, SEAC (1944–1945). He later became Assistant Controller of Supplies in the Ministry of Supply (1946–1949) before retiring in 1949. He died in 1964.

Percival, Lieutenant General Arthur Ernest
Born in 1887, Percival had served in Malaya as a General Staff Officer 1 (1936–1938) before serving in the UK and France. In 1940, he was appointed GOC, 43rd Division, and Assistant Chief Imperial General Staff at the War Office. He returned to Malaya in 1941 to serve as GOC, Malaya Command, where he is unfairly remembered as the general who lost the Malayan Campaign and who surrendered more than 100,000 British and Commonwealth

troops to Lieutenant General Tomoyuki Yamashita on 15 Febrary 1942 at the Ford Motor Factory in Singapore. A former prisoner of war (1942–1945), Percival retired in 1946 and was closely associated with the Far East Prisoners of War Association as well as the Red Cross until his death in 1966.

Power, Admiral Sir Arthur John
Born on 12 April 1889, Power did not see action in the First World War but was appointed CO of the *HMS Ark Royal* when the ship was under construction in 1938. Serving as the ship's First CO and Flag Captain, he was also Chief Staff Officer to Rear Admiral, Aircraft Carriers, Home Fleet (1938–1940). Briefly serving in the Admiralty and in Malta, Power was appointed Vice Admiral Commanding 1st Battle Squadron & Second-in-Command, Eastern Fleet (1943–1944), before becoming CinC, East Indies Station (1944–1945). After the war, he served in the Admiralty and in the Mediterranean before being promoted to Admiral of the Fleet in 1952 and being appointed Allied CinC, Channel and Southern North Sea Command (1952–1953). He retired in 1953 and died on 28 January 1960.

Roberts, General Sir Ouvry Lindfield
Born in 1898, Roberts served as Deputy Director of Military Operations & Intelligence, India (1939–1941), and as General Staff Officer 1, 10th Indian Division (1941), as well as CO, 20th Indian Brigade (1941). Appointed Brigadier General Staff, IV Corps (1943), he was later made GOC 23rd Indian Division, Burma (1943–1945). Prior to ZIPPER, he was appointed GOC, XXXIV Corps, Malaya (1945). After the war, he became a Deputy Adjutant-General in the War Office (1945–1947) and served as GOC, Northern Ireland; CinC, Southern Command, and finally as Aide-de-Camp General to the Queen (1952–1955). Roberts retired in 1955 and died in 1986.

Slim, Field Marshal Viscount William Joseph
Born in 1891, Viscount Slim served in Africa and the Middle East before becoming the GOC, Burma Corps, in 1942. He was then appointed GOC, XV Corps, Burma (1942–1943), before being made GOC, 14th Army, Burma (1943–1945). He then replaced Leese as CinC, Allied Land Forces Southeast Asia (1945) and was made Commandant of the Imperial Defence College after the war (1946–1947). Although he retired in 1948, he was recalled to serve his country as Chief Imperial General Staff (1948–1952), ending his career as Governor-General and CinC of Australia (1952–1960). He died in 1970.

Stopford, General Sir Montague George North
Born in 1892, Stopford served in France at the beginning of the war and was made GOC, XII Corps (1942–1943), before taking over as GOC, XXXIII Indian Corps, in Burma (1943–1945). He was also GOC, 12th Army, Burma (1945). Later he was appointed CinC, Allied Land Forces Dutch East Indies (1945–1946) and CinC, South-East Asia Land Forces (1946–1947) before serving as GOCinC, Northern Command (1947–1949) and also as Aide-de-Camp General to the King (1947–1949). He retired in 1949 and died in 1971.

Walker, Admiral Sir Harold Thomas Coulthard
Born on 18 March 1891, Walker served in the First World War and began his service in the Second World War as Flag Captain of the *HMS Barham* and as Chief Staff Officer to Vice Admiral Commanding, 1st Battle Squadron, in the Mediterranean (1939–1940). He then served in the Admiralty before becoming Rear Admiral Commanding, 5th Cruiser Squadron (1944), and was then appointed Flag Officer Commanding, 3rd Battle Squadron, and as Second-in-Command, East Indies Station (1944–1945). He later served as Vice Admiral Commanding, British Naval Forces in Germany, and as Chief British Naval Representative in the Allied Control Commission (1946–1947) before retiring in 1947. He was promoted to the rank of Admiral (Retd.) the following year. Walker died on Christmas Day 1975.

The Americans

MacArthur, General of the Army Douglas
Born in 1880, MacArthur served as CinC, South-West Pacific Area (1942–1945), and was CinC, US army forces in the Pacific (1945), as well as CinC, Allied Forces of Occupation, Japan (1945). After the war, MacArthur was made CinC, US Forces Far East (1947–1951), as well as CinC, UN Forces, Korea (1950–1951), retiring in 1951. MacArthur died in 1964.

Marshall, General of the Army George Catlett
Born in 1880, Marshall served as CoS, VIII Corps, in France (1918) and was CoS, US army (1939–1945). Retiring from the military in 1945, he was appointed Secretary of State in 1947. He is known for the Marshall Plan, which helped provide economic aid to post-Second World War Europe. He was also Secretary of Defense (1950–1951). He retired in 1951 and died in 1959.

Truman, Harry S.
Thirty-third president of the United States, Truman took over after President Franklin Delano Roosevelt died in office on 12 April 1945. Truman retired from public life in January 1953 and died on 26 December 1972.

Wainwright, Lieutenant General Jonathan Mayhew
Born in 1883, Wainwright was Commanding General, I Philippine Corps, in Philippines in 1942 and as MacArthur escaped to Australia, took on the role of CinC, Far East, before surrendering to the Japanese. A former prisoner of war (1942 – 1945), Wainwright and Percival were on board the *HMS Missouri* in Tokyo Bay to witness the Japanese surrender on 2 September 1945. Wainwright was made Commanding General of the 4th Army (1946–1947) before retiring in 1947. He died in 1953.

Wheeler, Lieutenant General Raymond Albert
Born in 1885, Wheeler served Mountbatten as Deputy Commander-in-Chief (DCinC), SEAC (1944–1945). He was also CinC, US Burma-India Theatre of Operations (1945), and was tasked by Mountbatten to come up with a quick plan to recapture Singapore. He later served as Chief of Engineers (1945–1949) before retiring in 1949. Wheeler died in 1974.

SPECIAL OPERATIONS EXECUTIVE (SOE) AND FORCE 136 MEMBERS AND AFFILIATED FIGURES [1]

Anstey, Brigadier John
Born on 3 January 1907, Anstey, who was a Territorial Army Officer in the Somerset Light Infantry and a well-liked junior manager in the Imperial Tobacco Company, had served in the War Office and in the SOE in the beginning of the Second World War before being promoted to the rank of Colonel and sent to Delhi in November 1944 as Deputy Head of the SOE India Mission/Force 136. After the war, Anstey was promoted to the rank of Brigadier and was awarded a Commander of the Order of the British Empire (CBE).

Broadhurst, Lieutenant Colonel Douglas Keith
Born on 28 June 1910, 'Duggie' Broadhurst served in the pre-war Malayan Police Force and joined Force 136 during the Second World War.

Broome, Major Richard Neville
Born on 19 June 1916, Broome was a District Officer in Perak when war broke out and became an original member of the SOE's Oriental Mission in Singapore. He later escaped the fall of Singapore with Davis and played a key role in clandestine operations in Japanese-

occupied Malaya. After the war, Broome was Secretary of the Chinese Section of the BMA.

Chapman, Lieutenant Colonel Frederick Spencer
Born on 10 May 1907, Chapman served at the 101ST guerrilla warfare school in Singapore. Sent behind enemy lines to organise reconnaissance and sabotage operations, he helped build up Force 136 in the Malayan jungles. At the end of the war he was promoted to the rank of Lieutenant Colonel and awarded a Distinguished Service Order (DSO). He went back to a career in teaching but as retirement approached, he was under increasing pressure from health and financial worries. Chapman shot himself on 8 August 1971.

Chin Peng
Born in Setiawan, Perak on 21 October 1924, Chin Peng (Ong Boon Hua) eventually led the Malayan Communist Party (MCP) in the late 1940s. Fleeing to the jungles of Thailand after losing the war against the Malaysian government, he continued to lead the MCP in exile, finally signing a peace agreement with the Malaysian government in 1989 At the time of writing, Chin Peng is yet again petitioning the Malaysian government to allow him to end his exile in Thailand and return to Malaysia, which has allowed many of his compatriots back in. The long-standing refusal to grant Chin Peng's applications to return to the country is partly due to his role in the 12-year communist insurgency and the racial massacres of 1945.

Chua Koon Eng @ Choy/Bill
Owner of a few fishing boats on Pangkor Island, Chua was key in ensuring the network's rendezvous with Force 136's submarines. Chua broke under interrogation by the Japanese military police, the *Kempeitai*, and revealed the names of the agents in the network. His betrayal led to Lim Bo Seng's eventual capture. As gratitude for his cooperation, the Japanese put all fishing boats on Pangkor Island under Chua, who survived the war.

Davis, Major (later Colonel) John L H
Like Broadhurst, Davis had also served in the pre-war Federated Malayan States Police Force and was a member of the SOE's Oriental Mission in Singapore. He, along with Broome, escaped the fall of Singapore and helped run agents and a clandestine organisation in Malaya. Davis played a key role in negotiations with the Malayan Communist Party (MCP) after the war but retired in 1947 before returning to Malaya to serve as a District Officer. He advised British forces during the Malayan Emergency.

Ivory, Lieutenant Colonel Basil Gerritsen
Born on 25 May 1901, Ivory was commissioned in the Royal Artillery (Territorial Army). He is believed to have served with the SOE in China and arranged the terms of service for Lim Bo Seng but not much else is known about his wartime role as his files are still classified.

Li Han Kwang/Lee Han Kwong @ Lee Ah Cheng/Lee Tsing
A nationalist Chinese who had joined Force 136, Lee was initially tasked with coordinating the monthly rendezvous but because of a clash with Davis, Lee became demoralised. However, his escape from the *Kempeitai* showed his resourcefulness. After the destruction of the network, Lee remained in the jungle camp for the rest of the Occupation.

Liang Yuan Ming @ Lee Chuen/Lee Choon
Another nationalist Chinese who joined Force 136, Liang was infiltrated into Malaya on 12 September 1943 as part of GUSTAVUS IV, led by Richard Broome. He remained in the jungle camps and served as a signals operator, the role for which he had been trained.

Lim Bo Seng @ Tan Choon Lim/Tang/Ah Lim
Born on 27 April 1909, Lim was trained by Force 136 to lead the Perak spy network. Captured after one of his agents broke under interrogation, Lim died on 29 June 1944. It took the British

Government more than three years after the war to recognise Lim's contribution with a reduced version of a promised pension to his widow and seven children. Lim is a national hero in Taiwan and Singapore.

Lung Chiu Ying @ Ah Long/Ah Loong
Another resourceful Force 136 agent, Lung replaced Li Han Kwang as the main rendezvous contact and went along with Chua to make the meetings with the monthly submarine visits. However, he was unable to make contact with the submarines from January to March and was on his way to the April rendezvous when he met Li on the way out of the jungle camp and was thus not captured. He survived the war.

Mackenzie, Colin Hercules
Born on 5 October 1898, Mackenzie was appointed head of the SOE India Mission in 1942 and was made Commander of Force 136 when the name of the organisation was changed.

Moh Wing Pun @ Muk Ching/Mok Kee/Lee
An ethnic Chinese journalist who worked for the Japanese in the Ipoh Information Department during the Occupation, Moh was recruited into the underground resistance movement in Malaya by Lim Bo Seng. He was the Force 136 representative in Ipoh and was captured with Lim along Gopeng Road as they tried to escape from the Japanese cordon that was tightening around Force 136 members. Tan Chong Tee had accused Moh of collaborating with the Japanese but action was never taken on this allegation.

Tan Chong Tee @ Lim Soong/Tan Thiam Seng/Ah Lim
A Force 136 agent recruited by Lim Bo Seng in Chungking, Tan was stationed in Lumut. He was also captured by the Japanese. Tan survived the end of the war and wrote his memoirs, describing the events surrounding the destruction of the spy ring. Tan went on to become a Singaporean hero on the badminton court.

Tan Kong Cheng @ Kong Ching
One of the first locals to begin helping the Force 137 spy network, Tan and his wife were eventually responsible for conveying food to the agents.

Wu Chye Sin @ Goh Meng Chye/Ah Ng/Wong Kwong Fai
Described by Davis and Broome as one of their best and most resourceful agents, Wu was also having an affair while operating as an agent for Force 136, a fact that upset some of his colleagues. He survived the war and was awarded an Order of the British Empire (OBE) for his services.

Yi Tian Song @ Tan Sek Fu/Tan Shi Fu/Chan Siak Foo
Recruited by Lim Bo Seng in Chungking, Yi arrived in Malaya on GUSTAVUS IV as well. Trained as a signal operator, he was based at Tapah. He was later captured by the Japanese but survived the war.

THE JAPANESE

Chudo, Admiral Kaigyo
DCoS to Field Marshal Count Terauchi, Chudo had commanded the 8th Section of the Japanese Navy General Staff and had been involved in the aborted plans to invade Australia.

Fukudome, Vice Admiral Shigeru
Commander of the 10th Area Fleet, Fukudome had been Director of the 1st Section (Plans and Operations) of the Japanese naval staff at the time of the attack on Pearl Harbour. He was one of the officers principally responsible for planning the destruction of the American fleet. Fukudome was executed as a war criminal in 1948.

Ishiguro, Lieutenant General Teizo

Appointed GOC, 28th Division (1940–1943), Ishiguro was later made GOC of the 6th Army (1943–1944). He ended his career as CinC of the Japanese 29th Army in Malaya (1944–1945).

Itagaki, General Seishiro

Born in 1885, Itagaki was CO of the 33rd Regiment in China (1928) and became DCoS of the Kwangtung army in Manchuria in 1934. A year later, he became CoS and then served as GOC, 5th Division, in China. He subsequently served as Minister of War (1938–1939) and then as CoS, China Expeditionary Army (1939–1941). He served a major portion of the war as CinC of the Chosen Army in Korea (1941–1945) and as CinC, 17th Area Army, in Korea before being posted as CinC, 7th Area Army, in Singapore as well as the Japanese Governor of Johor State. After signing the 4 September and 12 September surrenders, Itagaki was tried, condemned to death and hanged as a war criminal in 1948.

Kimura, General Hyotaro

Kimura was appointed Vice War Minister (1941–1944) and was also a member of the Supreme War Council (1943) before being appointed Commander of the Japanese army in Burma (1944–1945). Kimura was executed as a war criminal in 1948.

Numata, Lieutenant General Tokazo

CoS of the Japanese 2nd Area Army in the Celebes, Numata was later appointed as CoS of the Japanese southern army (1944–1945).

Terauchi, Field Marshal Count Hsiaichi

CinC of the Japanese southern army, Terauchi based his final headquarters in Saigon in 1944. He had suffered a debilitating stroke early in 1945 and as a result of its after-effects, was unable to surrender to Mountbatten in Singapore in September 1945. Mountbatten accepted Terauchi's surrender in Saigon in November 1945 before the Field Marshal was transferred to Singapore where he died in 1946. His ashes are located in a special shrine at the Japanese Cemetery in Singapore.

Tojo, General Hideki

Born on 30th December 1884, Tojo became head of the Kwantung army's military police in September 1935, following which he was appointed CoS to the Kwantung army (1937–1938). In July 1941, Tojo was appointed Minister of War and became prime minister on 16th October 1941. Tojo also held the posts of Minister of War, Home Minister and Foreign Minister. From February 1944, he was also CinC of the General Staff. He ordered the attack on Pearl Harbour on 7 December 1941. Tojo resigned from office July 1944 and tried to kill himself by shooting himself in the chest as Allied forces tried to arrest him in 1945. Tojo survived, was tried as a war criminal and executed on 23 December 1948.

Uozumi, Rear Admiral Jisaku

Having served in the First World War, Uozumi was Captain of the Japanese cruiser *Haguro* in 1942. He saw action at the Battle of the Java Sea where the remnants of the British and Dutch naval forces were destroyed by a superior Japanese naval fleet. Uozumi had also served as a senior officer on the Japanese naval staff before being appointed Naval Commander of Penang Island in August 1944.

THE INDIAN NATIONAL ARMY (INA)

Bose, Rash Behari

An Indian independence leader, Bose had gone into exile in Japan after a failed attempt to assassinate the Viceroy of India, Lord Hardinge, on 23 December 1912. Bose was one of the founders of the Indian Independence League and played a key role in setting up the first INA. After a fallout with Mohan Singh, he ran the movement by himself until Subhas Chandra Bose's arrival.

Bose, Subhas Chandra
An Indian nationalist leader, Bose was president of the Congress Party but later broke ranks with Mahatma Gandhi and Jawaharlal Nehru. Bose fled to Germany and set up the Azad Hind Fauj, which fought with the Wehrmacht in North Africa. Following Japan's victory in the Far East, Bose came to Asia to assume command of the Indian Independence movement. He set up an Indian government-in-exile and believed the men of the INA would be able to liberate India through the battle in Burma. With the Japanese routed in Burma and the war lost in August 1945, Bose was attempting to fly to Russia when his plane is believed to have crashed in Formosa. Bose was said to have been killed. Many do not believe this and hold that he survived the end of the war. Nonetheless, the INA was disbanded and the men repatriated.

Singh, Captain Mohan
A member of the Indian army, Singh was captured during the Malayan Campaign and was convinced to lead the first INA. However, he disagreed with Rash Behari Bose and felt the Japanese were using the INA to achieve their own aims. He tried to disband the first INA, following which he was put under house arrest, where he remained until the end of the war.

CIVIL ADMINISTRATORS AND DIPLOMATS

Lee Kuan Yew
Born on 16 September 1923, Lee led Singapore to independence and served as its first prime minister. He led the country through merger and then separation from Malaysia and then made the republic an economic superpower. In 1990, he stepped down as prime minister though he remained in the cabinet as senior minister and, later, minister mentor.

Selkirk, Lord, Sir George Nigel Douglas-Hamilton, 10th Earl of Selkirk
Born on 4 January 1906, he succeeded in 1940 as the 10th Earl of Selkirk. He became the UK Commissioner General for Southeast Asia (1957–1963) and UK Commissioner for Singapore (1963). He was also the UK Council Representative for Seato from 1960 to 1963. For services rendered, he was made Knight of the Order of the Thistle (KT) and Knight Grand Cross of the Order of St Michael and St George (GCMG) and awarded the Grand Cross of the British Empire (GBE). Selkirk died on 24 November 1994.

Tunku Abdul Rahman
Known as the Father of Malaysian Independence, he was born on 8 February 1903. The seventh son and twentieth child of Sultan Abdul Hamid Halim Shah, the 24th Sultan of Kedah, the Tunku became Chief Minister of the Federation of Malaya in 1955 and the country's first prime minister at independence in 1957. He remained prime minister after Sabah, Sarawak and Singapore joined in 1963 to form Malaysia and after Singapore separated in 1965. Following the 1969 racial riots, the Tunku resigned as prime minister in 1970. He died on 6 December 1990.

Endnotes

1 Details on SOE personnel are sketchy as most personnel files are still classified.

Appendix F Part I: Reproductions of Original Documents

INSTRUCTIONS TO THE JAPANESE FORCES UNDER THE COMMAND OR CONTROL OF JAPANESE COMMANDERS SINGAPORE AREA

(COURTESY OF THE NATIONAL ARCHIVES, LONDON)

On board H.M.S. SUSSEX in position
01° 10' North, 103° 30' East.

4th September, 1945.

Sir,

I have the honour to report that the enclosed Agreement was signed at 1805 FG in the Admiral's fore-cabin on board H.M.S. SUSSEX. The original has been sent to the Supreme Allied Commander South East Asia by General Sir Philip Christison. One copy was handed to General Itagaki, General Commanding 7th Area Army and the other copy to Vice-Admiral Fukodome, Commander-in-Chief of the 10th Zone Fleet.

I have the honour to be, Sir,
Your humble and obedient servant,

Rear-Admiral.

Admiral Sir Arthur J. Power, K.C.B., C.V.O.
Commander-in-Chief East Indies Station.

INSTRUCTIONS TO THE JAPANESE FORCES UNDER COMMAND OR CONTROL OF JAPANESE COMMANDERS SINGAPORE AREA.

1. The Japanese Commanders, Singapore Area, being fully aware that all Japanese Sea, Land, Air and Auxiliary Forces have already been surrendered unconditionally at Tokio by the Japanese Government to the Allied Powers, and that hostilities have ceased, do hereby agree to put into force immediately certain measures to prepare for the acceptance of the surrender of the Japanese Forces in the Singapore Area. You are required to confirm by appending your signatures and seal below that the definitions given in Appendix "A" are understood, and that you will carry out the following instructions as directed in Appendices "B" and "C" attached.

2. These definitions and instructions are drawn up in the English language, which is the only authentic version. In any case of doubt as to the intention or meaning, the decision of the Supreme Allied Commander, South East Asia, is final.

3. Since the Japanese Commanders of the Singapore Area have had no instructions or orders as yet regarding saluting and the surrender of Officers' swords from the Supreme Japanese Commander, Southern Region, paragraph 6, Appendix "B" and paragraph 2 (c) Appendix "C" are temporarily held in abeyance until such instructions and orders are received by them.

XXXX) Representing the
Rear-Admiral) Supreme Allied
XXXX) Commander, South
Lt. General) East Asia.

XXXX

XXXX

4th September, 1945

APPENDIX "A"

DEFINITION OF TERMS USED IN THE INSTRUCTIONS CONTAINED IN APPENDICES "B" AND "C"

1. "The Singapore Area" means the area bounded on the North by a line including Mersing, KLUANG, Batu Pahat, on the South by the latitude of 00 30' North and on the East and West by the longtitude of 102 54' E and 105 00' E, but not including Sumatra..

2. "Japanese Forces" means all Japanese Army and Naval Forces.

3. "Japanese Army Forces" means all Japanese Land and Army Air Forces, including Administrative Troops, Para-Military organisations ancillary forces, Security Police, and Japanese Allied Forces in the Singapore Area, or under the command or control of the Japanese Army Commander, Singapore.

4. "The Japanese Army Commander" means the Senior Japanese Army Officer in the Singapore Area.

5. "Japanese Naval Forces" means all Japanese Naval ships and craft and all Naval personnel controlled by the Japanese Army or Naval Commander.

6. "Naval ships and craft" means all vessels of the Japanese Navy or Merchant Navy or controlled by the Japanese Army or Naval Commader. It includes submarines, auxiliary craft, coastal forces, tugs and powered harbour craft.

7. "Naval personnel" means all Japanese Naval and Mercantile personnel, Naval Air Force and Base personnel, and other personnel controlled by the Japanese Naval Commander.

8. "The Japanese Naval Commander" means the Senior Japanese Naval Officer in the Singapore Area.

9. Any orders issued regarding the Singapore Area in the name of the Senior British Naval or Army Commander by any British Officer or Subordinate Commander will be regarded as the Orders of the Supreme Allied Commander, South East Asia.

APPENDIX "B"

INSTRUCTIONS TO BE CARRIED OUT BY 0200 GREENWICH MEAN TIME ON WEDNESDAY, 5TH SEPTEMBER, 1945.

MAINTENANCE OF LAW AND ORDER AND FEEDING OF CIVIL POPULATION.

1. The Japanese Army and Naval Commanders Singapore will be responsible for the maintenance of law and order and the prevention of looting, and the maintenance of all essential public services, and for the care and feeding of the civil population until such time as the British Forces assume control.

2. The existing rationing and price control systems will be continued until further orders, and all books and documents thereto will be preserved and handed over intact.

3. To assist to maintain order and preserve public safety, the Military and Civil Police Forces and the Military, Naval and Civilian Fire Brigades will remain at their posts in a state of readiness.

MAINTENANCE OF JAPANESE FORCES.

4. The Japanese Army and Naval Commander Singapore will continue to be responsible for the maintenance of their Forces until such time as this responsibility is assumed by the British Commanders.

DISCIPLINE OF JAPANESE FORCES.

5. Japanese Commanders, at all levels, will be informed that, pending further instructions, they will be responsible for the maintenance of discipline among their own personnel, providing that no sentence of death or corporal punishment will be put into force without prior reference to the local Allied Commanders, who must not be below the rank of Brigadier or equivalent Naval rank. Should any Japanese commit offences against local inhabitants in the area, those actually committing the offence and their immediate and formation commanders will be subject to disciplinary action.

6. All Japanese Military and Naval personnel of whatever rank will salute all Allied Officers. Failure to do this will be an offence and will be dealt with. Allied Officers will return salutes.

PROHIBITION OF DESTRUCTION

7. All demolitions, destruction, damage and sabotage of all kinds whatsoever are prohibited. In particular, the following are to be placed under guard until taken over by British Forces:-

(a) Arms, equipment, tanks, vehicles, artillery, ammunition, explosives all warlike stores, and all supplies.

(b) Fortifications and their armaments, field works.

(c) All aircraft and equipment, and airfields.

(d) All signal communications of all kinds; all broadcasting stations, equipment and facilities.

(e) Civil stores, all food stocks, stocks of raw and prepared opium, all stocks of liquor and spirits, all land, water and air transportation and communication facilities and equipment, public utilities, workshops, and harbour facilities.

(f) All documents, records, archives, cyphers and codes, both Military and Civil. This is to include those prior to the Japanese occupation and during it.

(g) Charts of minefields, booby traps and other dangerous obstacles and Survey Maps.

(h) Plans of fixed and field defences.

(i) All stocks of petrol, oil, lubricants and other fuel.

(j) All stocks of material, whether raw or prepared.

(k) All ships and craft of any kind operated by the Japanese Forces.

(l) All radar stations and equipment, including detecting and counter-acting equipment.

8. The Japanese officers in charge of the guards placed in accordance with the preceding paragraph will be held personally responsible for the condition of installations, equipment, stores, buildings and papers in their care.

STAND FAST

9. All movements of Japanese Forces will cease except as ordered by the British Commanders, and to comply with paragraph headed "Withdrawal of Japanese Forces".

10. All aircraft will be grounded, and will remain grounded except as ordered by the British Commanders.

11. Any movements of troops, naval ships and craft, or aircraft without the authority of the British Commanders will be treated as a hostile act.

WITHDRAWAL OF JAPANESE FORCES.

12. All Japanese Forces will be evacuated from the areas marked "A", "B", "C", "D" and "E" on the attached map, and in addition the area to the South and inclusive of the Stamford Canal as far West on the junction of Paterson Hill Road and Grange Road, thence Irwell Bank Road - Kimsong Road to the Singapore River and the Cathay Buildings.

13. All Japanese Forces on Singapore Island will be withdrawn, in accordance with instructions to be issued, into the area on the mainland bounded on the North by the general line, all inclusive Mersing - Kluang, Batu Pahat and on the South by exclusive the Road Pontian Kechil - Skudai - Tebrau - Masai.

14. All Japanese Forces under command or control of 46 Division will concentrate within the above area.

15. The minimum forces necessary to maintain law and order, guard dumps, installations, public services, warehouses, etc., and to prevent looting and sabotage, will be left in evacuated areas. On being relieved by Allied Forces these guards will be despatched to join their parent units under arrangements made by the Allied Forces.

16. "Prove safe" parties of Japanese will be required, and will be left behind in the evacuated areas.

17. Every member of the Japanese Forces, including auxiliary personnel and police, who are left behind in any evacuated area, will wear a white arm band.

18. A small Japanese Military Staff, limited to 20 persons in all, for Adminstrative purposes, will remain in Area "A" for work with the Allied Force Headquarters. In addition, 30 English-speaking Japanese will be made available for interpretation and to act as guides for the Allied Forces. These interpreters will be located with the staff mentioned above, available to be called forward as required.

COMMUNICATIONS

19. (a) All communications in code and cypher are prohibited.

(b) All signal communications, other than those permitted in paragraph (c) below are prohibited.

(c) Communications in clear between Army and Naval Commanders, Singapore, and their subordinate commanders may continue, subject to such supervision as the British Commanders may decide.

(d) No W/T transmitters are to be used without the authority of the British Commanders.

MILITARY TRANSPORT

20. All Japanese motor transport, including civil transport requisitioned by the Japanese Forces, will be concentrated in Motor Transport Parks within the evacuated area "A", and 100 lorries, on Kallang Airfield, with drivers available and filled with petrol and oil. Allied Forces will take over control of all such Motor Transport.

21. All the above vehicles will have a white flag flying.

22. No Civil or Military vehicles will move within the evacuated area on the day of occupation, except those used in the handing over proceedings and others authorised by the British Commanders.

ORDER OF BATTLE

23. The Order of Battle and Location Statementsoof all Japanese Forces located in the Singapore Area, as defined in Appendix "A" will be submitted to Headquarters 15th Ind. Corps on the first day of occupation.

CURFEW

24. A curfew, confining all persons to their houses and forbidding any movement outside, from 1800 hrs. to 0600 hrs. will be enforced until further orders, starting on the day of occupation. The Japanese Commander will be held responsible for the promulgation of the Curfew to all personnel, including the civilian population, on the first day of the occupation.

NAVAL SHIPS AND CRAFT

25. No personnel are to leave their ship or craft and Commanding Officers are to be on board to hand over their ships.

26. All special attack craft are to be rendered harmless and placed under guard.

27. All guns are to be unloaded and the breech blocks are to be removed and placed alongside the guns.

NAVAL SHIPS AND CRAFT - (CONTD.)

28. All torpedoes are to be unloaded and their warheads removed.

29. All explosives are to be struck down to the magazine; the magazines are to be locked and the keys held by the Commanding Officers.

30. Japanese ships and craft are to hoist and keep flying until further orders, a white ensign over their national flag. If this is not possible, a black flag only is to be flown at the masthead.

31. All minesweeping Forces are to keep their full crews and equipment on board, and are to be at the disposal of the British Naval Commander for the clearance of minefields. All ammunition in minesweepers is to be thrown over the side.

PRISONERS OF WAR AND INTERNEES

32. (a) The Japanese Commander will ensure the protection, good treatment, care and feeding of all Prisoners of War and Internees until such time as the British Commanders take over the responsibility.

(b) Ensure that all APWI are relieved forthwith of all forms of work.

(c) All records concerning Prisoners of War and Internees are to be kept intact and handed over to the British Army Commander.

CIVIL PRISONERS

33. All occupants of the civil prisons are to remain there, and the prisons are to be kept under guard. All records in connection with the occupants are to be kept intact and handed over to the British Army Commander.

HOSPITALS

34. All hospital staffs are to remain at their hospitals in charge of their patients until further orders are given. All drugs and equipment in hospitals will be left in position.

HEADS OF SERVICES

35. The Senior Representative of the Port Organisation, Civil Administration and Public Utility Services are to remain at their posts, and are to be instructed to assist in maintaining their particular service, and preventing sabotage.

36. The existing Japanese Civil Administration (including the Shonan Special Municipality) and all Japanese concerned therewith, will continue to function and remain at their posts until further orders.

TECHNICIANS.

37. All technical personnel of dockyard, port installations, public utility services and wireless stations will remain at their posts.

PILOTS

38. All the local port and harbour pilots are to be held at the disposal of the British Naval Commander.

PORT LABOUR

39. All available stevedores, gangers, and in addition 1,000 unskilled labourers to work the port will be made available at one hour's notice on instructions from the British Commanders.

TREATMENT OF RESISTANCE FORCES

40. All personnel of all resistance and guerilla forces in all areas occupied by the Japanese Forces shall be treated by the Japanese Forces as if they were Allied Forces. All reprisals against such personnel, and all acrion which may harm or injure them is prohibited.

INFECTIOUS DISEASES

41. Japanese Commanders will be responsible for disclosing forthwith the nature, type and extent of outbreak of any infectious diseases within the territory under their control, and for ensuring that all possible steps are taken to prevent any spread of such diseases.

FINANCE

42. (a) All Treasuries, Banks and Financial Houses, whether State or private, will cease forthwith.

(b) All coin, notes, species, valuables of any kind (including bonds and securities) and all books of account and business documents to be safeguarded.

(c) The printing and issue of all further paper currency in prohibited.

POSTS AND TELEGRAPHS

43. All public business is to cease forthwith and premises to be closed to the public. No further handling of postal and telegraphic matter will take place. All stocks of stamps, currency,

POSTS AND TELEGRAPH - (CONTINUED)

postal and telegraphic matter, records and books of accounts to be safeguarded.

NEWSPAPERS, ETC.

44. The publication of all newspapers and other forms of propaganda will cease forthwith. All printing presses will be closed and safeguarded and their whereabouts disclosed.

APPENDIX "C"

FURTHER ACTION REQUIRED BY THE BRITISH COMMANDERS

DISARMAMENT

1. All Japanese Forces will disarm and will move to the concentration areas mentioned in Appendix "B", paragraph 13.

2. All Japanese Forces will disarm in accordance with the following principles:-

(a) Weapons, after cleaning and oiling, and ammunition will be put in central dumps each for not less than one battalion or equivalent where possible.

(b) Dumps will be guarded. These guards may retain rifles on the minimum scale necessary but not automatic weapons or grenades.

(c) All officers' weapons, including swords, will be given up whenever their unit or formation as a whole disarm.

(d) Japanese Commanders will arrange disarmament of all subsidiary forces armed by them, and will be responsible that the personnel of such forces are not permitted to disperse. In particular, the INA will remain in their units or formations under their own officers.

NAVAL SHIPS AND CRAFT

3. British parties will board all ships and craft and will inspect them removing breech blocks and such material as they deem necessary. Thereafter, a daily inspection of ships will be carried out by officers of the British Navy.

4. The provision of necessary supplies to Japanese personnel in ships and craft will be arranged by the British Naval Commander.

5. Orders for the disposal of ammunition will be issued later.

6. The crews of all ships and craft, except minesweepers, will be reduced to one-fifth complement, the disembarked personnel being removed to the area mentioned in Appendix "B" paragraph 13.

JAPANESE, GERMAN AND ITALIAN NATIONALS.

7. Lists will be compiled without delay in English of all German and Italian Nationals, whether Naval, Military, Air Force or Civil, and Japanese civilians, showing full names, sex, age, occupation, and place of residence in Singapore and in Japan or Germany or Italy. No such personnel will leave the Singapore Area.

8. All Japanese, German and Italian businesses (other than those essential to the life of the community) will cease public business forthwith. Premises will be closed to the public, and all cash, goods, stock in trade and books of accounts will be preserved.

9. Lists in English of all Japanese, German and Italian businesses in the Singapore Area will be compiled showing the name and nature of the business, address of the business permises, name of the manager or owner, number and names of Japanese, German and Italian employees, address of Head Office in Japan, Germany, Italy or elsewhere.

10. All German and Italian civilians not engaged on public services or work essential to the life of the community, are to remain in their residences until further orders.

MEDICAL

11. The Japanese Medical Authorities will

(a) Produce details of the sanitary arrangements and apparatues in existance.

(b) Produce detailed malaria charts of Singapore Island.

(c) State the location of all hospitals, laboratories, medical stores and installations.

(d) Give the names and locations of all Allied sick and wounded, who are in Japanese medical care, other than those in Prisoner of War Camps.

(e) Ensure that the Singapore General Hospital, located at New Bridge Road, will be emptied of all Japanese patients by 1130 Greenwich Mean Time on the day of occupation, except those unfit to be moved. The hospital will be clean and in every way fit for immediate use. All other property vacated by the Japanese will be left clean and ready for use.

RESTITUTION OF PROPERTY.

12. Everything of every nature whatsoever that may have been requisitioned, taken or otherwise acquired by the Japanese in territories occupied by Japanese Forces, or in territories which they have entered, shall be surrendered and restored in accordance with the direction of the Supreme Allied Commander, South East Asia.

Appendix F Part II: Reproductions of Original Documents

ORDERS OF THE COMMANDER OCCUPYING FORCE TO THE JAPANESE COMMANDER OF SINGAPORE

(COURTESY OF THE NATIONAL ARCHIVES, LONDON)

N.O. Action File ... TOP SEC SACSEA Mission 221 31 Aug 45

ORDERS OF THE COMMANDER OCCUPYING FORCE' TO THE JAPANESE COMMANDER OF SINGAPORE. 94

(a) All JAPANESE Forces to be withdrawn from SINGAPORE Island by hours on the day of occupation. Your order of battle and location statements of all troops under your command will be submitted to this Headquarters by hours on the day of occupation. Prior to their departure all arms and equipment to be left dumped in areas. This to include all small arms, automatics, grenades, dahs and all ammunition and stores connected therewith.

(b) All guns to have the breech blocks removed.

(c) Tanks to be parked in unit areas.

(d) Only minimum guards to be left on these dumps and parks to ensure their safety and good order.

2. (a) Every member of all branches of the JAPANESE Forces and their Puppet Forces remaining on the island to wear a white arm band.

(b) Personnel not surrendering will be outlawed, and escaping surrendered personnel will be severely dealt with.

3. The JAPANESE will be held responsible for the maintenance of Law and Order and for any looting or destruction prior to the arrival and taking over of the occupying Force.

4. (a) The minimum force necessary will remain in SINGAPORE Town and Island area to maintain Law and Order, to guard dumps, installations, public services, ware houses, docking equipment and to prevent all looting or sabotage.

(b) The existing JAPANESE civil administration (including the SHONAN Special Municipality and the Police) will continue to function, and all JAPANESE concerned therewith will remain at their posts until further orders.

(c) All Japanese and Civil Port Authorities and personnel will remain at their posts and will have ready all available stevedores, gangers and the necessary unskilled labour to work the port.

(d) All technical personnel who are operating company, public or other installations including Wireless Telegraphy, water, lighting, gas, sanitation etc., will remain until the occupying Force takes over control of the said installations.

5. (a) All gun sites and guns to be disclosed.

(b) All mines, booby traps to be disclosed and removed by JAPANESE personnel under supervision of occupying Force.

(c) "Prove Safe" parties of JAPANESE will be required (from the force in 4 (a) above).

(d) All hospital staffs to remain at their hospital until further orders.

(e) All Port Installations including cranes etc., to be handed over in good condition.

(f) A responsible guard or caretaker will be left in every building vacated by the JAPANESE Forces to ensure its safe keeping and to prevent looting.

(g) All BRITISH and JAPANESE administrative records will be safeguarded and their locations disclosed. None will be destroyed. This order includes, in addition to all other records:-
(i) The records of the British Custodian of Enemy Property, and of the Japanese Custodian of Property, the former including all records under the Trading with the Enemy Act.

3/8(a)

To Sheet TWO .. 2

221a

Sheet TWO .. 2

95

(g) (continued)

(ii) All Survey maps, charts and plans.
(iii) All titles and records of the Land Office, including all records of dealings with lands and of the issue of title to lands, during the Japanese occupation.

(h) All cash and currency, including money orders and stamps held in bulk by the Japanese Armed Forces and the Civil Administration will be frozen and further instructions as to it's disposal will be issued later.

6. (a) All JAPANESE motor transport including civil requisitioned by JAPANESE to be collected in Motor Transport Parks under guards and to be handed over in good condition.

(b) Of the motor transport specified in 6(a) above 500 lorries with drivers will be collected at Dock area by hours on the day of occupation and 100 lorries at KALANG Airfield. All these lorries and vehicles to have a white flag flying.

(c) 100 large staff cars in high class condition to be available on the second day of oc-cupation for use by occupying Force.

(d) No civil or military vehicles other than the above will move on the day of occupation except those used in the handing over proceedings.

(e) CLEMENCEAU AVENUE will be cleared of all vehicular and pedestrian traffic from dawn on the second day of occupation until further orders.

7. Arrangements to be made for the local civil authorities to be available from hours onwards on the day of occupation to contact the Commander of the occupying Force.

8. A curfew confining all inhabitants to their houses and forbidding any movement from sun set to sun rise will be enforced until further notice starting on the day of occupation, except for personnel employed on essential services who must have a signed permit.

9. All stocks and stores of spirits, liquor shops, breweries etc., will be closed and guarded. Any other large supplies will be disclosed.

10. All JAPANESE flags or tokens will be removed.

11. (a) A small JAPANESE Headquarters for Administrative purposes will remain in SINGAPORE Town for work with Force Headquarters.

(b) Four similar Headquarters will be required to work with minor formations in the Island Area and will be ready to move immediately when so ordered.

(c) In each of these Headquarters 20 interpreters and guides will be available.

12. No JAPANESE Officer above the rank of MAJOR will be employed in contact with disarmed JAPANESE and/or Puppet Forces. These will be concentrated under orders of the Commander, Occupying Force.

13. (a) The where-abouts and numbers of all Allied Prisoners of War and Civil Internee Camps, permanent and temporary, will be disclosed.

(b) You will report by hours on
(i) Numbers by nationalities giving in each case their location.
(ii) The number of sick at each location which cannot be moved.

(c) (i) All Allied prisoners will be relieved forthwith of all forms of work.
(ii) They will be fed by you until taken over by the occupying Force.
(iii) You are responsible that they come to no harm until taken over by the occupying Force.

To Sheet THREE ... 3

221b

96

Sheet THREE ... 3

DGS (O)
GSO I (N)
GSO I (S)
G II (X)
G III (X) 1
G III (X) 2
G III (X) 3
G II (N)
G III (N) 1
G III (N) 2
G II (S)
G III (S)

14. (c) Responsible representatives of the following departments will be available by hours on day of occupation and will be in possession of all relevant information in connection therewith:-

(a) Engineer Services.

(b) Supply (Food)

(c) Supply (Petrol)

(d) Inter-communication and Signals.

(e) Railways.

(f) Prisoners of War and Civilian Internees.

15. (a) A JAPANESE Medical Officer, with an interpreter with medical knowledge will be included in the Headquarters detailed in paragraph 11(a) above.
He will produce full details of the following matters relatiing to SINGAPORE Town and Island.
(i) The presence of any epidemic, endemic or infectious diseases and the measures taken to control them.
(ii) The sanitary arrangements and apparatus in existence.
(iii) Detailed malaria charts of SINGAPORE ISLAND.
(iv) The locations of all hospitals, laboratories, medical stores and installations.
(v) The names and locations of all Allied sick and wounded who are in JAPANESE Medical care (other than those in Prisoners of War Camps.)

(b) (i) SINGAPORE General Hospital located at NEW BRIDGE STREET will be emptied of all JAPANESE patients except those unfit to be moved, before occupation of the island by the Force.
(ii) This hospital will be cleaned and in every way prepared for immediate use by the Medical Services of the Force.
(iii) A small staff, with technical interpreters, will remain to operate the water supply, lighting, heating, disinfecting, electricity, and X ray apparatus and equipment.

(c) All other hospitals vacated by the JAPANESE Forces will be left clean and ready for use.

16. No aircraft will leave the ground.

17. All aircraft, stores and air-field equipment will be guarded and kept in good condition.

18. JAPANESE troops leaving the Island will take three days food with them, all other supplies, civil and military, will be guarded until arrival of the occupying Force and then handed over intact.

19. All JAPANESE Commanders will be held personally responsible for the behaviour and discipline of the troops under their immediate command.

20. If any doubt or dispute arises as to the meaning or interpretation of these orders, the decision of the Commander, Occupying Force will be final.
The English version of these orders are the authentic text.

E.C. Mansergh

MAJOR GENERAL.
COMMANDER OCCUPYING FORCE.

Appendix F Part III: Reproductions of Original Documents

INSTRUMENT OF SURRENDER OF JAPANESE FORCES IN SOUTHEAST ASIA

(COURTESY OF THE NATIONAL ARCHIVES, LONDON)

21A

3/43 (P)

SECRET. Copy No. 39

C.O.S. (45) 229.

26th September, 1945.

CHIEFS OF STAFF COMMITTEE.

INSTRUMENT OF SURRENDER OF JAPANESE FORCES IN SOUTH-EAST ASIA.

NOTE BY THE SECRETARY.

THE annexed copy of the Instrument of Surrender of Japanese forces under the command or control of the Supreme Commander, Japanese Expeditionary Forces, Southern Region, within the operational theatre of the Supreme Allied Commander, South East Asia, as signed at Singapore at 0341 hours G.M.T. on the 12th September, 1945, is circulated for information and record.

At Appendix "A" is a copy of the Supreme Allied Commander's statement made prior to the actual signature of the Instrument of Surrender, together with a copy of General Itagaki's credentials at Appendix "B."

(Signed) L. C. HOLLIS.

Offices of the Cabinet and Minister of Defence, S.W. 1,
26th September, 1945.

ANNEX.

INSTRUMENT OF SURRENDER OF JAPANESE FORCES UNDER THE COMMAND OR CONTROL OF THE SUPREME COMMANDER, JAPANESE EXPEDITIONARY FORCES, SOUTHERN REGIONS, WITHIN THE OPERATIONAL THEATRE OF THE SUPREME ALLIED COMMANDER, SOUTH-EAST ASIA.

1. In pursuance of and in compliance with :

(*a*) the Instrument of Surrender signed by the Japanese plenipotentiaries by command and on behalf of the Emperor of Japan, the Japanese Government, and the Japanese Imperial General Headquarters at Tokyo on the 2nd September, 1945;

(*b*) General Order No. 1, promulgated at the same place and on the same date;

(*c*) the Local Agreement made by the Supreme Commander, Japanese Expeditionary Forces, Southern Regions, with the Supreme Allied Commander, South-East Asia, at Rangoon on the 27th August, 1945;

to all of which Instrument of Surrender, General Order and Local Agreement this present Instrument is complementary and which it in no way supersedes, the Supreme Commander, Japanese Expeditionary Forces, Southern Regions (Field-Marshal Count Terauchi), does hereby surrender unconditionally to the Supreme Allied Commander, South-East Asia (Admiral the Lord Louis Mountbatten) himself and all Japanese sea, ground, air and auxiliary forces under his command or control and within the operational theatre of the Supreme Allied Commander, South-East Asia.

2. The Supreme Commander, Japanese Expeditionary Forces, Southern Regions, undertakes to ensure that all orders and instructions that may be issued from time to time by the Supreme Allied Commander, South-East Asia, or by any of his subordinate Naval, Military or Air Force Commanders of whatever rank acting in his name, are scrupulously and promptly obeyed by all Japanese

2

sea, ground, air and auxiliary forces under the command or control of the Supreme Commander, Japanese Expeditionary Forces, Southern Regions, and within the operational theatre of the Supreme Allied Commander, South-East Asia.

3. Any disobedience of, or delay or failure to comply with, orders or instructions issued by the Supreme Allied Commander, South-East Asia, or issued on his behalf by any of his subordinate Naval, Military or Air Force Commanders of whatever rank, and any action which the Supreme Allied Commander, South-East Asia, or his subordinate Commanders, acting on his behalf, may determine to be detrimental to the Allied Powers, will be dealt with as the Supreme Allied Commander, South-East Asia, may decide.

4. This Instrument takes effect from the time and date of signing.

5. This Instrument is drawn up in the English language, which is the only authentic version. In any case of doubt as to intention or meaning, the decison of the Supreme Allied Commander, South-East Asia, is final. It is the responsibility of the Supreme Commander, Japanese Expeditionary Forces, Southern Regions, to make such translation into Japanese as he may require.

Signed at Singapore at 0341 hours (G.M.T.) on the 12th September, 1945.

(Signed) SEISHIRO ITAGAKI,
for *Supreme Commander,*
Japanese Expeditionary Forces,
Southern Regions.
[Seal.]

(Signed) LOUIS MOUNTBATTEN,
Supreme Allied Commander,
South-East Asia.

[Field-Marshal Count Terauchi's Seal.]

APPENDIX "A."

STATEMENT BY SUPREME ALLIED COMMANDER, SOUTH-EAST ASIA, MADE AT SURRENDER CEREMONY HELD IN THE MUNICIPAL BUILDINGS, SINGAPORE, ON 12TH SEPTEMBER, 1945.

"I HAVE come here to-day to receive the formal surrender of all the Japanese forces within the South-East Asia Command. I have received the following telegram from the Supreme Commander of the Japanese forces concerned, Field-Marshal Count Terauchi :—

'The most important occasion of the formal surrender signing at Singapore draws near, the significance of which is no less great to me than to your Excellency. It is extremely regretful that my ill-health prevents me from attending and signing it personally and that I am unable to pay homage to your Excellency. I hereby notify your Excellency that I have fully empowered General Itagaki, the highest senior general in Japanese armies, and send him on my behalf.'

On hearing of Field-Marshal Terauchi's illness, I sent my own doctor, Surgeon Captain Birt, Royal Navy, to examine him, and he certifies that the Field-Marshal is suffering from the effects of a stroke. In the circumstances I have decided to accept the surrender from General Itagaki to-day, but I have warned the Field-Marshal that I shall expect him to make his personal surrender to me as soon as he is fit enough to do so.

In addition to our Naval, Military and Air forces which we have present in Singapore to-day, a large fleet is anchored off Port Swettenham and Port Dixon, and a large force started disembarking from them at daylight on the 9th September. When I visited the force yesterday, there were 100,000 men ashore. This invasion would have taken place on the 9th September whether the Japanese had resisted or not, and I wish to make it entirely clear to General Itagaki that he is surrendering to superior force here in Singapore.

I now call upon General Itagaki to produce his credentials."

3

APPENDIX "B."

CREDENTIALS OF GENERAL ITAGAKI.

(Translation.)

I, the undersigned, hereby authorise General Seishiro Itagaki, Commander of the Imperial Japanese Seventh Area Army, to make, for and in the name of myself, arrangements and sign an instrument or instruments, with the Supreme Commander of the Allied Forces, South-East Asia, concerning the formal surrender of all the Imperial Japanese Army, Naval, Air and Auxiliary Forces which are under my command or control and are within the operational theatre of the Supreme Allied Commander, South-East Asia.

Done at Saigon this 10th day of the 9th month of the 20th year of Showa, corresponding to the 10th of September, 1945, of the Christian era.

(L.S). HISAICHI TERAUCHI,
Field-Marshal, Count, Supreme Commander of the Imperial Japanese Force, Southern Region.

[Seal.]

Selected Bibliography

Primary Sources:

Great Britain, The National Archives (Public Records Office), London

ADM116 *Admiralty: Record Office: Cases. 1852–1965.*

ADM199 *Admiralty: War History Cases and Papers, Second World War. 1922-1968.*

CAB79 *War Cabinet and Cabinet: Chiefs of Staff Committee: Minutes. 1939–1946.*

CAB81 *War Cabinet and Cabinet: Committees and Sub-committees of the Chiefs of Staff Committee: Minutes and Papers. 1939–1947.*

CAB119 *War Cabinet and Cabinet Office: Joint Planning Staff: Correspondence and Papers. 1939-1948.*

CAB122 *War Cabinet and Cabinet Office: British Joint Staff Mission and British Joint Services Mission: Washington Office Records. 1940–1958.*

CAOG9 *Crown Agents for Oversea Governments and Administrations: Finance Departments: Registered Files, Funds, Loans and Investments. 1860–1981.*

DEFE2 *Combined Operations Headquarters, and Ministry of Defence, Combined Operations Headquarters later Amphibious Warfare Headquarters: Records. 1937-1963.*

FO371 *Foreign Office: Political Departments: General Correspondence from 1906. 1906–1966.*

FCO24 *Commonwealth Office, Far East and Pacific Department and Foreign and Commonwealth Office, South West Pacific Department: Registered Files (H and FW Series). 1967–1974.*

HS1 *Special Operations Executive: Far East: Registered Files. 1940–1947.*

HS9 *Special Operations Executive: Personnel Files (PF Series). 1939–1946.*

PREM4 *Prime Minister's Office: Confidential Correspondence. 1934–1946.*

PREM11 *Prime Minister's Office: Correspondence and Papers. 1944–1964.*

WO193 *War Office: Directorate of Military Operations and Plans, later Directorate of Military Operations: Files concerning Military Planning, Intelligence and Statistics (Collation Files). 1934-1958.*

WO203 *War Office: South East Asia Command: Military Headquarters Papers, Second World War. 1932–1949.*

WO259 *War Office: Department of the Secretary of State for War: Private Office Papers. 1937-1953.*

Great Britain, Imperial War Museum, London

Baker, C.M.S. *Personal Papers. 96/34/11.*

Brown, Lieutenant A. P. G. RNVR. *Personal Papers. 92/27/1.*

Cazalet, Vice Admiral Sir Peter. *Papers.*

Findlay, Major R.J. *Personal Papers. 91/13/1.*

Horne, Captain J.E.T. *Personal Papers. 83/53/1.*

MISC 53 (799). "To All Allied Prisoners of War".

MISC 223 (3215). "Instructions to the Japanese Forces Under Command Or Control of Japanese Commanders, Singapore Area".

Munby, R. *Personal Papers. 87/34/1.*

Sayer, Vice Admiral Sir Guy. *Personal Papers. P68.*

Secondary Sources

Official Histories

Kirby, Major General S. Woodburn. *The War Against Japan,* vols. 1 to 5. London: HMSO, 1965.

Books

Attiwell, Kenneth. *The Singapore Story.* New York: Doubleday, 1960.

Ban, Kah Choon & Yap Hong Kuan. *Rehearsal for War: The Underground War Against the Japanese.* Singapore: Horizon Books, 2002.

Barber, Noel. *A Sinister Twilight: The Fall of Singapore 1942.* Boston: Houghton Mifflin, 1968.

Braddon, Russell. *The Naked Island.* London: Werner Laurie. 1952.

Brett-James, Anthony. *Ball of Fire: 5th Indian Division in World War II.* Aldershot: Gale and Polden, 1951.

Brooke, Field Marshal Alan F., Lord Alanbrooke, 1st Viscount, Baron Alanbrooke Of Brookeborough. *War Diaries 1939–1945: Field Marshall Lord Alanbrooke. Edited by Alex Danchev and Daniel Todman.* London: Weidenfeld and Nicolson, 2001.

Bryant, Arthur. *Triumph in the West 1943–1946.* London: Collins, 1959.

Chapman, Lieutenant Colonel F. Spencer. *The Jungle is Neutral.* London: Chatto & Windus, 1949.

Cheah, Boon Kheng. Red Star Over Malaya: Resistance & Social Conflict during and after the Japanese Occupation, 1941-1946 (Third Edition). Singapore:Singapore University Press, 2003.

Chin, Kee Onn. *Malaya Upside Down.* Singapore: Jitts, 1946.

Chin, Peng. *My Side of History.* Singapore: Media Masters, 2003.

Churchill, Sir Winston S. *The Second World War,* vols. 1 to 6. Boston: Houghton Mifflin, 1950.

Commonwealth War Graves Commission, The. *The War Dead of the British Commonwealth and Empire; The Register of the Names of Those who Fell in the 1939–1945 War and have No Known Grave; The Singapore Memorial: Introduction to the Register.* London: The Commonwealth War Graves Commission, 1957.

Eden, Anthony R., 1st Earl of Avon, Viscount Eden of Royal Leamington Spa. *The Eden Memoirs: The Reckoning.* London: Cassell, 1965.

Falk, Stanley. *Seventy Days to Singapore.* New York: G.P. Putnam's Sons, 1975.

Farrell, Brian and Sandy Hunter (eds.). *Sixty Years On: The Fall of Singapore Revisited.* Singapore: Eastern Universities Press, 2002.

Gough, Richard. *The Jungle was Red.* Singapore: SNP Panpac, 2003.

Hack, Karl and C.C. Chin (eds.). *Dialogues with Chin Peng: New Light on the Malayan Communist Party.* Singapore: Singapore University Press, 2004.

Harrington, Joseph D. *Yankee Samurai: The Secret Role of Nisei in America's Pacific Victory.* Detroit: Pettigrew Enterprises, 1979.

Keay, John. *Last Post: The End of Empire in the Far East.* London: John Murray, 1997.

Kratoska, Paul H. *The Japanese Occupation of Malaya 1941-1945.* London: Hurst & Company, 1998.

Lau, Albert. *A Moment of Anguish: Singapore in Malaysia and the Politics of Disengagement.* Singapore: Times Academic Press, 1998.

Low, Ngiong Ing. *When Singapore was Syonan-To.* Singapore: Eastern Universities Press, 1973.

Mitchell. Austin. *Election '45.* London: Fabian Society, Bellew Publishing, 1995.

Morrison, Ian. *Malayan Postscript.* London: Faber & Faber, 1943.

National Heritage Board, National Archives of Singapore. *The Japanese Occupation 1942–1945: A Pictorial Record of Singapore During the War.* Singapore: Times Editions, 1996.

Owen, Frank. *The Fall of Singapore.* London: Michael Joseph, 1960.

Percival, Lieutenant General Arthur E. *The War in Malaya.* London: Eyre & Spottiswoode, 1949.

Show, Clara. *Lim Bo Seng: Singapore's Best-Known War Hero.* Singapore: Asiapac Books, 1998.

Smyth, John. *Percival and the Tragedy of Singapore.* London: Macdonald, 1971.

Stripp, Alan. *Codebreaker in the Far East.* Oxford: Oxford University Press, 1989.

Tan, Chong Tee. *Force 136: Story of a WWII Resistance Fighter.* Singapore: Asiapac Books, 1995.

Turnbull, Mary. *Dateline Singapore: 150 Years of the Straits Times.* Singapore: Singapore Press Holdings, 1995.

Articles

"'Oot!' Said Mackie and the Jap Colonel Fled". *The Zodiac,* November 1945.

"Japanese in Malaya Surrender in Singapore". *The Straits Times,* 13 September 1945.

"Obituary: The Rev. Guy Armstrong". *Daily Telegraph,* 15 January 2003.

Baxter, Christoper. "In Pursuit of a Pacific Strategy: British Planning for the Defeat of Japan, 1943–45". *Diplomacy & Statecraft,* vol. 15, no. 2, June 2004.

Corr, Gerard. "The War was Over—but Where were the Liberators?". *The Straits Times Annual 1976.* Singapore: Times Publishing Bhd., 1976.

Fursdon, Major General Edward. "Without Saluting the Japanese Came to Bargain but Soon the Sun Set on Their Empire". *The Daily Telegraph,* 12 August 1985.

Lam, Pin Foo. "Japanese Settlers were here before the War". *The Straits Times—Life,* 25 February 1998.

Miller, Harry. "An End to 1,318 Days of Terror". *The Daily Telegraph,* 12 August 1985.

Roberts, Major Frank. "With the Beach Groups in Malaya". *The Malayan Daily News,* 22 October 1945.

Stewart, Athole. "How History was Written at Singapore". *The Zodiac,* December 1945.

Newspapers

Syonan Shimbun, 1944–1945.

The Straits Times, 1945–1975.

The Malayan Tribune, 1945–1948.

The Times of London, 1945–1946.

Websites

Ammentorp, Steen. "Biography of Seishiro Itagaki". *The Generals of WWII.* Accessed 28 January 2005. Available from <http://www.generals.dk/general/Itagaki/Seishiro/Japan.html>.

Ammentorp, Steen. "Biography of Sir Alexander Frank Philip Christison". *The Generals of WWII.* Accessed 28 January 2005. Available from <http://www.generals.dk/general/Christison/Sir_Alexander_Frank_Philip/Great_Britain.html>.

Ammentorp, Steen. "Biography of Sir Frederick Arthur Montague Browning". *The Generals of WWII.* Accessed 28 January 2005. Available from <http://www.generals.dk/general/Browning/Sir_Frederick_Arthur_Montague/Great_Britain.html>.

Ammentorp, Steen. "Biography of Takazo Numata". *The Generals of WWII.* Accessed 28 January 2005. Available from <http://www.generals.dk/general/Numata/Takazo/Japan.html>.

Australian National Flag Association. "Timeline". *Australian National Flag Association.* Accessed 14 August 2004. Available from <http://www.australianflag.org.au/timeline.php>.

Chung, Chee Min. "The Japanese Surrendered at the V.I.—TWICE!". *The Victoria Institution Web Page.* Accessed 14 August 2004. Available from <http://www.viweb.freehosting.net/japsurr.htm>.

Cooper, Carol. "South East Asia Under Japanese Occupation: The Story of Changi". *The Children (& Families) of the Far East Prisoners of War (COFEPOW).* Accessed 13 February 2005. Available from <http://www.cofepow.org.uk/pages/asia_singapore_changi_story.htm>.

Dunn, Peter. "Was there a Japanese Invasion Planned to Occur between Townsville and Brisbane in Queensland during WW2?". *Australia @ War.* Accessed 28 January 2005. Available from <http://home.st.net.au/~dunn/japsland/invade02.htm>.

Fildew, L.G. *Looking back at Singapore 1945-1946.* Accessed 15 August 2004. Available from <http://www.geocities.com/lesfil2000/mypagetoo.html>.

Green, Ken. "Memories of Stoke-on-Trent People—Ken Green". *Stoke-on-Trent.* Accessed 10 September 2004. Available from <http://www.thepotteries.org/memories/green_ken5.htm>.

Houterman, Hans. *World War II Unit Histories and Officers.* Accessed 12 February 2005. Available from <http://houterman.htmlplanet.com/home.html>

Malaya Historical Group. "Operation Zipper". *Malaya Historical Group: Malaya—Wrecks Research Group: Malaysian Military & Aviation Research & Project.* Accessed 26 August 2004. Available from <http://www.geocities.com/malaya_hg/ops_zipper.htm>.

Nishida, Hiroshi. *Imperial Japanese Navy.* Accessed 4 February 2005. Available from <http://homepage2.nifty.com/nishidah/e/index.htm>.

Pang, Augustine and Angeline Song (eds.). "Meet Singapore's James Bond". *Headlines, Lifelines: Chee Beng's Start Page.* Accessed 15 November 2004. Available from <http://ourstory.asia1.com.sg/war/lifeline/bond7.html>.

Taylor, Ron. "Charles Thrale Paintings". *East Anglia Net.* Accessed 10 August 2004. Available from <http://www.ean.co.uk/Data/Bygones/History/Article/WW2/Painting_the_Horror/html/body_charles_thrale_paintings_15.htm>.

Watson, Graham. "Operation Zipper: The Invasion of Malaya, August 1945". *Orders of Battle.* Accessed 30 January 2005. Available from <http://orbat.com/site/history/historical/malaysia/operationzipper.html>.

Wong, Marjorie. "Force 136 in Malaya: An Excerpt from 'The Dragon and the Maple Leaf'". *Burma Star Association.* Accessed 10 August 2004. Available from <http://www.burmastar.org.uk/136malaya.htm>.

Photo Credits

Author: 137, 138

Brett-James, Antony. *Ball of Fire: 5th Indian Division in World War II.* Aldershot: Gale and Polden, 1951: 82, 86 (top), 86 (bottom), 87

Chapman, Lieutenant Colonel F Spencer. *The Jungle is Neutral.* Singapore: Times Editions–Marshall Cavendish, 2005: 29 (left), 29 (right)

Imperial War Museum: pages 5 (top), 5 (bottom), 93, 117, 119 (top), 119 (bottom), 120, 123 (top)

Gough, Richard. *The Jungle was Red.* Singapore: SNP Panpac, 2003: 50

MCIA: 135 (top), 142

Courtesy of The President and Mrs SR Nathan: 150

Tan, Chong Tee. *Force 136: Story of a WWII Resistance Fighter.* Singapore: Asiapac Books, 1995: 38, 45

Yap, Siang Yong, Bose, Romen, Pang, Angeline, Singh, Kuldip, Lim, Lisa, Foo, Germaine. *Fortress Singapore: The Battlefield Guide.* Singapore: Times Editions–Marshall Cavendish, 2005: 114 (top), 114 (bottom), 123 (bottom), 131, 135 (bottom)

www.geocities.com/malaya_hg/ops_zipper.htm: 106

Index

About the Author

A former Indochina Bureau Chief and correspondent for Channel NewsAsia, Romen Bose has written extensively on the Second World War in Singapore and has been involved in researching Singapore and the region's military history for close to two decades. His books include *Secrets of the Battlebox, Fortress Singapore: A Battlefield Guide* and *A Will for Freedom: The Indian Independence Movement in Southeast Asia.* He has also worked with the United Nations and more recently, the Singapore Tourism Board. Romen is presently a British Council Swire Cathay Pacific/Chevening Scholar pursuing a Master's at Goldsmiths College, University of London. He and his wife, Brigid, have two daughters, Lara and Olive.